# Student Manual for

# PSYCHOLOGY:
## Understanding Behavior

PAUL B. PAULUS
University of Texas at Arlington

ROBERT A. BARON
Purdue University

W. B. Saunders Company    Philadelphia, London, Toronto

W. B. Saunders Company:   West Washington Square
Philadelphia, PA 19105

1 St. Anne's Road
Eastbourne, East Sussex BN21 3UN, England

1 Goldthorne Avenue
Toronto, Ontario M8Z 5T9, Canada

Student Manual for
PSYCHOLOGY: Understanding Behavior                ISBN    0-7216-7108-X

Last digit is the print number:  9  8  7  6  5  4  3  2

To our wives

Laurie and Sandra

and our children

Christopher, Leigh, and Jessica

## ACKNOWLEDGEMENTS

This project benefitted greatly from the many suggestions of Baxter Venable, the psychology editor of W. B. Saunders. His help and cooperation in all phases of this project was invaluable and is greatly appreciated. Thanks are also due to Karen Cartier for her diligence and care in typing the manual and to Duane Martin for reading and commenting on the Study Tips section of the Preface.

PREFACE

## PURPOSE OF THE STUDENT'S MANUAL

This student manual has a number of aims. It is designed to help you in studying the text material, reviewing this material, and in checking your comprehension of it. It is not meant as a substitute for reading your text, but as an aid in mastering the text material. Most of the important points covered in the text are covered in the student's manual, but it was obviously not possible to cover all of the facts, ideas, and perspectives presented by the text. However, we do feel that your conscientious use of the student's manual along with careful study of your text, should help you do well in the course. We will now turn to a more detailed discussion of how to use the manual, and then consider some tips on how to improve your studying.

## HOW TO USE THE STUDENT'S MANUAL

### Learning Objectives: What You Should Know

This section indicates the major points covered by the chapter. You should examine it carefully before reading your chapter so that you will be mentally "ready" for the material. Keep the objectives in front of you while you are reading. As suggested in the study tip section, you may want to turn these objectives into questions and try to answer them as you read. You should return to these objectives as part of your review sessions and try to write out the information required by the objectives. This is especially important preparation if your instructor uses essay questions, because it should help you prepare for those kinds of questions.

### Study Tips: A Helping Hand

This section should also be read prior to reading the chapter in your text. Sometimes the study tips point out some sections in the chapter which you may find somewhat difficult, and may suggest ways in which these sections and others in the chapter should be approached. At other times, we may simply remind you of the best way to master the material in the chapter or suggest some memory aids.

### Step-By-Step: A Guided Review

This is the longest and most important section of the manual. It is designed to help you master the important concepts and facts in the textbook. Unlike some programmed manuals, this review is not designed as a substitute for reading the text. You should read the appropriate chapter prior to using the review. After you have read the chapter or a major section of it, go to the Guided Review in order to check on your knowledge of the material. This is very important. Studies have shown that material that is reviewed or rehearsed immediately after reading it is remembered much better than material which was not so rehearsed.

In using your Guided Review, you should employ the following procedures. You will notice that the review contains numerous blank spaces with the appropriate answers in the margin to the right. These answers should be covered while you are reviewing. Mentally fill in the blanks, then check your answers. In many cases, your answers should be exactly the same as those in the margin (such as names of techniques, parts of the body, scientists, etc.), but in other cases a word of similar meaning to the one in the margin will do. Do not write the word in the spaces provided since you will need to use this review section again later. Write in the spaces only if it is your last time to use the review section. One purpose of this review section is to get you actively involved in learning the material. Active learning has been found to be more beneficial than mere passive reading of material. If you have trouble with some of the material in the review make a note of this and go back to the text for further study of the appropriate sections. Items on which you make mistakes should also be noted by marking in margins so that you can go back to the text and check on the correct answers and make sure you won't make those mistakes the next time. The Guided Review should be used to review the material again several times before the exam and can, along with additional readings of the chapter, be used as a final review for an examination.

## A Personal Quiz

This is a multiple choice quiz that should be similar in form to the ones used by your instructor. It is intended primarily to be used by you prior to your class exam to check on your knowledge of the text material. Do not use this quiz until you are just about finished with your studies for the exam but still have a little time left for review. If you do well on the Personal Quiz, you probably have mastered the material quite well and should do well on your exam. If you miss four or more items on the quiz you will probably need to do more study. Page numbers are provided to help you locate the part of the chapter to which the item refers. Do not rely only on this quiz to assess your readiness for the exam. You should also have mastered the Learning Objectives, the Guided Review, and the Key Concepts and Terms.

## Key Concepts and Terms

One of your more difficult tasks in mastering the material in your textbook is learning the meaning of various concepts and terms. Most chapters contain a large number of these, and we have included most of them in this section. This section should be used after you have gained a pretty good grasp of the text material. In the space provided you should write either the appropriate definition or the appropriate description of the concept or term. Text page numbers are provided so that you can check on the accuracy of your answers. The Glossary in the back of your text will also contain many of these terms and their meanings.

## Psychology in Action: Projects and Demonstrations

This section will present several projects or demonstrations which you may want to carry out on your own, with friends, or as part of a class exercise. The first project in this section is usually an elaboration of the project described in the Psychology in Action box in your text. This section of the manual will provide extra details on how to carry out the project and in most cases will provide forms for you to use. These forms can simply be torn from this manual along the perforation. The other projects suggest additional activities which are related to the text material. Forms are also provided for many of these projects.

# SOME STUDY TIPS

In the psychology course for which you have enrolled, inevitably some students will do quite well and others will do poorly. This fact often leads us to assume that these students just differ in their intelligence or intellectual ability. While this may be the case to some extent, a large portion of these differences in performance is probably due to differences in the way in which students approach their studies. Some are not motivated to work hard and so spend little time in actual study. Others may spend a lot of time studying but may have bad study habits. Let's briefly discuss how each of these two problems can be overcome.

## Motivation to Learn

Unless you are motivated to learn or do well in a course, you are not likely to perform well in the course even if you have all of the best study habits. There are of course many obvious reasons to be motivated to do well in a course. Personal satisfaction at doing well, approval from your instructors, and the benefits derived from good grades (e.g., getting good jobs or gaining entrance to graduate or professional schools) are often sufficient to motivate many students. If these factors are not important to you (and even if they are) you should try to learn to derive satisfaction from the learning itself. The discovery of new ideas and facts and the mastery of new concepts is often a source of pleasure in itself. You can probably increase the satisfaction derived from the learning by relating these facts, ideas, and concepts to your everyday life.

## Study Habits

Let's assume you are highly motivated to do well in a course. You should now be strongly interested in the most efficient way to study. One of the important factors is where you study. It's important to study in a quiet area that is free from outside distractions and interruptions. A quiet corner in the library may do. Your own room may also be fine, if you can control your roommates and/or friends. Set up definite study periods and make others respect these. Make sure your desk is not cluttered with distracting material. You can listen to light instrumental music but avoid programs which involve talking. Do not study by the TV. It is best to study in the same place each time so that it will become a habit when you are there (don't do anything else there except study!). Also be sure you have good lighting. It is best to have your light off to the side so as to minimize glare.

The next problem is how to study. One concern is how long you should study at one time. All of us have a span of concentration. Some of us can study for hours without a break. Others feel the need for a break after 10 minutes of study. In general it is best not to study too long at one time since fatigue will set in and you won't be accomplishing very much anyway. So be sure to take breaks at appropriate times. You may need one every hour or every half-hour, or even every 15 minutes. In fact you can use these to reward yourself for studying certain amounts of material (see p. 119 in your text). Decide how much material you plan to cover before taking a break. Then make sure you finish this material before you do take the break.

Another way of scheduling that will help your study is to study different subjects during your study session. This will prevent you from getting bored with one kind of study and will help you avoid retroactive interference (see p. 158 in your text) due to the previous study of similar material. Another important factor is your technique of study. One of the most widely used and tested methods of study is the $SQR_3$ method (Robinson, 1970). This method involves five steps: Survey, Question, Read, Recite, and Review.

Survey

When you first begin with a chapter, glance through the entire chapter briefly to note the major topics covered. Use the headings contained in the chapters since they indicate the major points of the chapter. Also read the summary at the end of the chapter. Now you will know what you will have to learn in the chapter, and how to organize the material as you read it. You may want to study one section before going on to the next, especially if a section contains a lot of information.

Question

As you now read through the chapter, turn the headings into questions. This will give you an active and receptive set as you read through each section. An active learning set is very important in improving your learning. Also be sure to look at the Learning Objectives section of the manual for additional questions.

Read

Next you should read the material in the text to answer the questions you now have. Do not read as if you were reading a novel, but read as if preparing for a test (which of course you are!). Read in order to remember the material at a later time. Make sure to read everything as you go along. Don't omit the graphs, tables, and boxes since they are important additions to your chapter.

Recite

As you finish each section, you should see if you now can answer the questions you asked yourself at the beginning. You can do this verbally or by briefly jotting down the major points of the section. Then go back and see if you were correct. As you go through the chapter you may want to go back and recite the major points of each section. Recitation is also designed to make you an active and involved learner. It is one of the most important of the study techniques and should take up a good part of your study time (e.g., one-third to one-half). Continue to question, read, and recite until you finish the chapter.

Review

After you have finished the chapter, you should review all of the material immediately. You can use your notes of the main topics or the main headings for this. Try to briefly summarize the major points of each of these sections. This should take only 10 minutes or so. This review is very important. If material is not reviewed immediately, much of it is soon forgotten. This review should be repeated at spaced intervals (e.g., every few days) and just prior to the examination. Your reviews should consist of both recitation and re-reading of the material, depending on your level of mastery.

We have only been able to make a few suggestions on how to improve your studying. If you have serious difficulties with your studies or reading, you should try to take a study skills and reading course. Many colleges and universities offer such courses, and they may be well worth the required investment of time. You should also periodically come back to this section to remind yourself about the study techniques. However, if you follow the above study suggestions carefully, you won't need to be reminded and you should find yourself doing better than ever in your course work. Good luck!

Paul B. Paulus
University of Texas at Arlington

Robert A. Baron
Purdue University

REFERENCE

Robinson, F.P.: Effective Study. Harper & Row Publishers, New York, 1970.

# TABLE OF CONTENTS

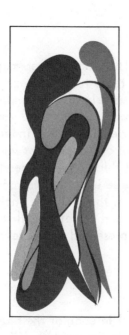

# Chapter 1

# PSYCHOLOGY:
Understanding
Behavior

## LEARNING OBJECTIVES: WHAT YOU SHOULD KNOW

After reading this chapter you should:

Be able to describe the historical development of psychology.

Be able to discuss the differences and similarities of structuralism, functionalism, and behaviorism.

Be able to discuss what psychologists do.

Know the basic features and the advantages and disadvantages of the experimental and correlational approaches to research.

Know some of the problems one encounters in trying to do reliable and valid research.

## STUDY TIPS: A HELPING HAND

This chapter should be relatively easy for you. There are not too many difficult concepts or theories, and there are a relatively small number of terms to remember. This chapter is very important, however, in that the subsequent chapters rely on your understanding of the concepts and issues considered within the introductory chapter. Be sure you understand the nature of the experimental method and the concepts of dependent and independent variable. Many students find the distinctions between independent and dependent variables confusing. To help remember the distinction between the two, just think of the dependent variable as being the factor whose value or level depends on what the experimenter does or manipulates (the independent variable). A thorough understanding of the problems encountered in interpreting the meaning of the results of both experimental and correlational studies is also important to enable a critical analysis of the research to be presented in the textbook.

## STEP-BY-STEP: A GUIDED REVIEW

After you have read the chapter, mentally fill in each of the blanks in the following section while covering the answers in the margin. Check your answer with that in the margin as you go along. While in many cases your answer should be the same as that in the margin, in other cases a word of similar meaning is acceptable. Do not write in the spaces until you are doing your final review.

1.  The idea of a scientific field of psychology did not take firm root until the end of the _____ century. Whether a field of study is considered scientific depends not on the topics under investigation but on the approach taken. This approach involves the use of _____ _____ and _____ _____ .

    nineteenth

    systematic obser-
    tion, direct ex-
    perimentation

2. The first psychology laboratory was established by _____   Wundt
   in _____. He held that the major task of psychology   1879
   was to analyze the contents of consciousness in order to
   determine the _____ of the mind. This   structure
   approach is called _____. The   structuralism
   method employed for this was _____.   introspection
   Wundt concluded that the mind is composed of three simple
   elements: _____, _____,   sensations, images,
   and _____.   feelings

3. Several groups of psychologists rebelled against this
   structuralist approach. One group emphasized that the
   functions of the mind and not its structure should be the
   object of study in psychology. This approach is called
   _____. Another approach proposed   functionalism
   that the proper subject matter for psychology was obser-
   vable behavior rather than unobservable conscious experiences.
   This approach is called _____ and was   behaviorism
   initially proposed by _____ and emphasized the   Watson
   use of direct _____ and controlled   experimentation
   _____.   observation

4. Physicians who, after completing their medical studies,
   specialize in the treatment of mental disorders are called
   _____. Psychologists receive their   psychiatrists
   training in departments of psychology, where some of them
   specialize in the study and treatment of mental disorders.
   This specialty is called _____ psychology.   clinical
   The principles governing the basic psychological processes
   are the primary concern of _____   experimental
   psychologists. Most psychologists are employed in
   _____ settings.   academic

5. The most powerful research technique of the psychologist is
   the _____ method. This   experimental
   method involves the systematic manipulation of the presence
   of strength of a particular factor (e.g., heat, shock, mood,
   etc.). The factor which is varied is called the
   _____ _____,   independent variable
   while the behavior which is studied is termed the
   _____ _____.   dependent variable

6. A research idea or suggestion is often termed a _____.   hypothesis
   A systematic set of assumptions regarding the causes and
   nature of a particular behavior is called a _____.   theory

7. When a psychologist conducts an experiment in which several different factors are varied at once, he/she can determine whether the effects of one factor are influenced by another. In other words, the possibility of _____ between the independent variables can be examined.

interaction

8. In order to determine whether a particular finding of differences between experimental groups is real, an experimenter may try to repeat or _____ the experiment, and he/she typically subjects the data to _____ analysis.

replicate

statistical

9. In generalizing the results from such research beyond the laboratory, it is important that the subjects employed constitute a _____ sample of the group to which generalizations are to be made.

representative

10. Another problem which can invalidate experimental results is that changes in behavior can be induced by events which accompany but are actually unrelated to the independent variables of interest. This problem is called the _____ effect. It is also possible for experimenters to accidentally communicate their expectation or hypothesis to the subject and thus produce results which are not a result of the independent variables but of the reactions of the subjects to the communicated information. This problem is often termed

_____ _____.

placebo

demand characteristics

11. The method which involves the observation of naturally occurring variations in two or more variables to determine whether they tend to occur together is called the _____ method. The strength of the observed relationship is often expressed statistically as a _____ _____.

correlational

correlation coefficient

12. When increments in one factor are accompanied by increments in the other, a _____ correlation coefficient is obtained. When increments in one variable are accompanied by decrements in another, a _____ correlation will be obtained. Correlation coefficients can range from _____ to _____.

positive

negative

+1.0, -1.0

13. The major problem with correlation is its lack of specificity as to the existence or nature of the _____ link. It is often difficult, if not impossible, to determine if an obtained correlation is due to the effect of one of the variables on the other or to a third underlying variable. This problem is demonstrated in the figure on the next page.

causal

FIGURE 1-11  Recent studies have shown that the more coffee individuals drink, the more likely they are to suffer heart attacks. Because these findings are of a correlational rather than experimental nature, they are open to at least three possible interpretations: (A) coffee drinking is a direct cause of heart attacks, (B) susceptibility to heart attacks somehow causes individuals to drink more coffee, and (C) the relationship between coffee drinking and heart attacks stems from the fact that both are related to an over-active life style (people who drink a lot of coffee also tend to worry, stay up late, over-work, etc.). While interpretation (C) seems most reasonable, (A) cannot be entirely ruled out. Interpretation (B) appears to make very little sense.

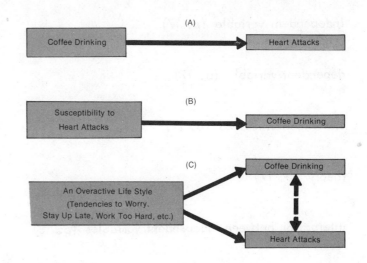

Figure 1 - 11

14. The study of a single person in great depth and detail in an attempt to uncover the roots of his or her current behavior is called the _____ _____ method.        case study
    However it is very difficult to reach any valid and general conclusions from such studies without additional experimental research.  Two additional techniques often employed in conjunction with correlational and experimental methods
    are _____ and _____.        surveys, tests

15. Animals are used in experimentation for a variety of reasons. One reason is that some types of research may be ethically or practically impossible to run with humans.


KEY CONCEPTS AND TERMS

        After you have finished your Guided Review, fill in the meaning of the following terms in your own words.  Check on your accuracy by consulting your text on the pages indicated or the Glossary.

structuralism  (p. 9)


functionalism  (p. 10)


behaviorism  (p. 10)


psychiatrist  (p. 13)

5

independent variable  (p. 17)

dependent variable  (p. 17)

experimental method  (p. 17)

theory  (p. 17)

interaction between independent variables  (p. 18)

representative sample  (p. 21)

placebo effect  (p. 22)

demand characteristics  (p. 24)

correlation coefficient  (p. 25)

A PERSONAL QUIZ

After you are about finished with your studies but still have some time left for review, take this quiz to check on your mastery. Fill in your answers in the spaces provided and after you are finished check their correctness with the answers provided.

____ 1.  Which of the following statements about the study of human behavior is considered correct by the authors of the text?  (p. 7-8)
   a.  psychology is simply a substitute for common sense
   b.  human behavior is an insoluble puzzle
   c.  human behavior is basically lawful
   d.  the scientific study of behavior has been around since the 15th century

____ 2.  The characteristics which define a field as scientific are  (p. 8)

   a.  systematic observation and direct experimentation
   b.  the topics under investigation
   c.  the use of particular scientific procedures and equipment
   d.  the use of naturalistic observation

____ 3.  The first psychological laboratory was established by Wundt in (p.8)
   a.  1910
   b.  1859
   c.  1815
   d.  1879

4. Wundt was the founder of structuralism which involved the determination of the structure of the mind employing the method of (p. 9)
   a. naturalistic observation
   b. observation of behavior
   c. introspection
   d. experimentation

5. The structuralists concluded that the mind was made up of all but one of the following elements: (p. 9)
   a. cognitions
   b. sensations
   c. images
   d. feelings

6. The approach in psychology which emphasizes the direct observation of overt actions instead of the study of conscious experience is called (p. 10)
   a. functionalism
   b. behaviorism
   c. empiricism
   d. structuralism

7. The founder of behaviorism was (p. 10)
   a. Skinner
   b. James
   c. Freud
   d. Watson

8. Which of the following statements about psychologists is false? (p. 13-16)
   a. psychologists have very diverse activities
   b. most psychologists are employed in academic settings
   c. a psychiatrist is a psychologist who specializes in treatment of mental disorders
   d. it is expected that there will be about 40,000 psychologists in the U.S. in the late 1970's

9. The most powerful tool of the research psychologist is the (p. 17)
   a. correlational study
   b. experimental method
   c. survey
   d. case study

10. In an experiment, the variable which is varied is called the _____ variable, while the behavior which is studied is called the _____ variable. (p. 17)
    a. independent, dependent
    b. dependent, independent
    c. control, observed
    d. stimulus, response

11. If one finds in an experiment that the presence of one factor influences the effects of the other, one has obtained a(n) _____ between the independent variables (p. 18)
    a. confounding
    b. relationship
    c. interaction
    d. correlation

12. Which of the following procedures would not enhance the reliability and validity of the results of an experiment? (p. 21-24)
    a. replication
    b. eliminating possible placebo effects
    c. representative sampling
    d. enhancing demand characteristics

13. When changes in behavior are induced by events which accompany but are unrelated to the manipulated independent variables one has obtained a(n) (p. 22)
    a. placebo effect
    b. demand characteristic effect
    c. experimenter bias effect
    d. valid result

14. When increased levels of one factor are accompanied by increased levels of another, one will obtain (p. 25)
    a. a negative correlation
    b. no correlation
    c. an increasing correlation
    d. a positive correlation

15. If one finds a positive correlation between degree of coffee drinking and the likelihood of heart attacks, one can conclude that (p. 26-27)
    a. coffee drinking causes heart attacks
    b. individuals prone to heart attacks are predisposed to drink a lot of coffee
    c. an active life style of certain people leads to both increased coffee drinking and an increased chance of heart attack
    d. none of the above

Answers:

| | | |
|---|---|---|
| 1. c | 6. b | 11. c |
| 2. a | 7. d | 12. d |
| 3. d | 8. c | 13. a |
| 4. c | 9. b | 14. d |
| 5. a | 10. a | 15. d |

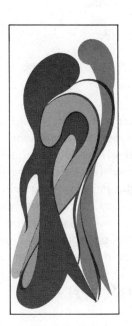

Chapter 2

# BIOLOGICAL BASES OF BEHAVIOR:
## A Look Beneath the Surface

## LEARNING OBJECTIVES: WHAT YOU SHOULD KNOW

After reading this chapter you should:

Know the basic characteristics of the neuron and how it works.

Be familiar with the different parts of the nervous system and their functions.

Be able to sketch the various parts of the brain and know what the functions of these parts are.

Be able to discuss the research on the split brain and its implications.

Know how eating and drinking behavior is controlled.

Be able to discuss the two different states of sleep and their characteristics and functions.

Know how the brain is involved in the control of emotions.

Be able to categorize the various drugs and their effects.


## STUDY TIPS: A HELPING HAND

This chapter is usually somewhat difficult for most students. Not only do you have to learn a lot of terms, but you also have to know the functions of the various structures of the nervous system and the brain. Learning this material will require frequent rehearsal of the chapter content. This fact makes the use of the manual (especially the Guided Review) doubly important. We have included almost all of the important material in this review. You should read the chapter in the text several times, employing rehearsal extensively, especially the second time. Next, work through the Guided Review repeatedly until you think you have mastered the material. Then try to complete the Key Concepts and Terms and take the Personal Quiz. One part of the chapter that you should pay some special attention to is the section on how neurons work. This chapter also provides a good occasion for the use of memory aids such as mnemonic devices as discussed in Chapter 5.


## STEP-BY-STEP: A GUIDED REVIEW

After you have read the chapter, mentally fill in each of the blanks in the following section while covering the answers in the margin. Check your answer with that in the margin as you go along. While in many cases your answer should be the same as that in the margin, in other cases a word of similar meaning is acceptable. Do not write in the spaces until you are doing your final review.

1.  The basic building blocks of the nervous system are called the
    _____. They generally possess three basic parts:     neurons
    the _____ _____, an _____ and several     cell body, axon
    _____.     dendrites

2. In many neurons the axon is covered by fatty material known
as _____ _____. The sheath is      myelin sheath
interrupted at several points by small gaps called _____      nodes
of _____.      Ranvier

3. Near its end the axon divides into several small branches known
as _____. These branches end in      telodendria
round structures known as _____ _____.      synaptic terminals

4. Can you locate the various parts of the neuron described above
on the figure below? If you're not sure, check the figure in the
text.

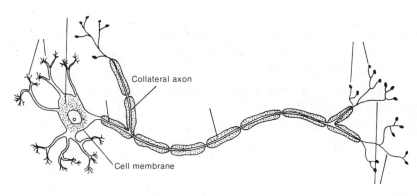

Collateral axon

Cell membrane

FIGURE 2-1  Structure of the neuron. Note the presence of several dendrites, a cell body, and,
in this particular case, one main and one collateral axon. (From Grollman, S.: *The Human Body*.
New York: Macmillan Co., Copyright © 1964.)

5. While the neurons are not actively engaged in transmitting information, the inside of the neuron has a slightly _____      negative
charge, often called _____ _____.      resting potential
This condition results because during such periods positively
charged particles, especially _____ _____,      sodium ions
exist in greater concentration outside the neuron than within it,
while negatively charged particles, especially_____      protein
molecules, exist in greater concentration inside.

6. When the neuron is stimulated in an appropriate fashion, the cell
membrane allows the entrance of a large number of sodium ions,
which results in the interior of the neuron becoming positively
charged. The resulting state is called _____ _____.      action potential
After a brief period of time, the neuron expels the sodium ions
which have entered and returns to its resting potential.

7. The action potential occurs only in an _____      all-or-none
fashion, which means that it either occurs at full strength or
not at all. Also, once the action potential is initiated, its size
and speed are _____ of the strength of the      independent
stimulus which evoked it.

8. Adjacent neurons approach each other closely in a region known as the _____. They pass information from one another across a narrow _____ _____.

synapse

synaptic cleft

9. When a neuron is stimulated, the action potential travels along its surface to the telodendria and _____ terminals. At this point the information is transmitted by complex physiological-chemical processes across the _____ _____. The synaptic terminals contain round structures known as synaptic _____ which empty chemicals known as _____ _____ into the synapse. When these transmitter substances reach the membrane of the second cell, they may either stimulate an action potential in this cell if they are _____ in nature, or they may make the conduction of an action potential more difficult if they are _____ in nature. The above communication process is depicted in the figure below.

synaptic

synaptic cleft

vesicles

transmitter substances

excitatory

inhibitory

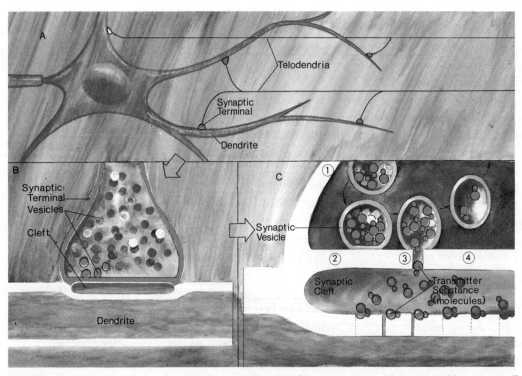

FIGURE 2-3 Communication across the synapse. (A) Several telodendria approaching the cell body or dendrites of a neuron. (B) A close-up view of the synapse showing a single synaptic terminal filled with synaptic vesicles. (C) A single *synaptic vesicle* (1) approaching the cell membrane, (2) reaching it, (3) releasing its contents *(transmitter substance)* into the synapse, and (4) returning to the interior of the cell. (After Eccles, 1965, pp. 58-62.)

10. The neurons are organized into a highly complex and special-
    ized system called the _____ _____.           nervous system
    This system can be divided into two portions, the
    _____ and the _____           peripheral, central
    systems. The peripheral system consists of bundles of axons
    or _____ and serves to conduct information             nerves
    from receptors to the central nervous system.

11. Some of the nerves in the peripheral system are concerned with
    the regulation of skeletal muscles, while others form a system
    which is concerned with the regulation of glands and internal
    organs and is called the _____ nervous system.         autonomic

12. The component of the autonomic system concerned with the
    readying of the body for vigorous physical activity is the
    _____ division. The                     parasympathetic
    portion of the autonomic system which has the opposite
    effect and stimulates internal processes of bodily restoration
    or regeneration is the _____ division.          sympathetic

13. The basic components of the central nervous system are the
    _____ and the _____.                  spinal cord, brain
    The basic function of the spinal cord is to conduct sensory
    information from the receptors (eyes and ears) to the brain
    and motor impulses from the brain to effectors (muscles and
    glands) by means of collections of axons or _____       white
    _____. The central portion of the spinal               matter
    cord consists of _____ matter and is concerned          gray
    with the regulation of spinal _____ (e.g.,              reflexes
    knee-jerks).

14. The brain consists of a variety of structures. Can you
    identify these structures on the schematic diagram below?
    Check the figure in your text if necessary.

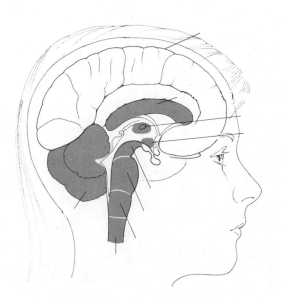

FIGURE 2-5 Basic structure of the human
brain. Note that in this illustration, the brain
has been split in two (just as you might slice
an apple from the stem to the bottom), and
you are looking at the inner surface of one of
the two halves. (For a color photo of an
actual brain, see Plate 4.)

15. The medulla and the pons are a continuation of the spinal
cord. In addition, both of these structures contain the

_____        reticular activating

system which plays a crucial role in sleep and arousal. The
medulla also contains several _____ which        nuclei
regulate vital processes such as breathing and the beating
of the heart.

16. The _____ is involved in the regu-        cerebellum
lation of motor activities. The _____        midbrain
contains an extension of the reticular activating system
and primitive centers for vision and hearing.

17. The diencephalon encompasses both the _____        hypothalamus
and the _____. The _____        thalamus, hypothala-
is involved in the regulation of emotional reactions, sexual        mus
behavior, eating and drinking, and control of body temperature. The thalamus is involved in transmitting sensory
information from lower regions of the brain to the

_____        _____.        cerebral hemispheres

18. The lymbic system is primarily concerned with the occurrence
of _____ reactions.        emotional

19. The cerebral hemispheres are quite large in man compared to
more primitive organisms. The surface of the hemispheres or
the _____ is folded into ridges or grooves called        cortex
fissures

_____.

20. The cortex can be divided into four distinct regions or lobes.
Can you identify these on the schematic below?

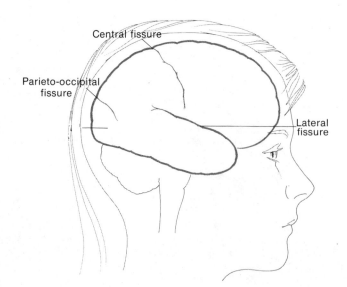

FIGURE 2-6 The cerebral cortex, showing
the location of the frontal, parietal, occipital,
and temporal lobes. (Note that the structures
shown in Figure 2-5 cannot be seen because
they are covered by the cortex.) (Adapted
from Grossman, 1973.)

21. The frontal lobe contains the _____      primary
_____ area which is concerned with the control      motor
of movement of various parts of the body. The parietal lobe
contains the primary somatic projection area which mediates
sensations from the _____. Damage to either of these      skin
two areas will result in only a partial loss of the related
functions since the brain appears to have a number of backup
systems for these same functions.

22. The occipital lobe and temporal lobe contain areas concerned
with _____ and _____,      vision, hearing
respectively.

23. The _____ areas of the brain appear      association
to be involved in complex cognitive processes (e.g., thinking
and memory).

24. Research on the split brain in which the _____      corpus
_____ has been severed suggests that there      callosum
may be a partial division of labor between the two cerebral
hemispheres with the left one superior in _____      verbal
tasks and the right one superior in the regulation of
_____ or motor abilities.      spatial

25. In one study by Gazzaniga it was found that if pictures or
words reached only the _____ hemisphere, subjects      right
were not able to read the words or identify the objects. However, they were able to select the appropriate object from an
array of objects by means of _____.      touch

26. Early research demonstrated that sensory information from the
stomach _____ (is/is not) essential to the control of      is not
eating. Instead the _____ appears      hypothalamus
to be involved in the regulation of food intake.

27. An area located in the _____ hypothalamus      lateral
appears to operate as a feeding center, initiating and facilitating food intake. Destruction of this region results in disturbances in eating behavior which are permanent and
irreversible.

28. The satiety or inhibitory center is contained in the
_____ hypothalamus. Lesions in      ventromedial
this area produce excessive eating or _____,      hyperphagia
which continues until the organism becomes greatly overweight.
Further, these animals will overeat only if their food is
_____, and they often refuse to work for food.      tasty

29. Although the above evidence suggests the existence of discrete feeding and satiety centers in the hypothalamus which facilitate and inhibit eating behavior in a direct manner, recent research has suggested some alternative possibilities. Some evidence suggests that eating is controlled by a diffuse system of neural pathways connecting _____ _____, while other research suggests that the regions of the hypothalamus function to set a _____ around which the body weight will be regulated. Damage to the ventromedial hypothalamus seems to _____ this setting, while damage to the lateral hypothalamus seems to _____ this setting, resulting in reduced food intake.

many systems

point

raise

lower

30. A second mechanism which seems to play an important role in obesity concerns the type of _____ which elicit eating behavior. Schachter has done a series of experiments which suggest that obese individuals have many similarities to rats whose ventromedial hypothalamus have been lesioned, in that they are _____ (more/less) sensitive to the taste of food than normals, are _____ (more/less) willing to work for food, and eat larger meals and eat more quickly than those of normal weight. One reason for overeating in rats and humans may reside in their inability to inhibit _____ ways of responding (such as eating).

cues

more

less

habitual

31. Drinking behavior seems to be largely regulated by the _____ in the _____ hypothalamus. These cells appear to be sensitive to changes in the level of water moving through their membranes, and feelings of thirst derive from their reactions to the reduction in the level of water in the body.

osmoreceptors, lateral

32. There appear to be two different states of sleep. The initial state of sleep involves _____ _____ or NREM sleep. This sleep state consists of four stages involving a gradual brain activity change from fast low magnitude _____ waves to a slower and higher magnitude _____ waves.

nonrapid eye movement

alpha

delta

33. The next sleep state is called _____ _____ or REM sleep. The electrical activity of the brain during this state resembles that of the _____ stage of NREM sleep, suggesting that the individual is close to a waking state. The _____ pattern is also interrupted by sudden bursts of high magnitude activity accompanied by rapid eye movements.

rapid eye movement

first
EEG

or electroencephelograph

34. REM sleep is also accompanied by _____ increased
(increased/decreased) muscular relaxation and
_____(increased/decreased) variations increased
in respiration and blood pressure. REM sleep alternates
with NREM sleep, with the duration of REM sleep
_____(increasing/decreasing) toward increasing
the end of the sleeping period.

35. Research has suggested that NREM sleep serves primarily a
restorative role in that many proteins and _____
appear to be synthesized during this sleep state. REM sleep RNA
may have a variety of functions. It may benefit regions
which would be harmed by long periods of deep (NREM)
sleep; it may help maintain _____ and in- memory
formation processing capacity; or it may provide the
nervous system the opportunity to recover from _____ stress
or _____. anxiety

36. The _____ _____ reticular activating
system seems to function as a waking center in that it produces
and maintains wakefulness. Sleep appears to be induced by
direct inhibition of the RAS system by _____ sleep
_____. The one primarily involved with centers
NREM sleep is the nuclei of _____. A second raphe
center is located in the _____ and seems to regulate pons
REM sleep.

37. Evidence _____(has/has not) supported the Freudian has not
notion that dreams serve as a safety valve for the release of
unacceptible wishes or impulses. Most dreams are quite
consistent with the waking behavior, thoughts, and needs of
the dreamers. There is some evidence that dreaming plays a
role in _____ _____ problem solving
and can be responsible for positive shifts in mood.

38. The control and integration of emotional reactions seems to
be centered primarily in the _____ hypothalamus
and the _____system (e.g., amygdala, limbic
hippocampus, septal area).

39. Destruction of the hypothalamus or its electrical stimulation
seems to produce a(n) _____ (increase/ increase
decrease) in emotional reactivity (such as aggressive behavior).
Removal of some limbic structures (e.g., the amygdala and
parts of the hippocampus) leads to a dramatic _____ reduction
(increase/reduction) in emotional reactivity (aggression and
fear) but a(n) _____(increase/decrease) increase
in sex. Destruction of the septal area produces heightened
emotional reactions.

40. Research by Olds and others has shown that direct electrical stimulation of certain portions of the brain have a powerfully _____ effect. The exact explanation for this effect remains unclear. Evidence suggests that such brain stimulation may in fact elicit feelings of _____ _____, _____ and _____. Possibly the arousal of such appetites by brain stimulation may in itself be rewarding, or brain stimulation may alternatively increase and decrease these feelings. The decrement in these feelings may be the rewarding element.

rewarding

sexual stimulation, hunger thirst

41. Drugs which increase the rate of neural activity and increase the tempo of many bodily functions are called _____. Some examples of this type of drug are _____, _____ and _____. They appear to work by stimulation of neurons in the _____ nervous system or by facilitating the release of _____ _____ at the synapse.

stimulants.
caffeine
nicotine, amphetamines
sympathetic
transmitter
substances

42. Alcohol is considered to be a _____. Although its consumption leads to an initial lowering of _____, increase consumption leads to drowsiness and loss of motor control. _____ are stronger depressants which lead to the slowing of mental and physical activity, feelings of drowsiness, and a lack of motor coordination.

depressant

inhibitions
Barbiturates

43. Substances which help fight pain are called _____. More powerful and addictive pain relievers such as _____ (e.g., heroin) seem to produce their effects by reducing responsivity of certain cells in the nervous system to pain and by affecting the activity in the brain in such a way that the experience of pain is no longer as unpleasant as usual.

analgesics

opiates

44. _____ drugs such as marijuana are used to produce positive shifts in mood. Marijuana is also reported by its users to increase absorption in one's activities, produce seemingly important insights, slow the perception of _____, and lead to increased enjoyment of _____. The exact effects appear _____ (to/not to) depend on the social context or the personality of the user.

Euphoric

time, eating
to

45. A famous artificial hallucinogenic drug is _____. Some of the effects of LSD are increased saturation of colors, _____ in the movement and shape of objects, a

LSD

change

sense of timelessness, _____ of thought          disordering
processes, and a blending of the senses known as _____ .   synesthesia
The phenomenon of synesthesia may be due to the stimulation
of neurons in the brain which connect the various senses but are
usually inactive.

46.  Studies of the effects of transcendental meditation or TM have
     found that such meditation produced physiological changes
     suggestive of reduced _____ .  Some      emotionality/anxiety
     of these changes are a(n)_____ (increase/         increase
     decrease) in alpha waves, a(n)_____                increase
     (increase/decrease) in skin resistance, and a drop in rate of
     respiration.  Other research has found that TM users have an
     increased ability to freely express their feelings and increased
     capacity for intimate contact with others, as well as a tendency
     to give up the use of drugs.

KEY CONCEPTS AND TERMS

         After you have finished your Guided Review, fill in the meaning of the
         following terms in your own words.  Check on your accuracy by con-
         sulting your text on the pages indicated or in the Glossary.

neurons (p. 38)


axon (p. 38)


dendrites (p. 38)


myelin sheath (p. 38)


nodes of Ranvier (p. 38)


telodendria (p. 38)


synaptic terminals (p. 38)


resting potential (p. 38)


action potential (p. 39)

synaptic cleft  (p. 40)

synaptic vesicles  (p. 40)

transmitter substances  (p. 40)

peripheral nervous system  (p. 42)

central nervous system  (p. 42)

autonomic nervous system  (p. 42)

parasympathetic division  (p. 42)

sympathetic division  (p. 42)

spinal cord  (p. 42)

white matter  (p. 43)

gray matter  (p. 43)

medulla  (p. 43)

pons  (p. 43)

reticular activating system  (p. 43)

cerebellum  (p. 43)

midbrain  (p. 43)

hypothalamus  (p. 44)

thalamus  (p. 44)

cerebral hemispheres  (p. 45)

cortex  (p. 45)

frontal lobe  (p. 45)

parietal lobe  (p. 46)

occipital lobe  (p. 46)

temporal lobe  (p. 46)

association areas  (p. 46)

split brain  (p. 46)

lateral hypothalamus  (p. 50)

ventromedial hypothalamus  (p. 50)

hyperphagia  (p. 50)

osmoreceptors  (p. 54)

REM sleep  (p. 55)

NREM sleep  (p. 55)

nuclei of raphe  (p. 58)

pleasure centers  (p. 63-64)

2  1

stimulants (p. 66)

depressants (p. 66-67)

euphoric drugs (p. 67)

analgesics (p. 67)

synesthesia (p. 69)

transcendental meditation (p. 69-72)

## A PERSONAL QUIZ

    After you are about finished with your studies but still have some time left for review, take this quiz to check on your mastery. Fill in your answers in the spaces provided and after you are finished check their correctness with the answers provided.

___ 1. The three basic parts of neurons are (p. 38)
    a. vesicles, gray matter, and the synapse
    b. telodendria, nodes of Ranvier, and synaptic terminals
    c. cell body, axon, and dendrites
    d. myelin sheath, cell body, and dendrites

___ 2. The stage in which the neuron has a slightly negative charge is called the (p. 38-39)
    a. dynamic stage
    b. steady-state stage
    c. action potential
    d. resting potential

___ 3. When a neuron is in the action potential stage it has a ____ charge due to the entrance of a large number of ____ into its interior. (p. 39)
    a. positive; sodium ions
    b. negative; protein molecules
    c. positive; protein molecules
    d. negative; sodium ions

___ 4. Information between adjacent neurons is passed across a (p. 40)
    a. transmitter cleft
    b. vesicle
    c. synaptic terminal
    d. synaptic cleft

___ 5. The chemicals which are emptied into the synapse by the synaptic terminals are called (p. 40)
    a. sodium ions
    b. transmitter substances
    c. protein molecules
    d. synaptic stimulants

___ 6. The portion of the nervous system concerned with the regulation of glands and internal organs is called the ____ nervous system. (p. 42)
    a. autonomic
    b. central

c. peripheral
d. somatic

___ 7. The component of the autonomic nervous system concerned with readying the body for vigorous physical activity is the _____ division. (p. 42)
a. central
b. sympathetic
c. parasympathetic
d. somatic

___ 8. Which of the following is not one of the functions of the spinal cord? (p. 42-43)
a. conduction of sensory information from the receptors to the brain
b. stimulating internal processes of bodily regeneration
c. conducting motor impulses from the brain to the muscles and glands
d. the regulation of reflexes

___ 9. The part of the brain concerned with the regulation of motor activities is the (p. 43)
a. cerebellum
b. midbrain
c. medulla
d. diencephalon

___ 10. The part of the brain concerned with the regulation of emotional reactions, sexual behavior, eating and drinking, and body temperature is the (p. 44)
a. cortex
b. midbrain
c. thalamus
d. hypothalamus

___ 11. Which one of the following is not one of the functions served by the various parts of the cerebral hemispheres? (p. 45-46)
a. mediation of sensations from the skin

b. involvement with vision and hearing
c. regulation of sleep
d. involvement with complete cognitive processes

___ 12. Research in which the corpus callosum has been severed suggests that (p. 46-48)
a. the two cerebral hemispheres serve essentially the same function
b. the two cerebral hemispheres perform somewhat different functions
c. the hemispheres control emotional behavior
d. none of the above

___ 13. Some research suggests that the initiation of eating is controlled by the _____, while the cessation of eating is controlled by the _____. (p. 49-51)
a. hypothalamus, ventromedial hypothalamus
b. hypothalamus, frontal lobe
c. thalamus, hypothalamus
d. limbic system, hypothalamus

___ 14. Lesions of the ventromedial hypothalamus produce (p. 50)
a. excessive eating
b. enhanced sociability
c. enhanced motivation
d. none of the above

___ 15. Which of the following is not characteristic of REM sleep? (p. 55-56)
a. increased muscular relaxation
b. increased variations in blood pressure and respiration
c. irregular and high magnitude delta waves
d. presence of low magnitude alpha waves

___ 16. NREM sleep's primary role seems to be (p. 57)

a. maintenance of memory
b. physiological restoration
c. synthesis of sodium ions
d. recovery from stress or anxiety

___ 17. Short sleepers tend to be (p. 57)
a. depressed
b. happy
c. neurotic
d. anxious

___ 18. The part of the brain which seems to function as the waking center is (p. 58)
a. limbic system
b. thalamus
c. reticular activating system
d. frontal lobe

___ 19. Destruction or electrical stimulation of the hypothalamus leads to ___ emotional reactivity; removal of some limbic structures leads to ___ emotionality. (p. 60-61)

a. increased; increased
b. decreased; decreased
c. increased; decreased
d. decreased; increased

___ 20. Alcohol is considered to be (p. 66-67)
a. a depressant
b. an analgesic
c. an euphoric drug
d. a stimulant

Answers:

| | | | |
|---|---|---|---|
| 1. c | 6. a | 11. c | 16. b |
| 2. d | 7. c | 12. b | 17. b |
| 3. a | 8. b | 13. a | 18. c |
| 4. d | 9. a | 14. a | 19. c |
| 5. b | 10. d | 15. c | 20. a |

## PSYCHOLOGY IN ACTION: PROJECTS AND DEMONSTRATIONS

### Remembering Your Dreams

In this exercise you will be recording descriptions of your dreams for six days. Be sure that you will have six days close together on which you can do this. Make sure that someone doesn't interrupt you during the time that you will be doing the recording.

Before retiring for the night place the dream recording forms and a pen near your bed. On the first morning lie quietly for about two minutes after waking (use a watch for this), and let any dreams you may remember pass through your mind. Do not actively try to recall them in great detail, because this may actually cause them to slip away. After the two minutes are up, enter a description of the dreams you recall in the first section of the forms. On the next morning, get up as soon as you awake, and immediately write down a list of all the important things you must do that day. Do this for two minutes (check your watch). Then record a description of your dreams in the same manner on the second section of the form. Continue alternating these procedures for six days, writing the dream descriptions in the appropriate spaces. At the end of six days, go back and look at the details of the dreams on the odd and even days. If activities which occur between your dreams and the recording of them interfere with recall of dreams, you should find that your descriptions were less detailed on the even days (when you made a list of the day's activities) than on the odd days (when you lay quietly in bed). This exercise may thus indicate one reason why we often have forgotten our dreams shortly after we get up.

## Need for Sleep

   Research suggests that sleep may serve as a means of "psychological restoration" by permitting the nervous system to recover from the ill effects of stress and anxiety. For example, it has been found that the need for sleep increases sharply at times when individuals experience stress, depression, or difficult mental activity, but decreases at times when everything is going quite well.

   You might like to see if you can observe the same relationships with your friends. Have 20 of your friends fill out the questionnaire on page 27. (You will need to have some copies made of this form.) Then determine the total number of affirmative responses (yes or stressful) given to items 1, 2, 3 and 5 by those friends who report more need for sleep and by those friends who report less need for sleep. Divide these two totals by the number of friends who fall into each of these two categories. So if you had 8 friends in one group you would divide that total by 8, and the total of the other group by 12. Do your results agree with those of your text?

## Day 1 - Lie Quietly

## Day 2 - Make a List of Activities

## Day 3 - Lie Quietly

## Day 4 – Make a List of Activities

## Day 5 – Lie  Quietly

## Day 6 – Make a List of Activities

# Questionnaire

1.  Have you recently changed jobs?

    yes ____                          no ____

2.  Are you presently experiencing increased physical or mental exertion at work or at home?

    yes ____                          no ____

3.  Are you presently somewhat depressed?

    yes ____                          no ____

4.  Are you presently needing more or less sleep than usual?

    more sleep ____                   less sleep ____

5.  Would you consider your present state of affairs a stressful one, or a time when everything is going well?

    stressful ____                    going well ____

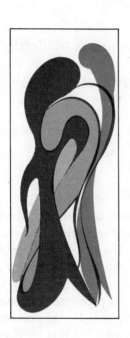

Chapter 3

PERCEPTION:
How the World
Outside
Gets Inside

## LEARNING OBJECTIVES: WHAT YOU SHOULD KNOW

After reading this chapter you should:

Have learned the various structures of the ear and the eye and their functions.

Be able to discuss signal detection theory.

Understand the various characteristics of sound and light energy.

Be familiar with the three major theories of pitch and how they explain the missing fundamental phenomenon.

Be able to discuss the various illusions and their causes.

Be able to discuss the studies which have provided evidence for the dominance of vision over the other senses.

Be familiar with the research on the stabilized image and its implications.

Be able to discuss the various studies on an infant's perception and the conclusions derived from these studies.

Know the different types of extrasensory powers and the results of research on them.

## STUDY TIPS: A HELPING HAND

In this chapter there are many terms to learn and a number of theories which you need to understand. Many of the terms that you need to know are related to the eye and the ear. We have included diagrams to help you with this task. The major theories discussed are signal detection theory, the three theories of pitch (place theory, periodicity pitch theory, and residue theory), and the Young-Helmholtz theory of color vision. Try to understand each of these theories and what they have to say about various perceptual phenomena. The section on the three theories of pitch and their relation to the missing fundamental effect may be somewhat difficult for you. Try to spend some extra time on this section. Again, as discussed in the Preface, the best approach to this chapter is to read it casually for understanding first, then go back and try to memorize the terms and understand the concepts and theories of each individual section of the chapter before going on to the next section. After you are finished going through the chapter for the second time, go to the study guide to check on your grasp of the chapter and for further review and drill. You may also want to employ some mnemonic devices or other memory aids to help with the memorization of lists of terms (see page 170 in the text). For example, the word has could be a reminder for the three parts of the middle ear (hammer, anvil, and stirrup). Also, to remember that cones, but not rods, are responsive to color, simply note that both cones and color start with co.

## STEP-BY-STEP: A GUIDED REVIEW

After you have read the chapter, mentally fill in each of the blanks in the following section while covering the answers in the margin. Check your answer with that in the margin as you go along. While in many cases your answer should be the same as that in the margin, in other cases a word of similar meaning is acceptable. Do not write in the spaces until you are doing your final review.

1. Psychologists call the process of knowing the world outside you by forming some mental impressions of it _____.          perception
Yet there is no direct one-to-one relationship between the image formed by your eye and your perception of that image. Accurate perception may often require a _____          combination
of _____. However, where unreliable cues conflict, the          cues
result is often an _____.          illusion

2. A device which changes energy from one form to another is a
_____.          transducer

3. When light enters your eye it first passes through the _____          cornea
and the _____ _____. The size of the          pupil opening
pupil opening is controlled by the _____ and determines the          iris
sharpness and amount of light allowed. The curvature of the lens
is changed by the _____ muscle. The change in          ciliary
the curvature is called _____ and          accommodation
depends on the distance of the object to be viewed. The lens
bends light rays to focus them on the _____ in the back          retina
of the eye.

4. The two kinds of receptor cells on the retina which respond to
light are _____ and _____. Rods are more sensi-          rods, cones
tive to light than cones, and only _____ can detect          cones
color differences. On the retina the light energy is transduced
by a photochemical process into nerve impulses on the _____          optic
_____.          nerve

5. A small region in the retina which contains only cones is called
the _____. This region allows the greatest perception          fovea
of detail or visual acuity.

6. Can you identify the various structures of the eye on the figure
at the top of the next page?

7. The eardrum or _____ _____          tympanic membrane
separates the external ear from the _____ ear.          middle
The middle ear contains three tiny bones, the _____,          hammer
the _____ and the _____. In conjunction          anvil, stirrup
with the tympanic membranes, these bones amplify the sound
from the external ear into the inner ear. The resulting vibrations
in the fluid of the inner ear are transduced into nerve impulses by
the _____. Hair cells on the _____          cochlea, basilar

31

of the cochlea are responsible for this         membrane
transduction. The various parts of the ear are shown in the
second figure below.

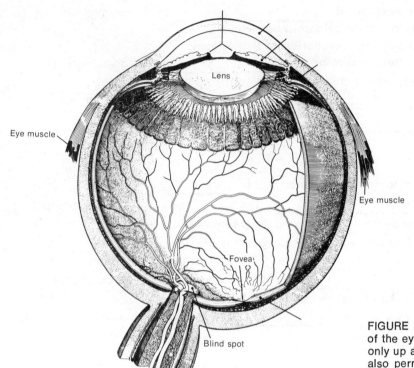

FIGURE 3-3   Looking down at a cross-section
of the eye. The eye muscles move the eye not
only up and down as well as left and right, but
also permit a limited amount of twisting. The
rest of the parts of the eye are discussed in
the text. (From Grollman, S.: *The Human Body*.
New York: Macmillan Co., Copyright © 1964.)

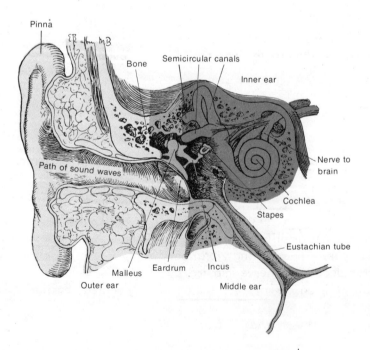

FIGURE 3-6   Inside the ear. The different
shadings identify the outer or external ear,
the middle ear, and the inner ear. The semi-
circular canals are not organs of hearing but
instead contribute to the detection of motion
and balance. The Eustachian tube permits
equalization of pressure on both sides of the
eardrum. (From Gardner, E.: *Fundamentals of
Neurology*. Philadelphia: W. B. Saunders Company, 1971.)

8. A theory of perception which has generally replaced the threshold view is _____ theory. According to this theory, external energy must first be transduced in nerve impulses, and then a

_____ is consulted before a final conclusion about perception can be reached.

signal detection

decision mechanism

9. The detection of a stimulus or _____ is often more difficult by the presence of random disturbances or _____. Signal detection theory argues that in discriminating between noise and signal one must take into account the _____ and _____ or payoff associated with your decision. A correct detection of a signal is called a _____, while the incorrect detection of a signal when only noise is present is called a

_____ _____.

signal

noise

costs, benefits

hit

false alarm

10. Taste depends not only on one's taste buds but also on _____, _____, and _____. The taste buds are sensitive to four basic qualities of taste: _____, _____, _____, and _____.

texture, smell
temperature
sweet
salty, bitter, sour

11. Knowing what kind of event occurs in the external world is called the _____ problem. The chapter discusses this problem in regard to sound and color. Sound consists of regular motion of air molecules transmitted in the form of pressure variations. Such pressure variations can be represented graphically by a _____ wave.

identification

sine

12. The height of the sine wave is called the _____ and controls the _____ of the sound. This sound intensity is measured in _____.

amplitude
intensity
decibels

13. The distance between two successive peaks of a sine wave is called the _____ and determines the pitch of the sound wave. Pitch is measured by the _____ of the wave in units of cycles per second. A frequency of one cycle per second is called a _____, that of 1000 cycles per second is called a _____.

period
frequency

Hertz (Hz)
kiloHertz (kHz)

14. Differences in the sound quality of the same frequency from different instruments is called _____. The lowest frequency in a complex sound wave is called the _____. Frequencies greater than that of the fundamental are called _____ and occur at integer multiples of the fundamental frequency

timbre

fundamental
harmonics

(e.g., 440, 880, etc.). An artificial wave form from which the fundamental frequency has been electronically eliminated is called a _____ _____.

missing fundamental

15. The three major theories of pitch perception are _____ theory, _____ _____ theory, and _____ theory. Place theory proposes that pitch perception is due to the vibration of a specific location on the _____ membrane. This theory's major proponents are _____ and _____.

place
periodicity pitch
residue

basilar
Helmholtz
Von Bekesy

16. Periodicity pitch theory argues that the firing of auditory nerve cells reflects the _____ of excitation rather than the place of excitation. Residue theory suggests that low frequency tones in a complex tone are heard as separate tones, while the high frequency components or _____ are jointly perceived as a single unit. _____ theory provides the simplest explanation of the missing fundamental effect, while _____ theory cannot easily explain it.

pattern

residue
Residue
place

17. Light energy is measured by its wavelength in units of _____ (one millionth of a millimeter). Exposure to a dark environment for a period of time will result in _____ _____ because the cones are not employed in dim light.

_____ _____ results from exposure to a bright surface. The light adapted eye is most sensitive to the color _____, while the dark-adapted eye is most sensitive to _____. This phenomenon is called _____ shift.

nanometer

dark adaptation

Light adaptation

green
blue
Purkinje

18. The three colors which can be combined to create almost all colors are _____, _____ and _____.

They are called the _____ colors.

According to the _____ theory, color vision results from activation of a specific kind of cone which is attuned to a specific wavelength (red, green, or blue). A person who lacks one of these types of cones is called a _____ or color-blind.

blue, green, red

primary

Young-Helmholtz

dichromat

19. Illusions result from inconsistent or ambiguous stimuli. Illusions capitalize on our knowledge of the external world which we use to interpret the input received. For example, we tend to see familiar objects as being the same size, regardless of their distance from us. This is called _____ _____. Tricking people about distances can thus result in _____.

size constancy
illusions

20. Other illusions of interest are the Ames distorted room, the impossible figures, the Moire pattern, and the Mach bands. The apparent movement illusion which results when two patterns are superimposed slightly out of alignment is called the _____ _____.

    Moire pattern

    This illusion may be due to attempts by the eye to focus on the pattern or _____.

    accommodation

21. _____ _____ is the phenomenon of perceiving the brightness of some stimulus incorrectly because of the brightness of the surrounding stimulus. _____ _____ result because when a particular visual mechanism is stimulated for a lengthy period of time, you tend to see the opposite when the stimulus is removed.

    Simultaneous contrast

    Visual aftereffects

22. Research on the interrelationship between the senses has found that _____ dominates other sense modalities. This phenomenon is called _____ _____. For example, Gibson found that individuals who wore prisms which made straight lines appear curved also reported that straight edges felt curved.

    vision
    visual
    capture

23. The constant motion of your eye is called _____. When this movement is stopped by special optical devices, a _____ _____ which remains in a constant location on the retina occurs. This technique results in the fading of the image and its eventual reappearance. Various types of fragmentations of the images also occur. Since the rate of fading is related to the shape and the orientation of the image, investigators have taken this as evidence for the existence of specialized _____ _____ systems in the brain which analyze such features as tilt, shape, and color.

    nystagmus

    stabilized image

    visual analyzer

24. Research on extreme sensory deprivation has shown that such experiences may lead to changes in size constancy and _____.

    hallucinations

25. Special polarizing goggles combined with two polarized light sources create a _____ _____, which is an apparent but not real object. When infants see such an image, they will reach out and become _____ when they cannot touch it. This research has led investigators to conclude that the dominance of vision over other senses is an _____ (innate/learned) phenomenon.

    virtual image

    upset

    innate

26. Gestalt psychologists proposed that the brain has innate organizing tendencies which can explain perception. For example, objects which are close together may be seen as related. This is called the rule of _____.       proximity

Research with infants _____(has/ has not) supported       has not
the Gestalt view.

27. The experiment by Gibson and Walk using the visual cliff found that infants _____(do/ do not) perceive depth. Other       do
research by Bower and associates has supported the view that
depth perception is _____(innate/learned).       innate

28. Extrasensory perception (ESP) takes many apparent forms.
_____ is knowing what is in someone       Telephathy
else's mind, and _____ is the ability       clairvoyance
to perceive objects without using normal perceptual stimuli.
The ability to manipulate physical objects mentally is called
_____. Research thus far _____       psychokinesis,
(has/ has not) supported the existence of extrasensory powers.       has not

## KEY CONCEPTS AND TERMS

After you have finished your guided review fill in the meaning of the following terms in your own words. Check on your accuracy by consulting your text on the pages indicated and in the Glossary.

transducer (p. 77)

iris (p. 78)

rods (p. 78)

cones (p. 78)

fovea (p. 79)

cochlea (p. 82)

basilar membrane (p. 82)

signal detection theory (p. 82-84)

pitch (p. 86)

fundamental (p. 86)

missing fundamental (p. 68)

place theory (p. 88)

periodicity pitch theory (p. 89)

residue theory (p. 89)

visual capture (p. 97)

stabilized image (p. 98)

sensory deprivation (p. 99-100)

hallucinations (p. 100)

virtual image (p. 101)

visual cliff (p. 102)

telepathy (p. 104)

clairvoyance (p. 104)

psychokinesis (p. 105)

Purkinje shift (p. 90)

# A PERSONAL QUIZ

After you are about finished with your studies but still have some time left for review, take this quiz to check on your mastery. Fill in your answers in the spaces provided and after you are finished check their their correctness with the answers provided.

___ 1. A device which changes energy from one form to another is called a (p. 77)
   a. transmitter
   b. decoder
   c. transducer
   d. transformer

___ 2. The size of the pupil opening is controlled by the (p. 78)
   a. iris
   b. cornea
   c. ciliary muscle
   d. retina

___ 3. The curvature of the lens of the eye is controlled by the (p. 78)
   a. diaphragm
   b. iris
   c. accommodator
   d. ciliary muscle

___ 4. The vibrations in the fluid of the inner ear are transduced into nerve impulses by the (p. 82)
   a. signal generator
   b. anvil
   c. stirrup
   d. cochlea

___ 5. Which of the following statements about signal detection theory is correct? (p. 82-84)
   a. it emphasizes the threshold concept
   b. signal detection is a random process
   c. it emphasizes the costs and benefits involved in discriminating between noise and signal
   d. it does not employ mathematical formulas

___ 6. Taste depends (p. 84)
   a. on one's taste buds and the smell, temperature, and texture of food
   b. only on one's taste buds
   c. only on smell and texture of the food
   d. only on the taste buds, smell, and temperature

___ 7. When opposite sides of the tongue are stimulated by taste qualities, the two sensations sometimes fuse to produce a taste sensation in the middle of the tongue. Only one of the following pairs of taste qualities can be fused. Which one? (p. 84-85)
   a. sweet and salty
   b. bitter and sweet
   c. salty and bitter
   d. sweet and sour

___ 8. Continuous exposure to an odor can result in a ____ reduction in sensitivity. (p. 85)
   a. 10%
   b. 50%
   c. 75%
   d. 25%

___ 9. The pressure variations of sound can be represented graphically by (p. 85-86)
   a. a straight line
   b. a Hertz wave
   c. a wave with very sharp peaks
   d. a sine wave

10. The difference between two successive peaks of a sine wave is called (p. 86)
    a. a Hertz
    b. the amplitude
    c. the period
    d. a decibel

11. The lowest frequency of a complex sound wave is called a(n) (p. 86)
    a. fundamental
    b. residue
    c. harmonic
    d. integer

12. Which one of the following statements about place theory is correct? (p. 88)
    a. it argues that pitch perception is due to the vibration of a specific location on the basilar membrane
    b. it proposes that the firing of auditory nerve cells reflects the pattern of excitation
    c. it proposes that high frequency components of a complex tone are perceived as a unit
    d. Helmholtz is its major detractor

13. Light energy is measured in terms of units of (p. 90)
    a. Hertz
    b. Avis
    c. decibels
    d. nanometer

14. The light adapted eye is most sensitive to the color _____ while the dark adapted eye is most sensitive to the color _____. (p. 90)
    a. blue, green
    b. green, blue
    c. red, green
    d. green, red

15. The above phenomenon is called the _____ shift. (p. 90)
    a. color
    b. inversion
    c. Purkinje
    d. Helmholz

16. The three primary colors are (p. 90)
    a. green, red, and yellow
    b. blue, green, and red
    c. blue, red, and brown
    d. blue, green, and yellow

17. The apparent movement illusion which results when two patterns are superimposed slightly out of alignment is called the (p. 94)
    a. Ames illusion
    b. visual aftereffects illusion
    c. Moire pattern
    d. Mach band illusion

18. Research using the stabilized image paradigm has suggested the existence of specialized systems which analyze such features as tilt, shape, and color. These systems are called (p. 98-99)
    a. detectors
    b. integrators
    c. pattern analyzers
    d. visual analyzers

19. Research with infants using a virtual image has led investigators to conclude that (p. 101)
    a. vision dominates touch
    b. touch dominates vision
    c. the domination of one sense over the other is learned
    d. infants do not have depth perception

20. Research on sensory deprivation has shown that such deprivation (p. 100)
    a. can lead to hallucinations
    b. is relatively pleasant
    c. does not affect visual perception
    d. produces hallucinations only toward the end of the deprivation period

Answers:

| | | | |
|---|---|---|---|
| 1. c | 6. a | 11. a | 16. b |
| 2. a | 7. b | 12. a | 17. c |
| 3. d | 8. d | 13. d | 18. d |
| 4. d | 9. d | 14. b | 19. a |
| 5. c | 10. c | 15. c | 20. a |

## PSYCHOLOGY IN ACTION: PROJECTS AND DEMONSTRATIONS

### How Does Your Brain Know Where Your Eyeball Is?

See your text for this demonstration.

### Do You Have ESP?

Much controversy exists about the existence of ESP. Many supposed demonstrations of ESP were flawed by methodological problems or cheating. However, there do exist several carefully designed demonstrations of ESP. One such study was done by McConnell, Snowden, and Powell (1955). They were concerned with the question of whether mental events (e.g., wishes) may influence the occurrence of events in the physical world. The following proposed demonstration is based on that study.

Collect a pair of dice, a cup, and a flat surface covered with felt or other soft material. Before you throw the dice, make a wish for a certain number to be shown on top of the dice when they come to rest. After you have thrown the dice, record your wish and the numbers showing on top of each dice on the sheet provided. Do this 120 times. Record the total number of times the wished numbers appear in each set of 30 throws in the spaces provided, and compare this with the numbers expected by chance (10 for each 30 throws).

McConnell and his colleagues found that more of the wished for numbers occurred on the early trials (e.g., 1–30), while fewer than expected occurred on the later trials (e.g., 91–120). What do you find? You might also want to try this with friends. If your results do not come out as McConnell's, don't be too surprised. His study was done under carefully controlled conditions with 393 subjects performing a total of 170,000 tosses of the dice. Even under those conditions the results were not very strong. In any case, we think you will have fun trying to see how well you can make your wishes come true.

### REFERENCES

McConnell, R.A., Snowden, R.J., and Powell, K.F.: Wishing with dice. J. of Exp. Psych. 50: 269–275, 1955.

40

# ESP Form

Record your wished for number and the actual numbers obtained in the spaces provided.

| | Wish | Result | | Wish | Result | | Wish | Result | | Wish | Result |
|---|---|---|---|---|---|---|---|---|---|---|---|
| 1. | ___ | ___ ___ | 31. | ___ | ___ ___ | 61. | ___ | ___ ___ | 91. | ___ | ___ ___ |
| 2. | ___ | ___ ___ | 32. | ___ | ___ ___ | 62. | ___ | ___ ___ | 92. | ___ | ___ ___ |
| 3. | ___ | ___ ___ | 33. | ___ | ___ ___ | 63. | ___ | ___ ___ | 93. | ___ | ___ ___ |
| 4. | ___ | ___ ___ | 34. | ___ | ___ ___ | 64. | ___ | ___ ___ | 94. | ___ | ___ ___ |
| 5. | ___ | ___ ___ | 35. | ___ | ___ ___ | 65. | ___ | ___ ___ | 95. | ___ | ___ ___ |
| 6. | ___ | ___ ___ | 36. | ___ | ___ ___ | 66. | ___ | ___ ___ | 96. | ___ | ___ ___ |
| 7. | ___ | ___ ___ | 37. | ___ | ___ ___ | 67. | ___ | ___ ___ | 97. | ___ | ___ ___ |
| 8. | ___ | ___ ___ | 38. | ___ | ___ ___ | 68. | ___ | ___ ___ | 98. | ___ | ___ ___ |
| 9. | ___ | ___ ___ | 39. | ___ | ___ ___ | 69. | ___ | ___ ___ | 99. | ___ | ___ ___ |
| 10. | ___ | ___ ___ | 40. | ___ | ___ ___ | 70. | ___ | ___ ___ | 100. | ___ | ___ ___ |
| 11. | ___ | ___ ___ | 41. | ___ | ___ ___ | 71. | ___ | ___ ___ | 101. | ___ | ___ ___ |
| 12. | ___ | ___ ___ | 42. | ___ | ___ ___ | 72. | ___ | ___ ___ | 102. | ___ | ___ ___ |
| 13. | ___ | ___ ___ | 43. | ___ | ___ ___ | 73. | ___ | ___ ___ | 103. | ___ | ___ ___ |
| 14. | ___ | ___ ___ | 44. | ___ | ___ ___ | 74. | ___ | ___ ___ | 104. | ___ | ___ ___ |
| 15. | ___ | ___ ___ | 45. | ___ | ___ ___ | 75. | ___ | ___ ___ | 105. | ___ | ___ ___ |
| 16. | ___ | ___ ___ | 46. | ___ | ___ ___ | 76. | ___ | ___ ___ | 106. | ___ | ___ ___ |
| 17. | ___ | ___ ___ | 47. | ___ | ___ ___ | 77. | ___ | ___ ___ | 107. | ___ | ___ ___ |
| 18. | ___ | ___ ___ | 48. | ___ | ___ ___ | 78. | ___ | ___ ___ | 108. | ___ | ___ ___ |
| 19. | ___ | ___ ___ | 49. | ___ | ___ ___ | 79. | ___ | ___ ___ | 109. | ___ | ___ ___ |
| 20. | ___ | ___ ___ | 50. | ___ | ___ ___ | 80. | ___ | ___ ___ | 110. | ___ | ___ ___ |
| 21. | ___ | ___ ___ | 51. | ___ | ___ ___ | 81. | ___ | ___ ___ | 111. | ___ | ___ ___ |
| 22. | ___ | ___ ___ | 52. | ___ | ___ ___ | 82. | ___ | ___ ___ | 112. | ___ | ___ ___ |
| 23. | ___ | ___ ___ | 53. | ___ | ___ ___ | 83. | ___ | ___ ___ | 113. | ___ | ___ ___ |
| 24. | ___ | ___ ___ | 54. | ___ | ___ ___ | 84. | ___ | ___ ___ | 114. | ___ | ___ ___ |
| 25. | ___ | ___ ___ | 55. | ___ | ___ ___ | 85. | ___ | ___ ___ | 115. | ___ | ___ ___ |
| 26. | ___ | ___ ___ | 56. | ___ | ___ ___ | 86. | ___ | ___ ___ | 116. | ___ | ___ ___ |
| 27. | ___ | ___ ___ | 57. | ___ | ___ ___ | 87. | ___ | ___ ___ | 117. | ___ | ___ ___ |
| 28. | ___ | ___ ___ | 58. | ___ | ___ ___ | 88. | ___ | ___ ___ | 118. | ___ | ___ ___ |
| 29. | ___ | ___ ___ | 59. | ___ | ___ ___ | 89. | ___ | ___ ___ | 119. | ___ | ___ ___ |
| 30. | ___ | ___ ___ | 60. | ___ | ___ ___ | 90. | ___ | ___ ___ | 120. | ___ | ___ ___ |

Total of Wished Numbers ___          Total of Wished Numbers ___          Total of Wished Numbers ___          Total of Wished Numbers ___

Chapter 4

# LEARNING ABOUT THE WORLD:
Classical Conditioning,
Instrumental Conditioning,
and
Observational Learning

## LEARNING OBJECTIVES: WHAT YOU SHOULD KNOW

After reading this chapter you should:

Be able to discuss the various characteristics of classical conditioning.

Know the basic features of instrumental conditioning, how it differs from classical conditioning, and the present consensus on the distinctions between the two types of conditioning.

Know the various schedules of reinforcement and their effects.

Be familiar with the effect of partial reinforcement and the various interpretations of this effect.

Be able to compare and contrast escape learning, avoidance learning, and punishment.

Understand the two factor theory of avoidance learning.

Be able to discuss and evaluate the research on the control of internal bodily processes by instrumental learning.

Understand the implications of the phenomena of instinctive drift and bait-shyness for classical and instrumental conditioning.

Be able to discuss observational learning and its role in the socialization of children.

## STUDY TIPS: A HELPING HAND

This chapter is potentially a confusing one for students. You are confronted with several types of learning, and within these types of learning you will be exposed to a variety of terms and phenomena. Again, it would probably be best to attain mastery of one major section of the chapter before attempting mastery of another. First make sure you understand the essentials of classical conditioning. Students often get conditioned and unconditioned stimuli and responses confused, so be sure to have these terms straight. Next, try to learn the various findings discussed in your text in regard to classical conditioning. Then go on to instrumental conditioning and repeat this process. Make sure you understand positive and negative reinforcement. Students also tend to have some difficulty with the schedules of reinforcement.

## STEP-BY-STEP: A GUIDED REVIEW

After you have read the chapter, mentally fill in each of the blanks in the following section while covering the answers in the margin. Check your answer with that in the margin as you go along. While in many cases your answer should be the same as that in the margin, in other cases a word of similar meaning is acceptable. Do not write in the spaces until you are doing your final review.

1. Any relatively permanent change in behavior produced by experience is termed _____. The type of learning **learning** in which a stimulus which is initially incapable of eliciting a particular response gradually acquires the ability to do so through repeated pairing with another stimulus which can elicit such reactions is called _____ **classical** _____. **conditioning**

2. Classical conditioning was first studied by _____. **Pavlov** He used dogs as subjects and studied the conditioning of _____. In this experiment a previ- **salivation** ously neutral stimulus such as a bell, termed the

   _____ _____ **conditioned stimulus** or CS, was paired with a stimulus which had a strong effect on salivation (e.g., meat powder), termed the

   _____ _____ **unconditioned stimu-** or US. Repeated pairings of these stimuli are called **lus**

   _____ _____. **conditioning trials**

3. Subsequent trials on which the bell was rung but no meat was presented (_____ trials) were designed to determine **test** if the bell itself had acquired the ability to induce salivation. Such salivation in response to the bell was indeed observed and was termed a _____ _____. **conditioned response** Salivation which occurred in response to the meat powder was termed an _____ _____, **unconditioned res-** since it occurred automatically. Research has shown that **ponse** conditioned and unconditioned responses are frequently _____ (different/ identical) in nature. **different**

4. Situations in which conditioned stimuli are paired with a new neutral stimulus and serve as a basis for further conditioning are said to involve _____ _____ **higher order** conditioning (e.g., second and third order conditioning).

5. As shown in the figure below, classical conditioning may be the basis for the acquisition of prejudice, sexual hangups, and strong fears.

| | On First Occasion When CS and US Are Paired | | | | After Repeated Pairings of CS and US | | | |
|---|---|---|---|---|---|---|---|---|
| Acquisition of an "Irrational" Fear | CS | Response to CS | US | Response to US | CS | Response to CS | US | Response to US |
| | Harmless Pet | None (or Approach) | Loud → Noise | Fear | Harmless → Pet | Fear | Loud → Noise | Fear |
| Acquisition of a Sexual "Hang-Up" | CS | Response to CS | US | Response to US | CS | Response to CS | US | Response to US |
| | Article of Clothing | None | Nude Body → of Lover | Sexual Arousal | Article of → Clothing | Sexual Arousal | Nude Body → of Lover | Sexual Arousal |

FIGURE 4-4 The role of classical conditioning in the acquisition of an "irrational" fear and one type of sexual "hang-up" (fetishism). In both cases, stimuli initially capable of eliciting strong reactions acquire this ability through repeated pairing with unconditioned stimuli.

7.  The strength of conditioning increases with _____
    pairings of the CS and US. The strength of conditioning
    is usually measured in terms of the _____,
    _____ and _____
    of occurrence of the conditioned response.

    increased

    magnitude

    latency, probability

8.  With repeated pairings the course of acquisition increases
    rapidly at first and then begins to _____.

    level off

9.  The interval between the presentation of the CS and US is
    also an important determinant of degree of conditioning.
    The optimal interval for many responses seems to be _____.
    However, some studies have shown that intervals can be much
    longer and still produce conditioning.

    0.5 sec.

10. If after being conditioned to one stimulus an organism also
    responds to similar stimuli, _____
    _____ has been exhibited.

    stimulus
    generalization

11. When a conditioned stimulus is repeatedly present without
    the unconditioned stimulus it was formerly associated with,
    the conditioned stimulus gradually loses its ability to
    elicit conditioned responses. This process is called
    _____. However, at some point
    after the extinction has been completed, the conditioned
    stimulus may again evoke the conditioned response. This is
    known as _____ _____.
    Some classically conditioned responses such as strong

    _____
    are often difficult to extinguish.

    extinction

    spontaneous recovery

    emotional reactions

12. When one of two similar stimuli is consistently followed by
    an unconditioned stimulus, while the other is not, individuals
    will often be able to _____
    between these two stimuli.

    discriminate

13. In a study by Liddell it was found that when animals who
    have learned to discriminate between two types of stimuli
    are confronted with examples of such stimuli which they
    cannot discriminate, they may exhibit extreme distress or

    _____ _____.

    experimental neurosis

14. The process by which we learn to behave in ways which result
    in positive outcomes and avoid actions which lead to negative
    outcomes is called _____ or
    _____ conditioning. The earliest systema-
    tic investigations of this type of learning were conducted by
    _____ using puzzle boxes.

    instrumental

    operant

    Thorndike

15. Based on his research, Thorndike proposed the _____ of _____. This law proposed that responses which produce satisfying consequences are _____ while those which produce unsatisfying consequences are _____. The first part of this law has been supported, but the second part should probably be modified to say that unsatisfying consequences lead to _____ or _____ responses.

Law
Effect
strengthened

weakened


avoidance, escape

16. Any event which serves to strengthen responses preceding its occurrence is generally called a _____. Any event which strengthens responses leading to its termination or removal is called a _____.

positive
reinforcer

negative reinforcer

17. Reinforcers which seem to naturally be able to exert strong effects on behavior and are often closely related to basic physiological systems are called _____ reinforcers (e.g., sex, food, and water). Reinforcers which acquire their influence over behavior through association with primary reinforcers are called _____ reinforcers (e.g., love, praise, and money).

primary


secondary

18. In considering the effects of various factors on instrumental conditioning, one needs to take into account the distinction between learning and performance. Essentially, learning involves relatively _____ changes in behavior, while performance involves more _____ changes. This distinction played an important role in the theory of Hull and Spence who proposed that performance on any task is a joint function of both learning and other temporary factors such as _____.

permanent
temporary


motivation

19. One of the major factors which affects instrumental learning is the number of times that a reinforcement is obtained. As with classical conditioning, instrumental learning increases _____ at first and then _____ _____ as the number of reinforced trials increase.

rapidly
levels off

20. The other major factor affecting instrumental learning is the _____ of reinforcement. The greater the delay, the _____ the learning.

delay
poorer

21. Two factors which appear to have effects primarily on performance of the conditioned response, but not the rate at which it is learned, are level of _____ (e.g., deprivation of food) and magnitude of _____ (e.g., amount of food presented).

motivation
reward

22. Rules which govern the occurrence of reinforcements are called _____ of reinforcement.    schedules
    Researchers have investigated the effects of such schedules of reinforcement on the rate of occurrence of simple but freely emitted responses known as _____    operants
    and often employ the term _____ conditioning    operant
    in place of instrumental conditioning.

23. When a reward follows every response, _____    continuous
    reinforcement is being employed. The schedule which involves the delivery of reinforcement only after a certain number of responses is called a _____    fixed-ratio
    schedule. This schedule leads to _____ (high/low)    high
    rates of responding, with a brief pause after each reinforcement.

24. In the case of a _____    variable-ratio
    schedule, the number of responses required for a reinforcement varies randomly around some average value. This schedule leads to a uniformly _____ (low/high)    high
    level of responding.

25. When reinforcements are presented only after the passage of a particular interval of time, a _____    fixed-
    _____ schedule is being employed.    interval
    This schedule leads to a very _____ (low/high) rate of    low
    responding immediately after the presentation of the rein-
    forcement, but a _____ (low/high) level of responding    high
    when the time for reinforcement approaches.

26. In _____ schedules    variable-interval
    the period of time which must elapse before reinforcement is presented varies around some average value. This schedule produces a very constantly _____ (low/high)    high
    rate of responding. The figure below summarizes the effects of the different schedules.

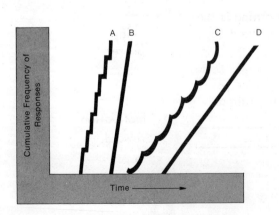
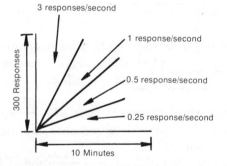

FIGURE 4-12 Patterns of behavior produced by (A) fixed-ratio, (B) variable-ratio, (C) fixed-interval, and (D) variable-interval schedules of reinforcement. The steeper the lines, the higher the rate of responding by subjects.

27. When different schedules are either presented in alternation or simultaneously, they are called _____ schedules.

compound

28. Research has shown that partial reinforcement leads to _____ (greater/less) resistance to extinction than continuous reinforcement. One explanation for this partial reinforcement effect is that individuals trained on partial schedules persist longer during extinction because it is harder for them to recognize that extinction has begun than is the case for continuously rewarded subjects. This is called the _____ hypothesis.

greater

discrimination

29. Another explanation proposed by Amsel is that the partially reinforced subjects have learned to continue responding in the face of _____ stemming from nonreinforcement, while the continuously rewarded subjects have not.

frustration

30. The procedure in which one tries to train an organism to perform a certain desired _____ _____ by administering reward only for responses closer and closer to the ones desired (_____ approximations) is called _____. This procedure is used in modifying a wide variety of behavioral problems in humans.

terminal
response
successive
shaping

31. Instrumental learning can also be based on the presentation of aversive, negative reinforcers. The two basic situations which have been studied are those in which an organism learns to _____ from aversive treatment once it has started, or those in which it learns to _____ the onset of an aversive event. These types of instrumental learning should be distinguished from _____ which involves organisms learning to refrain from performing responses which result in negative outcomes.

escape
avoid

punishment

32. Research has shown that organisms exposed to aversive stimuli from which they cannot escape often exhibit evidence of feelings of _____ which lead to passivity and resignation even in situations where escape from such aversive stimuli is possible. For example, in one study by Seligman and Maier dogs exposed only to inescapable shocks tended to fail to escape in a situation where escape was possible, while dogs which had received both escapable and inescapable shocks readily learned to do so.

helplessness

33. Most research on avoidance conditioning has used a
_____ _____ apparatus. Typically a               shuttle box
neutral stimulus is presented a few seconds before the shock
is presented in one compartment of the box. If the subjects
jump to the other compartment in response to the signal,
they can avoid the presentation of shock.

34. One explanation of avoidance learning discussed in the text
is _____ _____ theory. According to this           two factor
theory the neutral stimuli presented prior to the aversive events
(such as shock) acquire strong fear eliciting properties through
_____ conditioning. Since the performance      classical
of avoidance responses terminates these aversive stimuli, such
reactions are followed by a sharp reduction in _____.           fear
Since this fear reduction is _____               positively
reinforcing, the avoidance reactions are strengthened.

35. Some studies have shown that under conditions where the
aversive stimuli are extremely painful, the avoidance reactions are so strongly developed that they extinguish very
slowly, if at all. This type of learning maybe is responsible
for many of our _____ which have no realistic basis.       fears

36. Although early research suggested that punishment was not
effective in controlling behavior, recent research has suggested
that punishment can exert lasting and strong effects on behavior.
For punishment to be effective it has to be _____        contingent
on the subject's behavior so that it always follows a specific
response, and responses being punished should not also be
_____. Other conditions which are              rewarded
important for effective punishment are that it should be
_____, _____ and individuals           immediate, severe
should be provided with alternative means of obtaining reinforcement.

37. Studies of parents who abuse children indicate that they are
apparently _____ psychologically. They         abnormal
often suffer from feelings of _____,             depression
_____, and isolation. They also                  inferiority
tend to have _____ expectations for              unrealistic
their children, and often their parents abused them.

38. It is important to keep the distinctions between escape,
avoidance and punishment straight. The chart on the next
page should help you in your review of their essential
characteristics.

| PUNISHMENT | | | Result |
|---|---|---|---|
| Instrumental Response<br>(speeding on the interstate) → | Presentation of<br>Aversive Stimulus<br>(traffic ticket) | | Instrumental response<br>is suppressed |

| ESCAPE | | | Result |
|---|---|---|---|
| Presentation of<br>Aversive Stimulus<br>(nagging mother-in-law<br>on phone) → | Instrumental<br>Response →<br>(hanging up phone) | Escape from<br>Aversive Stimulus<br>(escape from nagging) | Tendency to perform<br>instrumental response<br>is strengthened |

| AVOIDANCE | | | Result |
|---|---|---|---|
| Presentation of Dis-<br>criminative Stimulus →<br>("dirty look" from spouse<br>at party) | Instrumental<br>Response →<br>(changing topic<br>of conversation) | Avoidance of<br>Aversive Stimulus<br>(avoidance of embarrassing<br>argument with spouse) | Tendency to perform<br>instrumental response<br>in presence of discrim-<br>inative stimulus is<br>strengthened |

FIGURE 4-18 The conditions existing in punishment, escape, and avoidance situations. In the case of punishment, individuals learn to refrain from performing a response which leads to negative consequences, while in escape and avoidance they learn to perform responses which allow them to either terminate or avoid unpleasant outcomes.

39. Recent evidence has suggested that internal body processes, such as heart rate and blood pressure, _____ (can/can not) be affected or controlled by instrumental learning. An early study by Miller and Carmona demonstrated that cats could be made to control their _____ through the presentation of a positive reinforcer. However, it is possible that such visceral responses can be controlled indirectly by changes in _____ tension or _____ rate.

can

salivation

muscle

respiration

40. Demonstration of direct control requires the use of the drug _____ since this prevents voluntary control of the skeletal muscles and respiration. Research by Miller and his colleagues, employing this drug and _____ as a reinforcer, demonstrated that heart rate, intestinal contractions, ear blushing, and urine formation in the kidneys could be affected by direct control. Later research has sometimes failed to replicate these findings, and the issue of _____ voluntary control over visceral responses remains unresolved.

curare

brain stimulation

direct

41. Humans have also demonstrated the ability to control their bodily reactions through _____ conditioning. A study of a Yogi found that this individual was able to reduce his consumption of oxygen to less than _____ its normal rate.

instrumental

one-fourth

42. A technique which involves the detection, amplification, and display in some form of changes within the body or brain to the individual using sophisticated electronic equipment, is called _____. Using this kind of

biofeedback

feedback, most individuals can readily learn to alter such bodily functions as _____ _____, _____ _____, _____ _____, and _____ _____.

blood pressure heart rate, skin temperature, alpha waves

43. When animals tend to increasingly emit innate responses instead of previously conditioned patterns of behavior, they are said to display _____ _____. This phenomenon suggests that _____ differences play an important role in learning and that to fully understand and predict behavior of organisms, one needs detailed information about their _____ behaviors.

instinctive drift

species

innate

44. Research by Garcia and associates has shown that rats will learn to avoid a sweet-tasting liquid if they become quite sick at their stomachs afterwards through the injection of a drug. This phenomenon is called _____. They also found that presentation of a buzzer prior to such an injection led to a _____ (greater/lesser) degree of avoidance of this stimulus. This research is interpreted by psychologists to mean that due to _____ predisposition, all associations between stimuli and responses are not formed with equal ease.

bait-shyness

lesser

innate

45. In the past it was assumed that classical conditioning affected automatic, reflexive responses termed _____, while instrumental conditioning affected voluntary actions or _____. At the present time there appears to be a consensus that respondents _____ (can/cannot) be instrumentally conditioned (e.g., Miller's work), while operants may be classically conditioned to specific stimuli.

respondents

operants
can

46. Classical conditioning of operants is suggested by a phenomenon called _____ in which organisms such as pigeons have been found to respond to neutral stimuli (e.g., peck at a light) which preceded reinforcement, even though this behavior did not affect the delivery of the reinforcement.

autoshaping

47. Learning which occurs through mere observation is called _____ learning or _____. This learning is often _____ (more/less) efficient than instrumental learning which often involves a lot of trial-and-error.

observational, modeling, more

48. Observational learning also plays an important role in child _____, the process whereby children acquire many of the behaviors required to function as adults.

socialization

In fact, some research has shown that children are _____ (more/less) affected by the deeds of their parents than their verbal statements.

more

49.  Research has shown that televised violence _____ (leads/does not lead) to the learning of aggressive or violent behavior by both children and adults.

leads

## KEY CONCEPTS AND TERMS

After you have finished your Guided Review fill in the meaning of the following terms in your own words. Check on your accuracy by consulting your text on the pages indicated or the Glossary.

classical conditioning (p. 111)


conditioned stimulus (p. 112)


unconditioned stimulus (p. 112)


conditioned response (p. 113)


unconditioned response (p. 113)


higher order conditioning (p. 114)


stimulus generalization (p. 117)


extinction (p. 117)


spontaneous recovery (p. 117)


discrimination (p. 118)


experimental neurosis (p. 118)


instrumental conditioning (p. 119)

Law of Effect  (p. 119)

positive reinforcer  (p. 120)

negative reinforcer  (p. 120)

primary reinforcer  (p. 120)

secondary reinforcer  (p. 120)

learning  (p. 121)

performance  (p. 121)

operants  (p. 124)

respondents  (p. 124)

fixed-ratio schedule  (p. 125)

variable-ratio schedule  (p. 125)

fixed-interval schedule  (p. 125)

variable-interval schedule  (p. 126)

compound schedules  (p. 127)

partial reinforcement effect  (p. 127)

shaping  (p. 128)

escape  (p. 131)

learned helplessness (p. 131)

avoidance (p. 132)

two-factor theory (p. 134)

punishment (p. 134)

biofeedback (p. 140)

instinctive drift (p. 143)

bait-shyness (p. 143)

autoshaping (p. 145)

observational learning (p. 146)


## A PERSONAL QUIZ

After you are about finished with your studies but still have some time
left for review, take this quiz to check on your mastery. Fill in your
answers in the spaces provided and after you are finished check their
correctness with the answers provided.

___ 1. The type of learning which involves
the pairing of conditioned and unconditioned stimuli is called (p. 112)
   a. observational learning
   b. instrumental learning
   c. classical conditioning
   d. experential learning

___ 2. In Pavlov's experiment on classical
conditioning the meat powder was
the ____ stimulus and the bell was
the ____ stimulus. (p. 112)
   a. conditioned, unconditioned
   b. unconditioned, conditioned
   c. primary, secondary
   d. secondary, primary

___ 3. Research has shown that the conditioned response is frequently
   ____ the unconditioned response.
(p. 113)
   a. different from
   b. identical to
   c. stronger than
   d. weaker than

___ 4. Which of the following statements
is correct about the strength of
classical conditioning? (p. 115-
116)
   a. repeated pairings of the CS and
   US increase acquisition, especially at the later stages

of training
b. repeated pairings of the CS and US do not affect conditioning
c. the optimal interval between the US and the CS for many responses seems to be 0.5 second
d. the optimum interval tends to be about 1 second

___ 5. If after being conditioned to a stimulus, an organism also responds to similar stimuli, the organism is exhibiting (p. 117)
a. response generalization
b. spontaneous recovery
c. extinction
d. stimulus generalization

___ 6. Research on instrumental conditioning has shown that unsatisfying consequences or negative outcomes (p. 120)
a. lead to avoidance or escape responses
b. strengthen responses
c. weaken responses
d. have no effect on behavior

___ 7. Any event which serves to strengthen the response preceding its occurrence is termed a _____ while one which strengthens behavior by allowing escape or avoidance of unpleasant stimuli is termed a ____. (p. 120)
a. negative reinforcer, positive reinforcer
b. primary reinforcer, secondary reinforcer
c. positive reinforcer, negative reinforcer
d. secondary reinforcer, primary reinforcer

___ 8. Which of the following two factors have effects primarily on the performance of the conditioned response in instrumental conditioning, but not the rate of learning of the response? (p. 122-123)

a. delay of reinforcement, frequency of reinforcement
b. level of motivation, frequency of reinforcement
c. magnitude of reward, delay of a reinforcement
d. level of motivation, magnitude of reward

___ 9. The reinforcement schedule which involves the delivery of reinforcement only after a certain number or responses is called a _____ schedule. (p. 125)
a. fixed-interval
b. fixed-ratio
c. variable-ratio
d. variable-interval

___ 10. The two reinforcement schedules which lead to uniformly high levels of responding are (p. 125-126)
a. variable-ratio and variable interval
b. fixed-ratio and fixed-interval
c. variable-ratio and fixed-interval
d. variable-interval and fixed-ratio

___ 11. Research on partial reinforcement has shown that partial reinforcement (p. 127)
a. increases the discriminability between acquisition and extinction
b. reduces tolerance for frustration
c. leads to less resistance to extinction than continuous reinforcement
d. leads to greater resistance to extinction than continuous reinforcement

___ 12. The situation in which an organism learns to refrain from performing responses which result in negative outcomes is called (p. 134)

a. escape
b. avoidance
c. punishment
d. none of the above

13. Organisms who are exposed to aversive stimuli from which they cannot escape often exhibit (p. 131)
    a. anxiety
    b. feelings of helplessness
    c. experimental neurosis
    d. enhanced motivation

14. Most research on avoidance conditioning has used the (p. 133)
    a. shuttle box
    b. maze
    c. runway
    d. free operant situation

15. One of the major interpretations of avoidance learning is (p. 134)
    a. frustration theory
    b. discrimination theory
    c. two-factor theory
    d. successive-approximation theory

16. For punishment to be effective it should have all but one of the following characteristics (p. 135)
    a. it should be contingent on the subject's behavior
    b. it should be mild
    c. it should be immediate
    d. responses punished should not also be rewarded

17. Which of the following statements about the recent research on the control of internal bodily processes, such as heart rate and blood pressure, by instrumental conditioning is true? (p. 139)
    a. the issue of voluntary control of internal bodily processes remains unresolved
    b. it has been demonstrated definitively that individuals

can control their bodily processes
c. findings in this area are readily replicated
d. individuals can control their heart rate but not their blood pressure

18. When animals tend to increasingly emit innate responses instead of previously conditioned patterns of behavior, they are displaying (p. 143)
    a. autoshaping
    b. respondent behavior
    c. instinctive drift
    d. extinction

19. Present day consensus is that operants (can/cannot) be classically conditioned, and respondents (can/cannot) be instrumentally conditioned. (p. 145)
    a. cannot, cannot
    b. cannot, can
    c. can, cannot
    d. can, can

20. Research on observational learning has shown all but one of the following: (p. 146-148)
    a. television violence leads to the learning of aggressive behavior
    b. children are more affected by the verbal statements of the parents than their deeds
    c. observational learning plays an important part in child socialization
    d. observational learning of often more efficient than instrumental learning

Answers:

| | | | |
|---|---|---|---|
| 1. c | 6. a | 11. d | 16. b |
| 2. b | 7. c | 12. c | 17. a |
| 3. a | 8. d | 13. b | 18. c |
| 4. c | 9. b | 14. a | 19. d |
| 5. d | 10. a | 15. c | 20. b |

# PSYCHOLOGY IN ACTION: PROJECTS AND DEMONSTRATIONS

## No Trial, No Error: Demonstrating the Efficiency of Observational Learning

This project's purpose is to demonstrate the usefulness of observational learning in eliminating extensive trial and error learning. First acquaint yourself with the problem shown in Fig. 4-28. The task is to connect all nine dots by means of four straight lines without lifting the pencil off the paper. The solution is also shown in Fig. 4-28, and you should be sure to master it thoroughly before proceeding. Once you have memorized the correct movements , take the form provided on page 60 and cut out each of the sets of nine dots. Show one of these to a friend who has never solved it before. Tell this person that you will assist him/her in this task by saying the word "warmer" each time he/she makes a correct move. Essentially, you will place your friend in an instrumental learning situation in which correct responses are rewarded by your verbal comments. As the friend begins to work on the problem, glance at your watch and time the performance in a discreet manner. If the friend fails to attain the solution within five minutes, stop and provide the solution. Note the time required for solution on the paper used by your friend.

Next, find another friend who has not solved this problem previously, and simply demonstrate the correct solution for your friend once with a new set of dots. After this, let him/her attempt the problem himself/herself and again time the performance and note the time required on the paper used by your friend. Repeat these procedures with additional friends if possible. A total of five subjects in each group would be a nice number. You can use the extra dot sheets for this but you may have to make some additional sets of dots yourself.

After you have finished, compare the average amount of time required to solve the puzzle by individuals in the two conditions. The results should provide you with a convincing demonstration of the efficiency of observational learning: the friends for whom you demonstrated the correct solution should require much less time than those for whom you provided verbal reinforcement.

## The Power of Positive Reinforcement

In this experiment you are going to try to demonstrate the effect of verbal reinforcement on behavior. Engage one of your friends in a conversation, preferably on the phone. Try to keep your friend talking for 15 minutes. During the first five minutes of your conversation keep a record of the number of times the friend makes a statement of opinion. Try not to react either positively or negatively to these statements during this period. You might simply say "I see" or state your own opinions in response to your friend's statements, if a response is needed at all. You should try to play a largely passive role during your entire conversation so it would be best if you picked a relatively talkative friend. During the second five minutes period begin reinforcing your friend's opinion statements by saying "mm-hmm" "yes, that's right," or similar positive statements whenever an opinion statement is made. Pay no attention to the contents of the opinions. Reinforce them whether you personally agree with them or not. Be careful during this period not to make too many statements of your own. Just continue your role as passive as possible. During the last five minutes stop providing verbal reinforcement for your friends opinion statements.

During the entire conversation you should be keeping a record of the number of opinion statements being made in each of the three five minute periods. A form for this is provided on page 61 . When you have finished collecting the data, be sure to explain to your friend what you have been doing since ethical standards for research require that you follow such procedures.

After you hang up, compare the total number of opinions uttered by your friend during each of the three five minute periods. If you have done a good job of delivering verbal reinforcement, you should find that the frequency of opinion statements was relatively low in the first period, rose sharply during the second, and then dropped again during the third period.

Data Sheet

Simply put a slashmark through the appropriate number each time your friend makes an opinion statement.

1.  First Phase

1 2 3 4 5 6 7 8 9 10 11 12 13 14 15 16 17 18 19 20

2.  Second Phase

1 2 3 4 5 6 7 8 9 10 11 12 13 14 15 16 17 18 19 20

3.  Third Phase

1 2 3 4 5 6 7 8 9 10 11 12 13 14 15 16 17 18 19 20

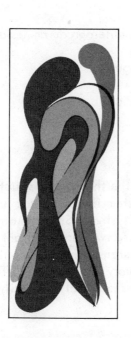

# Chapter 5

# MEMORY
# AND
# LANGUAGE

## LEARNING OBJECTIVES: WHAT YOU SHOULD KNOW

After reading this chapter you should:

Know the three basic storage systems of memory and how they function.

Understand retroactive and proactive interference.

Know how retrieval cues can facilitate free recall.

Know the findings in regard to primary and recency in free and serial recall.

Be able to discuss the relationship between recognition and free recall.

Be able to discuss some of the mnemonic devices employed to improve memory and how they work.

Be able to differentiate between retrograde amnesia, anterograde amnesia, and the mnemonist.

Know the basic concepts and levels of analysis of linguistics.

Understand the network and feature-list models of semantic memory.


## STUDY TIPS: A HELPING HAND

A major part of this chapter is concerned with the three basic structures of memory. Taking one system at a time, try to learn for each system in turn how it functions and what some of the evidence is which supports this analysis of the system. Students often confuse proactive and retroactive interference, so be sure you keep these two terms straight. You should also pay attention to the free recall and serial recall research so that you do not confuse the findings in these areas. The section on semantic memory is somewhat difficult and too complicated to present adequately in the study guide. You should rely primarily on your text for an understanding of this phenomenon.


## STEP-BY-STEP: A GUIDED REVIEW

After you have read the chapter, mentally fill in each of the blanks in the following section while covering the answers in the margin. Check your answer with that in the margin as you go along. While in many cases your answer should be the same as that in the margin, in other cases a word of similar meaning is acceptable. Do not write in the spaces until you are doing your final review.

1.  The three basic structures or storage systems of memory are

    _____  _____ ,              sensory storage
    _____ , and _____ .         short-term, long-term

2. The sensory storage system can hold information for less than a _____ . If visual stimuli are involved this system is called _____ memory, while it is termed _____ if the stimulation is auditory.

second
iconic
echoic

3. An experiment by Sperling investigated iconic memory. He presented three rows of letters on a _____ for less than one-tenth of a second. Each row contained three to six letters. When observers were asked to report as many letters as possible from the display, they could report only about _____ . However, with the use of a _____ report technique, in which subjects were asked to report only a single line, subjects could almost remember the entire line.

tachistoscope

4 or 5
partial

4. Apparently in the above study while the subject is reporting one line or set of letters, the memory representation or _____ of the others fades rapidly. No matter how many lines subjects were asked to report, they could only report roughly one line. The fact that the introduction of a delay between the presentation of the pattern and the time of partial report also hindered memory provides further support for the existence of _____ memory. Similar results have been obtained with auditory materials, suggesting the existence of _____ memory.

trace

iconic

echoic

5. The maintenance of information in short-term memory is maintained by a process called _____ . This option is _____ (not/also) available in short-term sensory storage.

rehearsal
not

6. Two major explanations exist to explain the loss of information from memory. The _____ _____ hypothesis states that information in short-term memory simply fades over time unless it is rehearsed. The _____ hypothesis suggests that forgetting is due to confusion among the various items in short-term memory.

trace decay

interference

7. Until recently, the study of memory involved the use of long lists of _____ syllables or words. Lists of nonsense syllables were first used by _____ , who studied his improvement in memory by assessing the time required to relearn previously memorized lists. This memory improvement is called _____ .

nonsense
Ebbinghaus

savings

8. _____ first postulated the existence of short-term and long-term memory and stimulated the study of memory for individual items. In a study of single-item memory, Peterson and Peterson required subjects to count

Broadbent

backward to prevent rehearsal during the _____     retention
_____, or the period between the presen-     interval
tation of the item and its recall. They found that memory
for three components, such as a three-letter nonsense syllable
or three words, but not for single words, _____ _____     goes down
markedly during a retention interval of 18 seconds. This
could be taken as evidence for the _____     trace
_____ hypothesis.     decay

9. When learning some present task interferes with the memory
for something you knew, you have experienced backward
or _____ interference. When some-     retroactive
thing you have learned in the past interferes with your
present learning or performance you are experiencing forward or _____ interference.     proactive

10. Using the backward counting procedure, Melton demonstrated
that as the number of consonants of the item to be remembered
increased, memory _____. He argued that     decreased
the increased forgetting due to the additional consonants
was due to _____ interference produced by     proactive
these consonants on the letters which they precede.

11. Information in short-term memory is coded _____,     acoustically
even if it was originally presented visually. Evidence for
this is derived in part from research which shows that a
series of letters which sound alike are _____ (more/less)     more
difficult to recall than letters which sound different.

12. Information is transferred from iconic storage into short-
term memory by a _____ mechanism which ex-     scanning
amines components from _____ to _____.     left, right
This scanning mechanism attaches an auditory name to one
component (e.g., letter) at a time and then scans the next
component. The rate of scanning is increased with increased
_____ of the units. This suggests the     familiarity
scanning mechanism results partly from a _____     learned
process.

13. The major problem with the long-term memory is obtaining
the information from wherever it is stored. This process is
called _____. In long-term memory,     retrieval
rehearsal _____ (is/is not) necessary to prevent forgetting.     is not
Any information in long-term memory is considered potentially
rememberable or _____, but only     retrievable
information which is actually remembered is considered
_____.     accessible

14. While interference in short-term memory occurs among acoustically related units or components, interference in long-term memory occurs among _____ related words. Short-term memory has a(n) _____ (limited/unlimited) storage capacity, while long-term memory has a(n) _____ storage capacity.

semantically
limited

unlimited

15. A general model of memory is illustrated below.

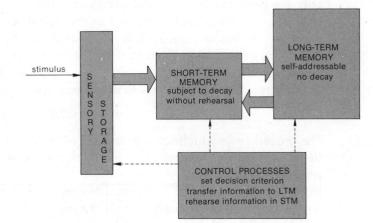

FIGURE 5-4 The "three-box" model of memory. Heavy arrows indicate the flow of information among the three memory systems. Dotted lines indicate the action of control processes upon these memory systems. (Adapted from Shiffrin and Atkinson, 1969.)

16. It is believed that in long-term memory the same plan which was used originally to store information is also used to retrieve information at a later time. This feature of long-term memory is termed _____.
External commands which generate activity in the memory systems are called _____ _____.
One such control process, _____ _____ _____ governs the decision of whether to stop or continue searching after some information has been located in long-term memory.

self-addressable

control signals
set decision
criteria

17. The technique in which subjects are asked to remember information as it comes to mind with no constraints on the order in which the items must be recited is called _____ _____.

free
recall

18. If a list of words contains various categories of words such as weapons, utensils, etc., representation of the category names of the words tends to _____ (facilitate/hinder) free recall. These category names are called _____ cues since they aid in making accessible information which is available but not retrievable without the category names.

facilitate

retrieval

19. A study by Slamecka found that when subjects were given some of the words from a list they had just learned in order to help them remember other words, their recall was
_____ (facilitated/hindered). Apparently     hindered
this procedure may interfere with the retrieval plan which the subject establishes during the learning of the list.

20. The study of the recall of integrated stories showed that only the general outline of the story was recalled as time passed. Individuals often fill in the details based on their own beliefs and stereotypes. Research has shown that if subjects are asked to learn various lists of words in succession they will have a _____ (lower/higher)     lower
level of recall at a later time than subjects who made stories with the words of each of the lists.

21. The procedure in which subjects are asked to recall the items on a list in the same order in which they were presented is called _____.     serial recall
In both serial recall and free recall the position of an item on the list to be remembered is called the _____     serial
position. For both types of recall, memory is _____     better
(better/worse) for items at the beginning (_____     primacy
effect) and the end (_____ effect) of the list.     recency

22. When recall is plotted on a graph as a function of serial position, the resulting U-shaped graph is called the

_____ _____ _____.     serial position curve
With free recall, the recency effect is _____     larger
(larger/smaller) than the primacy effect. (See Fig. 5-6 below)

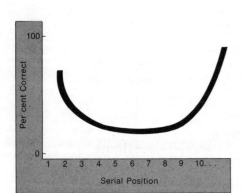

FIGURE 5-6  A typical serial position curve for free recall tasks. Recall is best at the early and late serial positions. While free recall has a large recency effect, as shown here, serial recall tasks show a larger primary effect.

23. According to the model presented previously in Figure 5-4, the primacy effect is due to the greater degree of _____     rehearsal
of the items in the lower serial positions. The recency effect is attributed to the contribution of _____     short-term
memory to the last few items. This interpretation of the recency

effect is supported by a study by Peterson and
Peterson in which subjects were given delayed recall
and were prevented from rehearsing during the delay.
Under these conditions the recency effect _____.          disappeared

24. In _____ tests previously presented          recognition
information is embedded among other items, and the subject
is asked to indicate which alternative is the correct one.
Theorists who believe that recall and recognition work the
same way are called _____          single-process
theorists. These theorists explain the usual finding of
better recognition than recall by proposing that recognition
is a more sensitive measure than recall. Most psychologists
favor a _____ approach which assumes          dual-process
that recall and recognition are two qualitatively different
processes.

25. Research has shown that recognition for pictures of faces
is _____ _____. However          very accurate
some studies have shown that recognition can under certain
conditions be worse than recall. The superiority of recognition to recall which is often reported may be due more to
the obvious differences in the recognition alternatives than
the inherent superiority of the recognition process.

26. A formal scheme designed to improve your memory is called
a _____. The          mnemonic device
mnemonic device which involves learning a list of places
and associating with them what you want to remember is called
the _____ of _____. In laboratory          method, loci
experiments using this technique students improved their
performance from two to _____ times.          seven

27. A system in which a list of objects is associated with a number
of digits and these are in turn related to a list of items to be
remembered is called the _____ _____          numeric pegword
system. This system works best when a strong _____          visual
_____ can be formed in response to the peg-          image
word. The reason for the effectiveness of the method of loci
apparently lies in its provision of an effective retrieval
scheme.

28. Research has shown that competing visual activities (such
as visual pointing) _____(facilitate/hinder)          hinder
visual imagery and vice versa.

29. When individuals cannot remember certain kinds of information as a result of brain injury they are said to have

_____.          amnesia, Retrograde
amnesia refers to a failure in long-term memory and is

characterized by forgetting of events that occurred some time prior to a traumatic injury. If the retrograde amnesia covers only a very short period of time, the time for recovery from amnesia is generally _____. In    short
recovery, older memories return before more recent ones.

30. _____ amnesia is a deficit in    Anterograde
short-term memory in which the individual is unable to
retain new information for any length of time. Someone
who has difficulty forgetting is called _____.    mnemonist

31. The discipline which studies the formal properties of
language is called _____. Linguists    linguistics
are interested in a person's ability to form linguistically
correct sentences and phrases based on the person's understanding and knowledge of the rules of a language. This
is referred to as _____ in language.    competence
Psychologists are interested in the actual language behavior
used or _____.    performance

32. The basic units of spoken language are termed _____.    phonemes
They are part of the _____ structure of language    surface
but do not convey any meaning in themselves. Phonemes are
combined to form _____, which are very    morphemes
similar to words. Most morphemes can convey meaning, but
they are still considered part of the surface structure of
language.

33. The next linguistic level is the phrase or sentence, which
consists of morphemes arranged to satisfy the rules of some
particular language. Diagramming a sentence according
to the arrangement of the parts of speech is called _____    parsing
the sentence. Such a diagram represents the _____    surface
_____ of a sentence.    structure

34. The surface structure of a sentence is not sufficient to indicate
the meaning of the sentence. To derive its meaning one has
to analyze its _____ structure. The relationship    deep
between meaning and surface structure is called _____.    semantics

35. Our knowledge of conceptual relations about the world is
termed _____ memory. Our personal record    semantic
of individual experiences is termed _____    episodic
memory. Various theoretical models of semantic memory have
been developed. Collins and Quillian suggest that semantic
concepts are stored in a _____    hierarchical
arrangement, while Smith and his colleagues propose that the
meaning of a word derives from a list of semantic features
associated with it. This is called the _____    feature-list
model.

36. The notion that language molds the way we think and perceive
is called _____ _____.                    linguistic relativity

This idea was proposed by Whorf. Experimental research
_____ (has/has not) supported this theory. One       has not

study by Heider and Oliver showed that even though the Dani
and Americans have _____ criteria for the           different

naming of color, their memory for the actual colors is very

_____.                                              similar

## KEY CONCEPTS AND TERMS

After you have finished your Guided Review, fill in the meaning of the
following terms in your own words. Check on your accuracy by consulting your text on the pages indicated or the Glossary.

sensory storage system  (p. 154)

short-term memory  (p. 156)

long-term memory  (p. 154)

iconic memory  (p. 154)

echoic memory  (p. 154)

trace decay hypothesis  (p. 156)

interference hypothesis  (p. 156)

retroactive interference  (p. 158)

proactive interference  (p. 158)

scanning mechanism  (p. 160)

retrieval  (p. 160)

set decision criteria  (p. 162)

free recall  (p. 162)

serial recall  (p. 167)

primacy  (p. 167)

recency  (p. 167)

serial position curve  (p. 167)

recognition tests  (p. 169)

single-process theory  (p. 169)

dual-process theory  (p. 169)

mnemonic device  (p. 170)

method of loci  (p. 170)

numeric pegword  (p. 171)

retrograde amnesia  (p. 173)

anterograde amnesia  (p. 173)

mnemonist  (p. 175)

linguistics  (p. 176)

language competence  (p. 176)

language performance  (p. 176)

phonemes  (p. 176)

surface structure  (p. 176)

morphemes  (p. 177)

parsing  (p. 177)

deep structure  (p. 178)

semantics  (p. 178)

semantic memory  (p. 178)

episodic memory  (p. 178)

feature-list model  (p. 179)

linguistic relativism  (p. 182)


## A PERSONAL QUIZ

After you are about finished with your studies but still have some time
left for review, take this quiz to check on your mastery.  Fill in your
answers in the spaces provided and after you are finished check their
correctness with the answers provided.

____  1.  Which of the following is not one
of the three basic storage systems of
memory? (p. 154)
   a.  trace
   b.  sensory storage
   c.  short-term
   d.  long-term

____  2.  The sensory storage system (p. 154)
   a.  is called echoic if auditory
       stimuli are involved
   b.  is called iconic if visual stim-
       uli are involved
   c.  can hold information for less
       than a second
   d.  all of the above

3. In an experiment on iconic memory Sperling presented rows of letters on a tachistoscope for less than one-tenth of a second. He found that (p. 155)
   a. when subjects are asked to report as many letters as possible, they report only 2 or 3
   b. subjects report 4 or 5 letters when asked to report as above
   c. with the use of partial report subjects could remember only 2 or 3 letters
   d. whole report is superior to partial report

4. Information in short-term memory is maintained by (p. 156)
   a. imagery
   b. proactive interference
   c. rehearsal
   d. echoic mechanisms

5. In studies of memory with nonsense syllables it has been found by Melton that if rehearsal is prevented by making subjects count backwards, memory for the items decreases as the number of consonents increased. This was interpreted as support for a _____ interpretation of forgetting. (p. 158-159)
   a. trace decay
   b. proactive interference
   c. retroactive interference
   d. none of the above

6. Evidence that a series of letters which sound alike are more difficult to recall than letters which sound different suggests that (p. 159)
   a. a scanning mechanism exists
   b. information is stored visually in short-term memory
   c. familiarity hinders memory
   d. information is stored acoustically in short-term memory

7. Which of the following statements about long term memory is not correct? (p. 160-161)
   a. the major problem with long term memory is rehearsal
   b. interference in long term memory occurs along semantic dimensions
   c. the storage capacity of long term memory is unlimited
   d. long term memory is self-addressable

8. Free recall of words which fall into various categories, such as weapons, utensils, etc., tends to be (p. 163)
   a. facilitated by provision of the categories of the words during testing
   b. hindered by such a procedure
   c. facilitated by provision of some words on the list
   d. none of the above

9. Research on primacy and recency effects in memory have found that (p. 167)
   a. only primacy occurs in free recall
   b. only recency occurs in serial recall
   c. recency and primacy occur in serial recall but not free recall
   d. recency and primacy occur in both free and serial recall

10. With _____ recall the recency effect is _____ than the primacy effect (p. 167)
   a. free, larger
   b. free, smaller
   c. serial, larger
   d. serial, smaller

11. The primacy effect is explained in the text as being due to (p. 167)
   a. attentional strategies
   b. short term memory

c. rehearsal
d. initial anxiety

12. Research comparing recognition and recall has shown that (p. 169)
   a. recognition is always superior to recall in terms of accuracy of recall
   b. recall is superior
   c. recognition can be worse than recall
   d. recognition is better than recall only in free recall

13. Laboratory experiments on the use of mnemonic devices in memory have found that these devices (p. 171)
   a. improve memory from 2 to 7 times
   b. hinder memory
   c. do not affect memory
   d. facilitate memory only in free recall

14. Which mnemonic device requires a strong visual image? (p. 172)
   a. the method of loci
   b. numeric pegword
   c. both of the above
   d. none of the above

15. If an individual is unable to retain new information for any length of time he is said to have (p. 173)
   a. anterograde amnesia
   b. retrograde amnesia
   c. post-traumatic amnesia
   d. mnemonism

16. In regard to language, linquists are interested in an individual's _____, while psychologists are interested in _____. (p. 176)
   a. style, competence
   b. competence, style
   c. competence, performance
   d. style, performance

17. The basic units of spoken language are termed (p. 176)
   a. semantic units
   b. phonemes
   c. morphemes
   d. words

18. To analyze the meaning of a sentence one has to (p. 178)
   a. diagram it
   b. parse it
   c. analyze its surface structure
   d. analyze its deep structure

19. Our knowledge of conceptual relations about the world is termed _____ memory. (p. 178)
   a. conceptual
   b. deep
   c. semantic
   d. episodic

20. The notion of linguistic relativism (p. 182)
   a. has not been supported
   b. has a lot of experimental support
   c. has yet to be investigated experimentally
   d. was proposed by Heider

Answers:

| | | | |
|---|---|---|---|
| 1. a | 6. d | 11. c | 16. c |
| 2. d | 7. a | 12. c | 17. b |
| 3. b | 8. a | 13. a | 18. d |
| 4. c | 9. d | 14. b | 19. c |
| 5. b | 10. a | 15. a | 20. a |

## Measuring Your Span of Apprehension

See your text for this demonstration.

## Retrieval Cues in Free Recall: Tell Me A Story

You will need two friends for this demonstration. Try to pick two of relatively equal mental ability. Find a quiet place so that you will not be disturbed. Cut out each of the five lists of words below. First, have one friend make up a story using the ten words in the first column. Note the amount of time your friend takes. Then take away the list of words and have your friend recall the words aloud while you mark whether or not he/she was correct on the data sheet. Repeat this procedure for the other four lists. Then ask your friend to recall all the words. Again mark the correctness of the answers on the data sheet.

Next have another friend try to memorize each list of words for the amount of time it took your first friend to make up the story. He/she should also try to recall the words of each list separately, and after all the lists have been memorized and recalled separately, recall for all words should be obtained. Again, a place is provided for you to record the data on page 78.

For each of the two friends total the number of words correctly recalled from each list separately and during the total recall phase. You should not find much difference in the immediate recall ability of your friends, but the friend employing the story should do much better on the recall of the entire list.

### Lists

| 1 | 2 | 3 | 4 | 5 |
|---|---|---|---|---|
| bottle | curtains | moon | window | hat |
| airplane | gun | tree | table | canoe |
| trowel | book | axe | lamp | chair |
| broom | telephone | radio | television | stereo |
| desk | doorknob | house | letter | bank |
| cup | glass | saucer | dish | sink |
| lion | tiger | fox | giraffe | elephant |
| boat | ferry | sail | train | car |
| bed | desk | typewriter | helmet | button |
| fish | lobster | snail | shrimp | turtle |

## Using Mnemonics to Improve Your Memory and Impress Your Friends

Memorize the numeric pegword list on page 172 in your text and read how it should be used. Find two friends who are willing to help you with your demonstration. Have one friend write a list of ten items on a piece of paper. Have him/her place this piece of paper in front of you and the other friend for one minute while the two of you try to memorize all 10 words. You should try to use your numeric pegword list in doing this. After the minute has elapsed, the list of words should be removed and both you and your friend should try to recall as many of the words as possible on a blank sheet of paper for a two minute period. If your mnemonic device worked for you, you should have been perfect (or almost so) in your recall, while your friend made a number of mistakes. If your demonstration worked well, try it with some other friends. If your friends do too well on this memory task, you might shorten somewhat the time that you are exposed to the list.

# Date Sheet

Instructions: Place a checkmark by each word recalled correctly. The first column of spaces is for the immediate recall trial, while the second column is for the delayed recall of the entire list.

## Subject Using Story

| 1 | | | 2 | | | 3 | | | 4 | | | 5 | | |
|---|---|---|---|---|---|---|---|---|---|---|---|---|---|---|
| bottle | ___ | ___ | curtains | ___ | ___ | moon | ___ | ___ | window | ___ | ___ | hat | ___ | ___ |
| airplane | ___ | ___ | gun | ___ | ___ | tree | ___ | ___ | table | ___ | ___ | canoe | ___ | ___ |
| trowel | ___ | ___ | book | ___ | ___ | axe | ___ | ___ | lamp | ___ | ___ | chair | ___ | ___ |
| broom | ___ | ___ | telephone | ___ | ___ | radio | ___ | ___ | television | ___ | ___ | stereo | ___ | ___ |
| desk | ___ | ___ | doorknob | ___ | ___ | house | ___ | ___ | letter | ___ | ___ | bank | ___ | ___ |
| cup | ___ | ___ | glass | ___ | ___ | saucer | ___ | ___ | dish | ___ | ___ | sink | ___ | ___ |
| lion | ___ | ___ | tiger | ___ | ___ | fox | ___ | ___ | giraffe | ___ | ___ | elephant | ___ | ___ |
| boat | ___ | ___ | ferry | ___ | ___ | sail | ___ | ___ | train | ___ | ___ | car | ___ | ___ |
| bed | ___ | ___ | desk | ___ | ___ | typewriter | ___ | ___ | helmet | ___ | ___ | button | ___ | ___ |
| fish | ___ | ___ | lobster | ___ | ___ | snail | ___ | ___ | shrimp | ___ | ___ | turtle | ___ | ___ |

Total
Correct ___ ___    ___ ___    ___ ___    ___ ___    ___ ___

Total correct for all five lists during immediate recall: _____.
Total correct for all five lists during the recall of the entire list: _____.

## Subject Not Using Story

| | 1 | | | 2 | | | 3 | | | 4 | | | 5 | |
|---|---|---|---|---|---|---|---|---|---|---|---|---|---|---|
| bottle | ___ | ___ | curtains | ___ | ___ | moon | ___ | ___ | window | ___ | ___ | hat | ___ | ___ |
| airplane | ___ | ___ | gun | ___ | ___ | tree | ___ | ___ | table | ___ | ___ | canoe | ___ | ___ |
| trowel | ___ | ___ | book | ___ | ___ | axe | ___ | ___ | lamp | ___ | ___ | chair | ___ | ___ |
| broom | ___ | ___ | telephone | ___ | ___ | radio | ___ | ___ | television | ___ | ___ | stereo | ___ | ___ |
| desk | ___ | ___ | doorknob | ___ | ___ | house | ___ | ___ | letter | ___ | ___ | bank | ___ | ___ |
| cup | ___ | ___ | glass | ___ | ___ | saucer | ___ | ___ | dish | ___ | ___ | sink | ___ | ___ |
| lion | ___ | ___ | tiger | ___ | ___ | fox | ___ | ___ | giraffe | ___ | ___ | elephant | ___ | ___ |
| boat | ___ | ___ | ferry | ___ | ___ | sail | ___ | ___ | train | ___ | ___ | car | ___ | ___ |
| bed | ___ | ___ | desk | ___ | ___ | typewriter | ___ | ___ | helmet | ___ | ___ | button | ___ | ___ |
| fish | ___ | ___ | lobster | ___ | ___ | snail | ___ | ___ | shrimp | ___ | ___ | turtle | ___ | ___ |

Total
Correct ___ ___    ___ ___    ___ ___    ___ ___    ___ ___

Total correct for all five lists during immediate recall: _____.
Total correct for all five lists during the recall of the entire list: _____

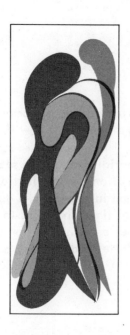

Chapter 6

# HUMAN INFORMATION PROCESSING: Engineering Approaches to Mental Life

# LEARNING OBJECTIVES: WHAT YOU SHOULD KNOW

After reading this chapter you should:

Know the basic concepts and characteristics of information processing models.

Be able to compare and contrast information processing and S-R approaches to behavior.

Understand Donder's methods of studying reaction time.

Know Hick's law.

Be able to discuss the various concepts of attention and how the different areas of research on attention relate to them.

Know the various models of problem solving and their relation to computer simulation.

Understand the "rational" model of decision making.


# STUDY TIPS: A HELPING HAND

This chapter deals with a variety of concepts and issues in the area of human information processing. Thorough understanding of this chapter requires that you know how flow charts and hierarchical structures can be used to represent behavior. This may require some extra effort and drill in the early part of the chapter. Another potentially confusing section is the one on attention. Each of the phenomenon discussed in this section has implications for several models of attention. So it is best to remember each phenomenon in terms of the degree of support they provide for these models. Some confusion arises at times in regard to the concepts of bit, utility, and expected value. Be sure you know how the terms information and uncertainty are used in reference to bits, and how expected value is defined and may differ from utility.


# STEP-BY-STEP: A GUIDED REVIEW

After you have read the chapter, mentally fill in each of the blanks in the following section while covering the answers in the margin. Check your answer with that in the margin as you go along. While in many cases your answer should be the same as that in the margin, in other cases a word of similar meaning is acceptable. Do not write in the spaces until you are doing your final review.

1.  Human information processing deals with a theoretical analysis of how we abstract and utilize information. Information processing differs from more traditional S-R learning theories in that the basic unit of information processing is _____.          larger

2.  Information theorists often use a series of boxes to represent
    sequential operations. This is called a _____ _____.          flow chart
    A flow chart which allows for different possibilities and
    different orders of possible events is called a _____           branching
    flow chart. The path between the boxes is called the _____.     loop

3.  The flow of information counter to the main flow is _____.      feedback
    A feedback control system involves the control of some
    _____. The output of the process is compared with               process
    the input by a _____. If the output does not                    comparator
    match the input (either too high or too low), the comparator
    sends the appropriate signal to the _____                       controller
    which leads to appropriate modification of the process. The
    feedback control system is depicted in the figure below.

FIGURE 6-5  A feedback control system. The comparator adds up the algebraic sum of the input signal and the feedback signal. If the two signals are equal, their algebraic sum is zero, and no signal is sent to the controller. If the signals are unequal, a correction is sent to the controller, which then alters the process until the proper relationship between input and feedback is obtained.

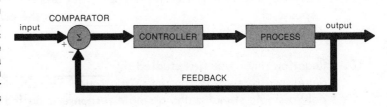

4.  The feedback system in which there is continuous path from
    any element of the system, around the loop, and back to the
    element is called _____ control                                 closed-loop
    system. If the feedback loop is broken, we have an
    _____ control system.                                           open-loop

5.  Information theory is a mathematical tool that quantifies the
    uncertainty in the world in units of information or uncertainty
    called _____. This is the information present in the            bits
    toss of a coin. Before one flips a coin one has one bit of
    _____. Afterwards one has gained one                            uncertainty
    bit of _____. Each time one doubles                             information
    the number of possible outcomes one adds _____ bit of           one
    uncertainty.

6.  Much behavior can be represented in hierarchical structures
    in which units of behavior can be broken down and represented
    diagrammatically with increasing numbers of smaller units. In
    diagramming hierarchical flow charts the text presents a form
    of feedback loop called a _____ unit. This represents          TOTE
    _____, _____, _____, and                                     Test, Operate
    _____. The Test phase functions like the comparator            Test, Exit
    previously discussed. The Exit of the TOTE unit leads to the
    next behavior to be performed and allows the combination of
    several feedback loops in succession.

7. The information processing approach to man is in conflict with the more traditional _____ approach. While the S-R approach implies that man is a passive creature subject to the forces of the environment, the information processing approach suggests that man is _____. Studies with _____ or purposive machines provide support for the information processing view.

S-R

purposive

automata

8. Another problem with the S-R approach is that the particular response to a stimulus depends on the set of potential external stimuli which may occur. Further, humans are capable of a variety of options and strategies in responding to stimuli.

9. Much research in information processing is concerned with the time required to complete different mental operations. The analysis of behavior in terms of time is called _____ analysis. The time between a signal onset and the subsequent response or _____ _____ is the primary dependent variable.

chronometric

reaction time

10. Reaction time was first studied by _____ who developed three reaction time situations. The situation involving only a single stimulus and a single response is called _____ reaction time and provides an estimate of time required for routine _____ _____. This reaction time provided the base line from which more complicated kinds of mental time could be estimated.

Donders

simple

mental processes

11. The situation involving more than one stimulus and response is called _____ reaction time. Donders believed this reaction time measured the mental operations of _____ and _____. The situation involving a number of stimuli, but only one of them calling for response, is called the _____ time and was presumed by Donders to reflect the mental operation of _____. Subtracting c-reaction time from choice reaction time gives a measure of the mental process of _____. Donder's subtractive method is summarized in the figure below.

choice
identification
selection

c-reaction
identification

selection

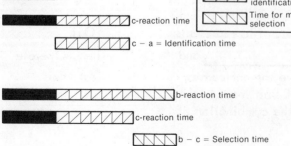

a-reaction time

c-reaction time

c − a = Identification time

Nervous system conduction time

Time for mental identification

Time for mental selection

b-reaction time

c-reaction time

b − c = Selection time

FIGURE 6-13 Donders' subtractive logic. Subtracting *a*-reaction time from *c*-reaction time (top panel) gives an estimate of mental identification time. Subtracting *c*-reaction time from *b*-reaction time gives an estimate of mental selection (bottom panel). The three different shadings show the proportion of reaction time allotted to each mental process.

13. As the amount of information in a set of alternatives
increases in a reaction time situation, the reaction time
_____. This relationship is termed _____     increases, Hick's
law. The effect of adding alternatives on reaction time is
_____ (less/greater) when the S-R relationships     greater
are incompatible or unnatural. This effect is shown in the
figure below.

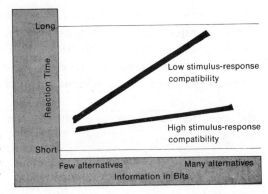

FIGURE 6-14 The Hick's function for two levels of stimulus-
response compatibility. The high compatibility relationship
is flatter, indicating that increases in the number of alternatives have a smaller effect than they do for low compatibility relationships.

14. In studies of reaction time, increased speed is generally
accompanied by _____ accuracy. This is          decreased
called the speed-accuracy trade-off.

15. When two or more tasks are performed simultaneously there is
usually a decrease in the efficiency of one or both of the tasks.
This is an example of _____                    information
_____. This can also be induced by pre-        overload
senting a series of stimuli and requiring responses at a rate
which exceeds the human's normal capabilities.

16. When two stimuli are presented in rapid succession, the
reaction time to the second stimulus is _____          increased
(increased/decreased). This is called the psychological
_____ _____ based on an    refractory period
early explanation that the effect was due to brief turning off
of the central processing mechanism after the presentation of a
stimulus. Research _____ (supports/            does not support
does not support) this model.

17. Broadbent explains this phenomenon by means of a _____       limited
_____ model.                                   capacity channel
This model assumes that your central processing system can
carry only a certain amount of information per second called
_____ capacity. Whenever a task requires more  channel
information capacity than the channel capacity can provide,
performance is slower and/or less accurate.

18. In a _____ _____ dichotic listening
task two separate messages are represented one to each ear.
Subjects are required to repeat the message presented to
one ear aloud and subsequently tested for their knowledge
of both messages. Research has shown that repeating the one
message _____ (interfered with/ interfered with
facilitated) the knowledge of the other message.

19. One explanation of this effect by Treisman argues that in
one's attention system a filter attenuates or weakens signals
as they pass through it. This filter leads to the weakening
of the unattended message. The degree of weakening depends
on the importance of the information. This is called an
_____ _____ model since early selection
the selection acts directly on the internal representation
of the stimulus.

20. In contrast with the early selection model, the _____ late
_____ model by Norman proposes that all selection
stimulus information reaches memory. However, repeating the
one message aloud interferes with the retention of the other
message.

21. In performing tasks simultaneously, as the information processing
requirements of one task increases, the performance of a
second task may _____. This suggests a deteriorate
limited _____ model of attention as proposed by capacity
Broadbent. This model predicts that as one or both tasks in
a time-sharing situation are made more difficult, performance
will become less accurate and slower because the information
processing channel can no longer handle the greater task demands.
This prediction has _____ (always/not always) been not always
supported.

22. The task in which one is presented with a color name printed in a
competing color of ink is called the _____ task. Stroop
Studies have shown that individuals find it difficult to ignore
the color name when asked simply to name the color of the ink.
A perceptual or _____ _____ early selection
view of this effect suggests that interference between the two
stimulus dimensions is the primary cause. A response conflict or
_____ _____ model argues that late selection
the interference is due primarily to the inability to emit
responses due to the competition between alternative responses.

23. Research favors the _____ response conflict
view since an experiment has shown that if individuals are asked
to respond with same or different to stimuli which either have the
same color name and ink or different color and name respectively,
their response times are _____ _____. the same

24. A number of psychological models are based on computer principles. This does not mean that psychologists view humans as computers. In computer simulation the _____, but not the machine itself, is the model for the behavior. Most computer simulation models deal with processes which do not have a _____ requirement in which decisions must be made rapidly.

program

real-time

25. The search process aimed at getting from some initial state to some desired final state by finding some pathway linking the two states is termed _____ _____.

problem solving

26. One can solve problems in two general ways. The search process which guarantees finding a successful solution if one exists is called an _____. In this case one employs a set of rules or operations which allow systematic examination of all possibilities. The other way to solve problems is by the _____ approach in which one takes kind of a best guess but has no guarantee that a solution will be found. Human problem solving and computer models thereof are based on _____.

algorithm

heuristics

heuristics

27. Heuristics are often preferred to algorithms because we may not know an algorithm for a particular problem, and algorithms may be impractical because of the time required by them.

28. If in a particular problem one is able to recognize when the search has been satisfactorily concluded, the problem is considered to be _____.

well-defined

29. One recognition difficulty in problem solving is _____ _____ in which problem solutions are impeded by the tendencies of individuals to fixate on a particular function of an object and not being aware of alternative functions of these objects.

functional
fixedness

30. One of the most successful computer programs of human problem solving is the General Problem Solver (GPS) developed by Newell and Simon. The program works by a kind of _____ analysis. This analysis involves the use of some means or series of operations required to deal with the objects of the problems in such a way as to reach the end or solution of the problem. In other words the solution requires the elimination of the _____ between the start and the finish of the problem.

means-end

differences

31. In trying to find some means for reaching its goal or end, GPS often establishes sub-goals. GPS tries to reach three kinds of goals. _____ goals involve changing one object into another, such as taking six people from one side of the river to the other. To do this GPS must find the difference between the

Transformation

two objects and then establish a sub-goal for reducing this difference.

32. _____ _____
    goals attempt to find some operation which is relevant
    to reducing this difference and then establish a sub-goal
    of applying this operation. _____
    _____ goals are concerned with
    ensuring that the proposed operation is allowable.

    Difference re-
    duction

    Operator
    applicator

33. An individual's verbal explanations of her/his attempted
    solutions as she/he work through a problem is called a
    _____ and can be compared to the
    GPS protocol. If these protocols are very similar, the
    computer program is considered to be a reasonable
    simulation of behavior.

    protocol

34. Computers perceive patterns _____(more/less)
    efficiently than people. One type of computer program
    for pattern recognition is called _____
    _____ since it involves the comparison
    of a standard figure with a test figure to determine the
    degree of correspondence. This technique involves a lot
    of technical difficulties since an infinite number of tem-
    plates are required for the wide variety of possible per-
    ceptual stimuli (e.g., handwritten letters).

    less

    template
    matching

35. Psychologists think that humans use a _____
    _____ approach in which particular sets
    of letter components are identified. A pattern is examined
    against a checklist of these features.

    feature
    testing

36. Mathematicians and statisticians have developed models
    which tell us what a _____ decision maker
    should do under specified circumstances. People often
    _____(do/do not) behave as rational decision
    makers. In considering how individuals make decisions one
    has to consider both _____ and
    _____ _____.

    rational

    do not

    utility

    expected value

37. The expected value of a behavior or act is calculated by
    multiplying the amount you will _____ times its
    probability minus the amount you can _____
    times its probability. The point at which the costs involved
    in engaging in the behavior and its expected value are equal
    is called the _____point.

    gain
    lose

    indifference

38. When the potential gains and losses involved in a particular
    act (e.g., betting) become very large, one has to consider

86

the _____ of the act since this                           utility
may not be identical with the expected value. That is,
utility tends to _____ (decrease/increase)                decrease
when large sums of money are involved.

39.  Another reason that individuals are not entirely rational
     decision makers is that they put _____                greater
     (less/greater) emphasis on the probability of a win than on
     the probability of a loss.

## KEY CONCEPTS AND TERMS

After you have finished your Guided Review, fill in the meaning of the
following terms in your own words.  Check on your accuracy by consulting your text on the pages indicated or the Glossary.

flow chart  (p. 187)

loop  (p. 187)

feedback  (p. 189)

closed-loop control system  (p. 190)

open-loop control system  (p. 190)

bit  (p. 199)

TOTE  (p. 192)

automata  (p. 193)

chronometric analysis  (p. 194)

simple reaction time  (p. 195)

choice reaction time  (p. 195)

c-reaction time  (p. 195)

Hick's law  (p. 195)

S-R compatibility  (p. 197)

psychological refractory period  (p. 200)

limited-capacy channel model  (p. 200)

early-selection model  (p. 202)

late-selection model  (p. 202)

dichotic listening  (p. 201)

real-time requirement  (p. 205)

algorithm  (p. 206)

heuristics  (p. 206)

General Problem Solver  (p. 208)

template matching  (p. 211)

feature testing  (p. 211)

utility  (p. 214)

expected value  (p. 214)

indifference point  (p. 214)

After you are about finished with your studies but still have some time
left for review, take this quiz to check on your mastery. Fill in your
answers in the spaces provided and after you are finished check their
correctness with the answers provided.

___ 1. When information theorists represent sequential operations they often
use a (p. 187)
a. comparator
b. controller
c. flow chart
d. S-R diagram

___ 2. The feedback system in which there
is a continuous path from any element of the system, around the
loop, and back to the element is
called a(n) (p. 190)
a. branching flow chart
b. closed-loop control system
c. open-loop control system
d. comparator system

___ 3. A bit is the information present
in (p. 190)
a. one toss of a coin
b. one throw of a dice
c. two tosses of a coin
d. two throws of a dice

___ 4. Each time one doubles the number
of possible outcomes one adds
_____ bit(s) of uncertainty.(p. 190)
a. 1
b. 2
c. 4
d. 8

___ 5. The TOTE feedback loop
a. is an automata
b. is an S-R hand
c. is an open loop
d. can be used in hierarchical
structures

___ 6. The information processing approach
to man assumes that he is (p. 193)

a. a passive creature
b. an automata
c. a purposive individual
d. a hierarchical structure

___ 7. The reaction time situation used
by Donders which involves a number of stimuli but only one response is called (p. 195)
a. complex reaction time
b. c-reaction time
c. choice reaction time
d. simple reaction time

___ 8. According to Donders, a measure
of the mental process of selection
can be obtained by subtracting
_____ reaction time from
_____ reaction time. (p.196)
a. simple; complex
b. simple; choice
c. simple; c
d. c; choice

___ 9. When two or more tasks are performed simultaneously, there is usually
a decrease in the efficiency of one
or both tasks. This is an example
of
a. information overload
b. Hick's law
c. speed-accuracy trade-off
d. none of the above

___ 10. When two stimuli are presented in
rapid succession, the reaction time
of the second is (p. 200)
a. unaffected
b. increased only with similar
stimuli
c. increased
d. decreased

11. Research suggests that the above phenomenon can best be explained by a(n) ___ model.(p. 200)
    a. refractory period
    b. limited-capacity channel
    c. interference
    d. late-selection

12. Research with a dichotic listening task has shown that repeating one message ___ the knowledge of the other message. (p. 201)
    a. interferes with
    b. facilitates
    c. has no effect on
    d. none of the above

13. Research on the Stroop task favors a ___ model (p. 204)
    a. limited channel
    b. early-selection
    c. response conflict
    d. stimulus substitution

14. Human problem solving and computer models thereof are based on the ___ technique of problem solving (p. 208)
    a. real-time
    b. heuristics
    c. algorithm
    d. chronometric

15. One of the most successful computer programs of human problem solving is the ___ by Newell-Simon. (p. 208)
    a. GPS
    b. CPA
    c. SPC
    d. PSP

16. This program involves all but one of the following goals: (p. 210)
    a. difference reduction
    b. operator applicator
    c. functional
    d. transformation

17. To determine whether a computer program is a reasonable simulation of behavior one needs to (p. 210)
    a. compare it with other programs
    b. observe problem solving behavior
    c. have subjects interact with the computer
    d. compare subject protocols with those of the program

18. Psychologists believe that people use a ___ approach to pattern perception. (p. 211)
    a. feature testing
    b. pattern testing
    c. template matching
    d. relational

19. Research on decision making has found that (p. 214)
    a. people are rational decision makers
    b. utility and expected value tend to be similar when potentially large gains are involved
    c. utility in betting tends to increase when large sums of money are involved
    d. individuals put more emphasis on the probability of a win than that of a loss

20. Expected value is expressed by which of the following formulas? (p. 214)
    a. probability of win x amount - probability of loss x amount
    b. probability of win x probability of loss
    c. amount of win - amount of loss
    d. probability of win x amount + probability of loss x amount

Answers:

| 1. c | 6. c | 11. b | 16. c |
|------|------|-------|-------|
| 2. b | 7. b | 12. a | 17. d |
| 3. a | 8. d | 13. c | 18. a |
| 4. a | 9. a | 14. b | 19. d |
| 5. d | 10. c | 15. a | 20. a |

## Getting the Bit in Your Teeth

Page 92 contains a figure with eight rows and eight columns. Give this page to a friend and have him/her put an X in one of the 64 squares. Your job is to locate the square with the X by asking only questions which can be answered by yes or no. Since the 64 alternatives correspond to 6 bits of information (Table 6-1), you should be able to locate the square by asking no more than 6 questions. Can you do it? The solution is shown in Figure 6-6 in your text. Make some extra copies of the checkerboard figure and try it on some other friends. You might compare some mathematics majors with some liberal arts majors to see if a math background facilitates performance of this task.

## Making Rational Decisions: Tennis or Sailing

See your text for this demonstration (p. 215).

## Problems with Problem Solving Sets

Often in problem solving we are hindered by sets picked up from past experience. These sets may hinder us in solving problems for which this set is wrong or another set is much better. A set of problems which was used by Luchins (1942) to demonstrate this phenomenon is the Water Jar Test. These problems are shown on page 93. You might want to try them on your friends. Give your friends a blank sheet of paper to work on the problems. Let them work about 2 1/2 minutes on each problem. If the first problem is not solved, show your friend the correct solution. In the case of problem 1 it is as follows: fill the left bottle first, then fill the right one three times with water from the left bottle. Then go on to problem 2. Again if necessary, demonstrate its solution. For problem 2 one must fill the middle jar, then fill the left jar once and the right jar twice with water from the middle one. This same solution applies to problems 3 through 6. Repeat your demonstration of it each time one of these problems is not solved. Problems 7 through 11 can also be solved by the solution used for problems 2 through 6, but a simpler solution is also availabe. For problems 7, 9 and 11, one can simply fill the left jar and then fill the right jar once from it. In the case of problems 8 and 10, one can simply fill both the left and right jars and pour this water into the middle one. Do your friends continue to use the more complex rule?

## REFERENCE

Luchins, A.S.,: Mechanization in problem solving: The effect of Einstellung. Psych. Monographs. 54, No. 6, Whole No. 248, 1942.

# Water Jar Test

| Problem | Given the following empty jars as measures | | | Obtain the required amount of water in one jar |
|---|---|---|---|---|
| 1 | 29 | 3 | | 20 |
| 2 | 21 | 127 | 3 | 100 |
| 3 | 14 | 163 | 25 | 99 |
| 4 | 18 | 43 | 10 | 5 |
| 5 | 9 | 42 | 6 | 21 |
| 6 | 20 | 59 | 4 | 31 |
| 7 | 23 | 49 | 3 | 20 |
| 8 | 15 | 39 | 3 | 18 |
| 9 | 28 | 76 | 3 | 25 |
| 10 | 18 | 48 | 4 | 22 |
| 11 | 14 | 36 | 8 | 6 |

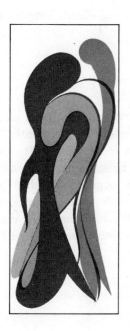

Chapter 7

MOTIVATION
AND
EMOTION:
Attempting
to
Explain Behavior

After reading this chapter you should:

Understand the different types of motivational explanations of behavior.

Know the basic ideas of the Hull-Spence theory of motivation.

Know how high anxiety affects the performance of individuals on tasks and tests.

Be able to discuss the factors involved in the control of arousal in both males and females.

Be able to discuss the effectance motive and the evidence for its existence.

Know how high achievement motivation develops and how it affects behaviors.

Be able to describe the research and problems in the area of identification of emotions in oneself and others.

## STUDY TIPS: A HELPING HAND

This chapter does not contain too many difficult concepts and ideas so you are primarily confronted with the task of remembering the research findings. Systematic rehearsal and the use of the Guided Review should enable you to master this material quite well. One of the major concepts in the chapter is Hull's drive concept. Be sure you know all its various features and how drive affects behavior. Remember that according to Hull's system, if there is no motivation, there will be no behavior. In the section on sexual arousal you may find it difficult to keep the male/female differences straight. Just remember that female sexual arousal is dependent on the internal hormonal factors and not much affected by external stimuli.

## STEP-BY-STEP: A GUIDED REVIEW

After you have read the chapter, mentally fill in each of the blanks in the following section while covering the answers in the margin. Check your answer with that in the margin as you go along. While in many cases your answer should be the same as that in the margin, in other cases a word of similar meaning is acceptable. Do not write in the spaces until you are doing your final review.

1.  The hypothetical internal process that provides the energy for
    behavior and directs it toward a specific goal is called
    _____. The subjective feeling state          motivation
    which involves physiological arousal and is accompanied by
    characteristic behaviors is called _____.          emotion

2. Three types of motivational explanations of behavior discussed in the text are _____, _____ and _____. Explanations of behavior in which humans are believed to act because there was a reason to do so are known as _____. The difficulty with rationalisms is that they are circular and provide no way to predict behavior. Such explanations are also not _____.

rationalism, mechanism empirical determinism

traditional rationalisms

testable

3. The _____ position is that human behavior has physical causes and that the knowledge of the machinery is all that science needs to obtain. _____ assumes that behavior is a natural phenomenon and that it is predictable. The goal of this approach is to determine the conditions under which behavior occurs rather than to discover some "deeper" explanation of behavior.

mechanist

Empirical determinism

4. The concept of drive was introduced by _____. Deprivation of physiological needs leads to _____ which supposedly activates the organism. Any behavior which leads to a reduction in the need reduces drive and is supposedly _____. Evidence indicates that _____(all/not all) reinforcement is based on drive reduction.

Hull
drive
arousal

reinforcing

not all

5. A variety of stimuli can become motivators by their association with drive reduction. Such stimuli are called _____. These stimuli may be positive or negative and may lead the organism to approach or avoid an object or situation.

incentives

6. Evidence that drive has a general _____ effect on behavior was obtained in part from studies in which spontaneous running activity in rats _____ when they were deprived of food. However, subsequent research has shown that the early findings were partly due to the accidental reinforcement of the running behavior by subsequent feeding. Moreover, research with a tilt cage has found that increase in drive level leads to a _____ in movement.

energizing

increased

decrease

7. In the Hull-Spence theoretical system, _____ and _____ were employed as the necessary determinants of behavior. Learning was represented by the concept of _____. This was presumed to increase whenever a stimulus-response combination was followed by _____.

learning
motivation

habit strength

reinforcement

Motivation was represented by the concept of _____ .     drive
This increases whenever a motivational state is not met. Hull
proposed that habit strength and drive _____     multiply
to produce response strength.

8. Research on Hull's theoretical system has primarily been concerned
   with predicting the probability of the conditioned response
   occurring when the conditioned stimulus is presented. This
   research _____ (has/has not) supported the notion that drive     has
   and habit strength jointly determine the probability of the
   conditioned response.

9. The Manifest Anxiety Scale was designed to measure differences
   in anxiety which would reflect differences in _____     drive
   level. In accord with the Hull-Spence theory, the probability
   of a conditioned eyeblink increases with increases in number of
   conditioning trials ( _____ )     habit strength
   and anxiety level ( _____ ).     drive strength
   This phenomenon is demonstrated in the figure below.

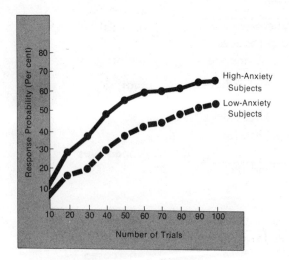

FIGURE 7-4 In a classical conditioning experiment, an air puff served as the unconditioned stimulus which was paired with a lighted disc as the conditioned stimulus; an eyeblink was the unconditioned response. After a series of such pairings, subjects tended to respond to the disc with an eyeblink. The probability of that conditioned response was heightened as the number of trials increased (habit strength) and was greater for anxious individuals than for nonanxious ones (drive strength). (Adapted from Spence, 1960.)

10. Subjects who score high on the Manifest Anxiety Scale
    tend to perform better than nonanxious subjects on _____     reaction
    _____ and simple _____ tasks but poorer on many     time, coding
    other tasks. This finding may be explainable by the notion that
    drive increases the response strength of all habits. When only one
    habit is evoked, higher drive would thus lead to _____     improved
    performance (as with simple tasks). When several habits are
    evoked at the same time, drive increases the response strength of
    each of the habits. The resulting competition between the right
    and wrong responses would lead to _____     decrements
    in performance (as with complex or poorly learned tasks).

11. In accord with the above line of reasoning, it has been found that when subjects are asked to learn a list of non-sense syllables, high anxious subjects make _____ (more/less) mistakes than low anxious subjects during the early stages of learning, while the reverse is true during the later stages (when the list is fairly well learned).

more

12. A study by Spielberger which examined the joint effects of academic ability and anxiety on grades found that high anxiety had a _____ (detrimental/ facilitory effect on grade point average, especially in the _____ range of academic ability. (See Figure 7-5 below) Another study found that while low anxious subjects were not affected by the addition of humor to an exam, high anxious subjects performed _____ (better/worse) on a humorous exam than on a nonhumorous exam. Apparently the humor _____ the anxiety level of the high anxious students.

detrimental

middle

better

reduced

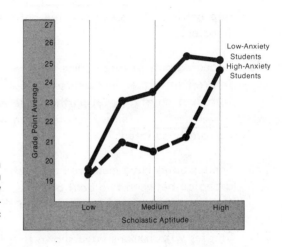

FIGURE 7-5 Though grade point average is determined in part by scholastic aptitude, motivational variables are also an important factor in college performance. High levels of anxiety are found to have a detrimental effect on grades for the majority of students who fall in the middle range of academic ability. (Adapted from Spielberger, 1966.)

13. Unless the hormone _____ is secreted six weeks after conception, all embryos naturally develop the _____ genital system. The male and female genital systems _____ (have/do not have) the same basic structures.

androgen

female
have

14. Infants and young children _____ (frequently/ seldom) display sexual activities. Harlow's research with monkeys has shown that _____ with others is necessary for the development of normal sexual interests and skills.

frequently

physical contact

15. Sexual changes at puberty such as physical changes in the genitals, development of breasts and pubic hair, as well as growth in height, are related to the production of _____. The need for _____ also shows a dramatic increase.

    sex hormones, sex

16. In most species, female sexual arousal seems to be primarily under the control of _____. In males, sexual activity tends to be related to a combination of _____ activity and external stimuli which are _____. The most common stimulus for male sexual arousal appears to be _____. Apparently, substances secreted in the female vagina called _____ are important for sexual arousal in mammals.

    hormones
    hormonal
    arousing

    smell
    pheromones

17. The strength of the sex drive is difficult to determine since it is dependent on both hormonal levels and external stimuli. For female animals the sex drive appears to increase and decrease throughout the _____ cycle. Number of days of deprivation increases sex drive only for _____(males/females).

    estrous
    males

18. Repeated acts of intercourse lead to _____ interest in further intercourse for both males and females. The introduction of a novel partner renews sexual desire for the _____ (male/female) even when the animal seems to be totally satiated.

    decreased

    male

19. Some studies have measured drive strength by giving the animal a choice between two goal objects. This research suggests that the _____ drive is stronger than the _____ drive.

    sex, hunger

20. Studies with humans have shown that increased sexual arousal is accompanied by a variety of physical and physiological changes in the body. However in higher animals such as humans, sexual arousal is less controlled by hormones and instinctive responses and more by the _____. _____. This means that human sexual arousal involves _____ to a greater degree.

    cerebral cortex
    learning

21. For humans many external stimuli can become _____ _____ when they are associated with various sexual activities. Another example of cognitive influence of sex in humans is that humans are able to respond to words, pictures, and ideas involving sexual matter. In fact, physiological measures of arousal of individuals watching a sex film are no different from those of individuals engaging in the initial stages of sexual intercourse.

    sexual
    incentives

22. One study showed that subjects who saw erotic slides of stories were _____ (less/more) aroused than those who were asked to imagine a series of erotic situations.

less

23. Other research has shown that sex criminals report _____ (more/less) frequent contact with pornography and a _____ upbringing than do normals. Exposure to pornography appears to lead to a slight _____ (increase/decrease) in usual sexual behavior, and an _____ (increased/decreased) interest in members of the opposite sex. A high degree of sexual arousal during exposure to explicit sex _____ (is/is not) related to a high level of subsequent sexual activity.

less
stricter

increase

increased

is

24. Psychologists have also been interested in the mechanisms underlying exploration, manipulation, and curiosity. Robert White conceptualizes this behavior as satisfying the _____ motive which leads organisms to learn to deal effectively and competently with the world around them.

effectance

25. Research suggests that visual exploration is _____ for animals. Other studies have shown that both animals and humans prefer a relatively _____ stimulus to a _____ one. If stimuli are too complex, however, individuals may react with _____. It has been found that individuals who are _____ and _____ enjoy novelty and complexity more than those who are not.

rewarding

complex

simple
anxiety

creative

intelligent

26. Animal studies seem to suggest that both humans and animals are naturally inquisitive. Rats and chimpanzees have been found to examine _____ objects. The _____ motive which underlies this manipulative behavior appears to be stronger when other motives (e.g., hunger, thirst) _____ (are/are not) strongly aroused. The primary functions of the effectance motive seems to be _____ about our world and _____ it.

novel, effectance

are not

learning
changing

27. Man has apparently acquired a large number of motives which are not based on physiological needs. These _____ motives come about through _____ _____ and _____ _____.

acquired
classical
conditioning,
instrumental
learning

28. The concern over competition and some standard of excellence is often explained by psychologists in terms of the _____ motive. This motive is frequently measured using the

achievement

Test. Individuals who score high on this test tend to be higher in _____ and _____ _____, and tend to get better grades in courses that are related to their future career.

29. Research has also shown that achievement motivation affects an individual's approach to games and tasks. Those individuals who are high in achievement orientation tend to prefer tasks of _____ difficulty or _____ odds, while those low in achievement motivation tend to prefer situations in which the chance of success is either almost _____ or rather _____.

intermediate

intermediate

sure, low

30. Achievement motivation appears to be most likely to develop in homes which stress _____ and _____ as the way to reach high standards. The parents tend to _____ the child whenever he/she does well. Mothers who respond with indifference to success but provide punishment for failure tend to produce children motivated by fear of _____.

excellence

competition
reward

failure

31. Families with extremely _____ fathers tend to produce low achievement motivation in children. While the sons of blue collar workers have only slightly _____ achievement motivation than the sons of white collar workers, the achievement motivation of sons of men with _____, _____ jobs is higher than that of sons of those in _____, _____ jobs. These findings are shown in Figure 7-16 below.

dominant

lower

independent
decision making

dependent,
routine

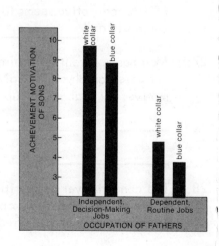

FIGURE 7-16 It has been found that a boy's level of achievement motivation is related to the type of job held by his father. Regardless of social class (white collar versus blue collar), the achievement motive was higher in boys whose fathers held independent, decision-making positions than in boys whose fathers held dependent, routine jobs. (Adapted from Turner, 1970.)

32. Emotions are similar to motivational states in that they can also _____ and direct behavior. Few psychologists agree on a definition of emotion, but emotions are generally classified according to the accompanying overt behavior (e.g., crying or laughing) and the subjective reports of the person experiencing the emotion.

energize

33. To try to determine how many different emotions there are, Bridges observed infants for two years. She found that by the time the children were two years old, _____ distinct emotions were observed. However this and other systems encounter the problem of having observers agree on the emotions being expressed.

eleven

34. Attempts to identify the basic emotions at the physiological level have also not been successful, leading some to suggest that emotions simply reflect some kind of general _____.

arousal

35. Research examining the relation of facial expressions to emotion have generally found that individuals have a _____ time determining another's emotional state on the basis of facial expression alone.

difficult

36. When individuals are asked to act out or portray various emotions, however, facial expressions have been found to vary along the dimensions of _____

and _____.

Apparently when individuals are asked to try to depict an appropriate emotion they tend to portray an expression that is more easily recognized in our culture as demonstrating a particular feeling.

pleasantness-unpleasantness
rejection–attention

37. Further research has suggested that one reason that we are often inaccurate in identifying emotions is that we need _____ information. Some facial expressions appear to be universal, reflecting inherited tendencies and are recognized across various cultures (e.g., _____). Other expressions, such as _____, appear to be learned since there is little crosscultural agreement about the expression of these emotions.

contextual

happiness
fear

38. Work by Schachter and Singer indicates that in trying to identify their own emotions, individuals utilize a combination of _____ _____

and _____ about the context in which the emotion occurs.

physiological
arousal
information

39. A theory of love by Berscheid and Walster suggests that an individual will interpret his/her emotional state as being love if his/her state of emotion occurs in situations which suggest the label of _____. For example, in studies where males have been aroused with the threat of shock, they have shown _____ _____ for females who were present at that time.

love

enhanced liking

40. Another study showed that when males were interviewed by a female on an arousal inducing bridge, they expressed more _____ on a Thematic Apperception Test and were more likely to _____ the experimenter afterwards than those interviewed on a nonarousing bridge. When the interviewer was male, the type of bridge had little effect on attraction.

sexuality

contact

## KEY CONCEPTS AND TERMS

After you have finished your Guided Review, fill in the meaning of the following terms in your own words. Check on your accuracy by consulting your test on the pages indicated or the Glossary.

motivation (p. 220)

emotion (p. 220)

rationalism (p. 221)

mechanism (p. 222)

empirical determinism (p. 223)

drive arousal (p. 223)

incentives (p. 223)

habit strength (p. 226)

Manifest Anxiety Scale (p. 226)

androgen  (p. 231)

pheromones  (p. 232)

estrous cycle  (p. 232)

effectance motive  (p. 238)

acquired motives  (p. 241)

achievement motive  (p. 242)

Thematic Apperception Test  (p. 242)


## A PERSONAL QUIZ

After you are about finished with your studies but still have some time
left for review, take this quiz to check on your mastery. Fill in your
answers in the spaces provided and after you are finished check their
correctness with the answers provided.

___ 1. Which one of the following is not
one of the three motivational
explanations of behavior discussed
in the text? (p. 220)
a. scolism
b. rationalism
c. empirical determinism
d. mechanism

___ 2. The approach which seeks to determine the conditions under which
behavior occurs rather than to
discover some deeper explanation
of behavior is (p. 223)
a. rationalism
b. scolism
c. empirical determinism
d. none of the above

___ 3. Which of the following is not one
of the features of the theoretical
system introduced by Hull?
(p. 223-226)
a. deprivation of physiological
needs leads to drive arousal
b. motivation and incentives are
the necessary determinants of
behavior
c. drive reduction is reinforcing
d. drive energizes behavior

___ 4. Which of the following statements
has the best research support?
(p. 226)
a. drive has a general energizing
effect on behavior
b. drive reduction is reinforcing
c. habit strength and drive multiply to produce response strength
d. habit strength and drive add
to produce response strength

5. Research on manifest anxiety has found that anxious subjects perform better than nonanxious subjects
   a. on complex tasks
   b. during the early stages of learning
   c. on poorly learned tasks
   d. on reaction time and simple coding tasks

6. Research on the relationship between anxiety and academic performance has found that (p. 228-230)
   a. highly anxious students have higher grades than low anxious students
   b. humor on an exam facilitates the performance of highly anxious students
   c. high anxiety has a detrimental effect on the grade point average of average students
   d. both b and c

7. Which of the following statements about sexual behavior is not correct? (p. 231-233)
   a. physical contact with others seems to be necessary for development of normal sexual skills and interests
   b. infants seldom display sexual activities
   c. female sexual arousal appears to be primarily under the control of hormones
   d. the hormone androgen is necessary for the development of the male genital system

8. The most common stimulus for male sexual arousal appears to be (p. 232)
   a. visual cues
   b. auditory cues
   c. olfactory cues
   d. none of the above

9. The substance secreted in the female vagina which is important for male sexual arousal is called (p. 232)
   a. pheromones
   b. androgen
   c. estrogen
   d. pubimones

10. Research on the strength of the sex drive has found that (p. 232-233)
    a. repeated acts of intercourse increase sexual interest
    b. the female sexual drive is relatively stable
    c. introduction of a novel partner increases the sexual interest of an apparently satiated male
    d. females have a stronger sex drive

11. In higher animals sexual arousal appears to be more controlled by _____ and less by _____ (p. 235)
    a. hormones and instincts, learning
    b. external stimuli, the cerebral cortex
    c. learning, hormones and instinct
    d. learning, the cerebral cortex

12. Research on the effects of erotic stimuli on human sexual arousal has found that (p. 236)
    a. sexual arousal during the watching of a sex film is different from the arousal involved in actual sexual intercourse
    b. imagining an erotic situation can be more arousing than viewing erotic slides
    c. erotic stimuli lead to sex crimes
    d. sex films lead viewers to try new techniques

13. The motive which leads an organism learn to deal effectively and competently with the world around them is called the (p. 238)
    a. effectance motive
    b. achievement motive
    c. competence motive
    d. anxiety motive

14. Research on exploratory behavior has found that
    a. relatively complex stimuli are preferred to simple ones
    b. intelligent individuals enjoy novelty and complexity more than less intelligent ones
    c. if stimuli are too complex, individuals may react with anxiety
    d. all of the above

15. The primary functions of the effectance motive seem to be _____ and _____. (p. 240)
    a. anxiety reduction, stimulation
    b. learning about the world, changing it
    c. providing structure, achieving competence
    d. enhancing curiosity, drive reduction

16. Acquired motives come about through
    a. observational learning
    b. classical conditioning
    c. instrumental conditioning
    d. both b and c

17. Which of the following does not characterize high achievement motivation individuals? (p. 243)
    a. they prefer tasks of intermediate difficulty
    b. they desire to enter high status occupations
    c. they are less creative than low achievement individuals
    d. they tend to be successful in business

18. The homes of high achievement motivated individuals tend to be characterized by (p. 244)
    a. fathers with independent, decision-making jobs
    b. dominant fathers
    c. punishment for failure
    d. none of the above

19. When individuals are asked to portray various emotions, facial expressions have been found to vary along the dimensions of _____ and _____.(p. 247)
    a. happiness-sadness; excitement-calm
    b. pleasantness-unpleasantness; rejection-attention
    c. excited-calm; rejection-attention
    d. happiness-sadness; pleasantness-unpleasantness

20. Research on emotions indicates that in trying to identify one's own emotions, an individual uses (p. 251)
    a. external cues
    b. physiological stimuli
    c. physiological arousal and information about the context
    d. none of the above

Answers:

| 1. a | 6. d | 11. c | 16. d |
|------|------|-------|-------|
| 2. c | 7. b | 12. b | 17. c |
| 3. b | 8. c | 13. a | 18. a |
| 4. c | 9. a | 14. d | 19. b |
| 5. d | 10. c | 15. b | 20. c |

# PSYCHOLOGY IN ACTION: PROJECTS AND DEMONSTRATIONS

## Reading the Emotions of Other – Using Your Personal Radar

First read the Psychology in Action box on page 249 in your text. After you have gone through the various exercises suggested for you, you can begin on the project described below and in your text.

Find fifteen individuals who would be willing to try their skill at judging emotions. Cut out the pictures and captions on page 109. Show five people only the pictures from the top of page 109 and ask them to write down on a piece of paper the emotions being expressed in each of the pictures. You may want to number the pictures to facilitate this procedure. Next, show five people the same pictures accompanied by the brief captions and have them write down the emotions being expressed. Finally, show five people the pictures from the bottom of page 109 and have them also write down the emotions being expressed. You should find large differences in the judgment of the emotions being expressed by the three groups since these emotions are being expressed in different contexts.

## Observing Manipulative Activities

This project's purpose is to make you more aware of the degree to which people engage in manipulative behavior (i.e., manipulation of objects in their environment). As indicated in your text, manipulative behavior in man and animal may reflect the effectance motive or the motivation to achieve competence. Choose a day on which you will be coming into contact with many different environments, such as school, home, stores, and parks. In each of these situations look for examples of manipulative behavior. For instance, you might come across children playing with toys, teenagers playing with pinball machines, students playing with pencils, and adults engaging in hobbies. A sheet is provided so that you can conveniently note the occurrence of such behaviors and the persons and situations involved. Do you notice any group of people that is most likely to exhibit such behavior? Are such behaviors found more frequently in some situations than in others?

Figure 7-19. How do you 'read' these people's faces? If you find the task at all difficult, there is a good reason. In real-life situations, you ordinarily are able to see not only a person's face but also the total situation or contest. You know what the person is doing and what is causing the emotional reaction. (Upper left photo by Brian Aris, Photo Trends; upper right photo by Horst Schafer, Photo Trends; lower left photo by Ben Ross, Photo-Trends; lower right photo from McGraw-Hill Films.)

FIGURE 7–20 *Now* how do you read these people's faces? (Photo credits: lower right, McGraw-Hill Films; all others, Photo Trends.)

## Manipulative Activity Form

| Specific behavior | By Whom | Where |
|---|---|---|
| 1. _____ | _____ | _____ |
| 2. _____ | _____ | _____ |
| 3. _____ | _____ | _____ |
| 4. _____ | _____ | _____ |
| 5. _____ | _____ | _____ |
| 6. _____ | _____ | _____ |
| 7. _____ | _____ | _____ |
| 8. _____ | _____ | _____ |
| 9. _____ | _____ | _____ |
| 10. _____ | _____ | _____ |
| 11. _____ | _____ | _____ |
| 12. _____ | _____ | _____ |
| 13. _____ | _____ | _____ |
| 14. _____ | _____ | _____ |
| 15. _____ | _____ | _____ |
| 16. _____ | _____ | _____ |
| 17. _____ | _____ | _____ |
| 18. _____ | _____ | _____ |
| 19. _____ | _____ | _____ |
| 20. _____ | _____ | _____ |
| 21. _____ | _____ | _____ |
| 22. _____ | _____ | _____ |
| 23. _____ | _____ | _____ |
| 24. _____ | _____ | _____ |

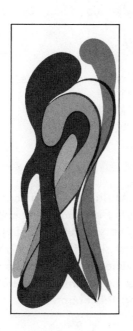

Chapter 8

# DEVELOPMENT AND GROWTH:
From Child
to
Adult

# LEARNING OBJECTIVES: WHAT YOU SHOULD KNOW

After reading this chapter you should:

Know the three distinct stages of prenatal development and their characteristics.

Know the effects of nutrition, disease, and drugs on prenatal development.

Know the basic characteristics of motor and perceptual development.

Be able to discuss the development and features of early speech.

Understand the three theories of language development.

Understand Piaget's theory of cognitive development.

Be able to describe Harlow's research on attachment behavior in monkeys.

Know how children acquire a sexual identity.

Be able to discuss sexual stereotyping and the research on sex differences.

Know the theories of moral development by Piaget and Kohlberg.

# STUDY TIPS: A HELPING HAND

Although the ideas and research in this chapter should not be difficult to understand, there are a lot of details you will have to master. Again, try to review and rehearse the chapter in sections. The Learning Objectives should give you an idea of the different parts of the chapter that you should focus on. Remember, first skim the entire chapter and note the important points. Then read the chapter a second time, rehearsing the material as you read. Go to the Guided Review for further drill. You may want to review the study tips at the beginning of the Student's Manual before starting this chapter.

# STEP-BY-STEP: A GUIDED REVIEW

After you have read the chapter, mentally fill in each of the blanks in the following section while covering the answers in the margin. Check your answer with that in the margin as you go along. While in many cases your answer should be the same as that in the margin, in other cases a word of similar meaning is acceptable. Do not write in the spaces until you are doing your final review.

1.  Growth prior to the actual moment of birth or _____          prenatal
    development is usually divided into three distinct stages.  During
    the period of the ovum, the fertilized ovum goes through the
    mother's reproductive tract toward the womb or _____.       uterus

During this interval of several _____, the ovum subdi-
vides into several dozen cells. The inner layer of cells develops into the _____, while the outer layer develops
into _____ and _____
structures.

days

child

protective, life-
sustaining

2. After _____ days the ovum becomes implanted in the
wall of the mother's uterus and becomes known as the
_____. During this period of the embryo the
outer cell layer of the embryo develops into protective membranes and the _____ _____. This
structure carries blood from the embryo to the _____.
The blood of the embryo and the mother exchange _____
and _____ in the placenta.

10 to 14

embryo

umbilical cord
placenta
nutrients
wastes

3. The inner layer also continues its growth to a full human form.
By the _____ week the heart has begun to beat. By
the _____ week the face, arms, and legs are developed. The major internal organs have begun to form, the
_____ glands begin to function, and the _____
system is developing rapidly.

third
eighth

sex, nervous

4. During the seven months after the period of the embryo the
unborn child is known as the _____. During this
period the hair, nails, skin, and eyes complete their development. If the child is born prior to the _____
month of life, it has little chance for survival. The newborn
child is called the _____.

fetus

seventh

neonate

5. A number of factors can interfere with prenatal growth and
produce abnormal conditions. Poor nutrition does not appear
to harm the fetus during the _____ part of pregnancy,
but during the _____ part of the pregnancy inadequate diets have been related to _____,
_____,
_____,
and _____.
Evidence suggests that these effects _____ (are/are not)
reversible.

early
later
premature births
physical abnormalities
susceptibility to di-
sease
lowered intelligence
are not

6. Diseases which can affect prenatal development include _____,
_____, _____, and _____.
For example, _____ or German measles can cause

Rubella
influenza, mumps,
smallpox
Rubella

blindness, deafness, or _____ _____,                    heart disease
especially if contracted _____ in pregnancy.                       early

7.  Drugs can also negatively affect prenatal development.  For
    example, in the 1960's the drug _____                          thalidomide
    led to the birth of deformed babies.  Cigarette smoking can lead
    to _____ _____.  Excessive                           premature birth
    use of aspirin can have harmful effects on the _____           circulatory
    system of the fetus.  Psychoactive drugs (e.g., LSD) may cause
    _____ damage in the mother.  The drugs                         chromosome
    _____ (have/do not have) to be taken during preg-             do not have
    nancy to affect the health of the fetus.

8.  Normally the release of the hormone _____ will                 androgen
    result in the development of male sexual organs.  In some cases
    of genetic malfunctioning, the cells of the male fetus are in-
    sensitive to the sex hormone created by its _____,             testes
    and consequently female sexual organs develop and the child
    appears to be a girl.  During adolescence when large doses of
    androgen are secreted the child may begin to develop _____     male
    characteristics.  Often an effective remedy to this problem is
    _____ or hormonal treatment.                                   surgery

9.  In some cases a genetic female may appear at birth to be a boy.
    This arises due to a genetic malfunctioning which causes the
    _____ glands to secrete a substance resembling                 adrenal
    androgen, resulting in the development of male sexual organs.
    During adolescence the secretion of the female sex hormone
    _____ causes feminine characteristics to develop.              estrogen
    This situation can also be counteracted by surgical and hormonal
    treatments.

10. At birth infants possess a number of simple _____,             reflexes
    but they are limited in their ability to move around and reach
    for objects.  However, motor development proceeds quite rapidly,
    and by about _____ months the infant is able to                fifteen
    walk.  The figure at the top of the next page summarizes some
    major points of motor development.

11. Some motor behaviors do not require practice or instruction but
    seem to come about by _____.  Motor                           maturation
    development and control seems to occur in a _____              head-to-toe
    and _____                                                     center-of-the-
    manner.                                                                 body-outward

114

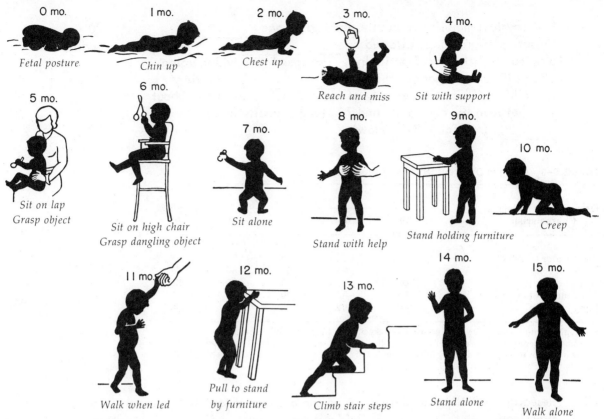

0 mo.
Fetal posture

1 mo.
Chin up

2 mo.
Chest up

3 mo.
Reach and miss

4 mo.
Sit with support

5 mo.
Sit on lap
Grasp object

6 mo.
Sit on high chair
Grasp dangling object

7 mo.
Sit alone

8 mo.
Stand with help

9 mo.
Stand holding furniture

10 mo.
Creep

11 mo.
Walk when led

12 mo.
Pull to stand
by furniture

13 mo.
Climb stair steps

14 mo.
Stand alone

15 mo.
Walk alone

Figure 8-2. Some milestones of infant motor development. (From the First Two Years: A Study of Twenty-Five Babies by Mary M. Shirley  Child Welfare Monograph No. 7, Vol. II. University of Minnesota Press, Minneapolis.  Copyright 1933 by the University of Minnesota.)

12.  In studying perceptual development psychologists observe differences in degree of gazing and the interruption of ongoing activity to determine whether an infant perceives the presence of stimuli.  Using such techniques it has been found that infants can discriminate _____ and _____      color, brightness
at birth.  Other research shows that infants prefer to look at the _____ _____ in contrast to other similar      human face
patterns.  In regard to sound, infants are quite sensitive to differences in _____ at birth and quickly develop the      pitch
ability to discriminate various sounds of speech.

13.  The growth of children begins to slow after about _____      two
years.  At about the age of _____ for girls and      11 or 12
_____ for boys, a period of sexual maturation      13 or 14
known as _____ occurs.  At this time the sex      puberty
glands which have developed slowly for a number of years show
renewed activity and boys and girls show rapid _____      growth
and various signs of sexual maturity.  Menstruation commences
in girls at about age _____ while boys produce sperm at about      13
age _____.  Research suggests that deficiency in diet can      15
_____ the average age of first menstruation.      delay

14. Full physical maturity is usually reached by age _____ .          20
    Cessation of growth is followed by _____ in            decline
    physical abilities and functioning. The speed with which aging
    affects different organs of the body _____ (varies/    varies
    is similar). While the velocity of nerve impulses decreases about
    10% between the ages of 30 and 70, lung capacity drops about
    _____ (see Table 8-3 below).                           50%

**TABLE 8-3  Aging in Different Organs of the Body**

| Organ or Physiological Characteristic | Age | | | | |
|---|---|---|---|---|---|
| | 30 | 40 | 50 | 60 | 70 |
| Nerve impulse speed | 100 | 100 | 96 | 93 | 91 |
| Body water content | 100 | 98 | 94 | 90 | 87 |
| Work rate | 100 | 94 | 87 | 80 | 74 |
| Heart output (at rest) | 100 | 93 | 83 | 70 | 58 |
| Efficiency of kidneys | 100 | 98 | 90 | 82 | 77 |
| Lung capacity | 100 | 92 | 78 | 61 | 50 |

While some organs quite rapidly lose their capacity to function with increasing age, others continue to operate at relatively high levels of efficiency for several decades. The figures shown for each age are percentages derived from a base line of 100 per cent functioning at age 30. (Based on data from Shock, 1962.)

15. Research by Philips has shown that among a group of famous
    Americans _____ individuals than expected died in       fewer
    the month prior to their birthday, while _____ of them   more
    than expected died in the month after their birthday. This
    effect was strongest with the _____ (least/most) famous. most
    This finding suggests that individuals may be able to control
    their bodily processes and hence delay death if they have a
    strong desire to live.

16. _____ and _____ are the only forms           Crying, cooing
    of communication of the child until about six months. At this
    point _____ occurs. This form of commun-                babbling
    ication contains all the sounds of human speech. Babbling can
    be increased by the use of _____ .                      reinforcement
    After about the age of 9 or 10 months, babbling involves pri-
    marily the speech sounds employed by the _____ .        parents
    Most children say their first word by age of _____ .    one year

17. By age two, children may already be using _____ words and at      200
    age three _____ words. However, the child's _____    1000, compre-
    of the speech of others is usually well ahead of the child's       hension
    _____ of the words.                                     production

18. One characteristic of early speech is the use of single word to
    express a variety of complex intentions and meanings. This is
    called _____ speech. When children at                   holophrastic

116

the age of 18-20 months begin to combine words into simple
sentences, they employ the _____ rules          grammatical
even in the absence of direct instruction.

19.  Early speech also tends to be _____          telegraphic
     in that words not essential to the overall meaning of a statement
     are omitted.  Early speech also involves _____         overgeneraliza-
     (the use of one word for a variety of different but related objects)   tion
     and _____                                    overdifferentia-
     (limiting the use of a word to too small a number of objects).  tion

20.  By the age of two and a half, children begin to attach appropriate
     endings to words (such as s and ed).  By age _____ they   three
     begin to construct sentences consisting of several words, and some-
     what later they start using _____ and         pronouns
     _____.  During the early school years they    prepositions
     start to master the meaning of words describing the relationship
     between people (e.g., friends).  Although large individual
     differences exist in the age at which these skills occur in children,
     their order of mastery is quite _____.        constant

21.  Research _____(suggests/does not suggest) the exis-   suggests
     tence of differences between members of differing racial and
     economic groups in language development.  A recent study of
     ghetto-reared black children suggests that such apparent differ-
     ences in language development are not due to deficiency in
     language mastery but the use of a somewhat different _____.  language

22.  One theory of language development by Skinner is that children
     learn to speak through the process of _____   operant
     _____.  Parents supposedly teach              conditioning
     their offspring to speak by selective _____           reinforcement
     of sounds resembling adult speech and by actively eliciting and
     rewarding _____ of their own verbal behavior.  imitation
     However this theory cannot account for the rapid growth in vo-
     cabulary in young children or the speed with which children master
     grammatical rules.

23.  Another explanation is that language is acquired by merely ob-
     serving the speech of others.  This is called _____    observational
     learning.  According to this position reinforcement and direct
     training are not necessary.  Some evidence for this position exists,
     but the fact that children often generate sentences or words not
     heard previously and comprehend complex rules of grammar not
     obvious from observed speech suggests that other factors must also
     be involved.

24.  In contrast to the position that language behavior is learned,
     Chomsky has argued that is partly _____.  He proposes   innate

that humans have a built-in neural system called _____     Language

                                                         or     Acquisition De-
LAD. This device supposedly enables children to intuitively     vice
grasp the basic rules of grammar.

25. The existence of the LAD is derived from three facts. In
learning language, children make _____     much fewer
errors than expected, all children go through the same stages
of language acquisition, and specific areas of the brain _____     are
(are/are not) involved in speech. So far no definitive evidence
exists to allow determination of the correctness of Chomsky's
position.

26. Although chimpanzees cannot learn to speak, they are capable
of mastering other types of language such as _____ language.     sign

27. Work by _____ has provided evidence that the     Piaget
cognitive processes of children and adults are     different
(similar/different). In Piaget's view, from birth on, cognitive
growth can be seen as an attempt to develop the abilities of
_____ _____ and     abstract reason-
    ing
_____ _____. This     logical thinking
development occurs through the conflict or tension between the
process of _____ and     assimilation
_____. The tendency to apply old     accommodation
ideas or habits to new objects or problems is _____.     assimilation
_____ is the tendency to acquire new     Accommodation
responses or change old ones. The continual tension between
these two processes leads to an increased ability of the child to
adapt to new situations.

28. Piaget proposes that children go through an orderly sequence of
_____ major stages toward cognitive maturity. In the     four
first stage or _____ stage, the infant knows     sensory-motor
his/her world only through _____ activities and _____     motor, sensory
impressions. The absence of mental representations during this
period results in infants acting as if objects they no longer see or
feel do not _____. The development of the concept that     exist
an object exists even if removed from view is called _____     object
_____.     permanence

29. Between the ages of 18 and 24 months infants acquire the ability
to form mental images of the world around them and begin to
think in _____ _____.     verbal symbols
This marks the beginning of the _____     preoperational
period. During this stage the capacity for _____     observational

learning appears. The thought processes at this level are still immature though. The infants are _____ in that they cannot imagine that others may perceive the world differently from themselves. They lack a true understanding of _____ terms (e.g., larger) and lack the ability to arrange objects in order along some dimension (i.e., _____).

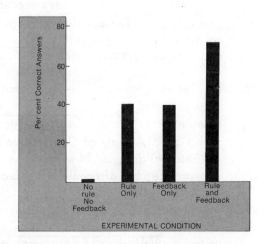

30. They also lack the principle of _____.    ~~~~~~on
By age _____ most children can solve the problems    seven
of the preoperational period and enter the period of
_____.    concrete opera-
During this period children develop the capacity for logical    tions
thought concerning objects directly in front of them.

31. At age 12 most children enter the stage of _____    formal
_____. At this point children demonstrate    operations
the ability to do careful scientific reasoning. They also show a
preoccupation with _____ itself.    thought

32. The basic notion of Piaget that children pass through different
stages of cognitive development is essentially _____    correct
(correct/incorrect). However, evidence suggests that children
_____ (can/cannot) be accelerated in their movement    can
from one stage to another. For example, Siegler and Liebert
were able to teach children the principle of conservation by
providing a formal rule and _____    accuracy
_____. These results are depicted in the    feedback
figure below.

FIGURE 8-11 Evidence that children as young as 5½ can acquire conservation. Mastery of this concept was facilitated both by the provision of a formal rule and by feedback regarding the accuracy of subjects' answers. (Based on data from Siegler and Liebert, 1972.)

33. The development of a strong affective bond toward another person
is called _____. One interpretation of the    attachment
development of attachment is _____    classical
_____ which assumes that through    conditioning
the association of pleasurable stimuli with another person, this
person becomes a conditioned stimulus for pleasurable stimuli.

34. Studies with monkeys by _____ have shown that
    classical conditioning is not a sufficient explanation. In
    various experiments Harlow found that the attachment of
    monkeys to their mother seems to depend primarily on the degree
    to which the mother satisfies their need for _____
    _____. Any object which satisfies this need
    for rubbing, touching, and clinging (such as a cloth mother) will
    become the source of attachment. Provision of nourishment by
    a wire mother _____ (produced/did not
    produce) attachment behavior.

    Harlow

    contact
    comfort

    did not produce

35. Other studies by Harlow showed that presence of cloth mothers,
    but not wire mothers, was able to _____
    of monkeys in the presence of strange objects. Having cloth
    mothers reject the baby monkeys by presenting various noxious
    stimuli (e.g., metal spikes) _____ (altered/
    did not alter) the attachment of the baby monkeys.

    reduce the fear

    did not alter

36. Although research has not been able to establish whether contact
    comfort is the basis for attachment of human infants, recent re-
    search suggests that infants from various species seem to form an
    attachment to the first object (e.g., mother) they encounter
    which allows them to perform their strongest or _____
    responses (such as following moving objects and clinging to
    objects). This is called _____.

    dominant

    imprinting

37. Several studies have shown that monkeys reared in isolation
    showed extreme deficiencies in _____ and
    _____ behavior. Apparently, _____
    _____ is necessary for normal social
    development. For monkeys who have been isolated more than
    six months, the effects are _____ (easy/
    difficult) to reverse.

    social
    sexual, social

    interaction

    difficult

38. Studies with humans have found that institutionally reared infants
    show retarded _____ and _____
    development. These effects appear _____ (to be/not to be)
    reversible. A study of Guatemalan children found that confinement
    of these children for 14 months in a dark hut led to a _____
    appearance, but afterwards they recovered quickly.

    social, cognitive
    to be

    listless

39. The process through which children come to acquire sexual identity
    is called _____. The two major conceptions
    as to how children acquire sexual identity are the _____
    _____ and _____ views.
    According to the social learning view, sex-typing is the result
    of _____ of models similar to oneself and
    the _____ of such behavior by one's parents.

    sex-typing
    social
    learning, cogni-
    tive
    imitation
    rewarding

The cognitive view suggests that the process starts when children learn to _____ themselves as a boy or a girl. They then adopt behavior which they perceive as being appropriate to their gender.

identify

40. Surveys of television offerings indicate that in children's programs _____ characters greatly outnumber _____ characters. The content of the programs seems to characterize females as _____ _____ and males as _____ _____. In children's books the ratio of male to female characters and the employment of sexual stereotypes is _____ (greater/ less).

male, female

passive followers

active leaders

greater

41. Research with children of age five and older has shown that they _____ (hold/do not hold) firm sexual stereotypes. Females are seen as appreciative, soft-hearted, and _____, while males are seen as strong, adventurous, and _____. These stereotypes _____ (increase/decrease) in strength from kindergarten through second grade and remain largely unchanged throughout later life.

hold

emotional

aggressive

increase

42. Research on differences between men and women has found that many frequently assumed differences _____ (do/do not) exist or that the extent of the differences is less than expected. Males have been shown to be more _____ and have greater _____ and _____ _____ ability than females, while females excell in _____ ability. Findings from research on male-female differences are summarized in the table below.

do not

aggressive

mathematical,

visual-spatial

verbal

TABLE 8-5   How Different Are the Two Sexes?

| Differences Borne Out by SOME Testing | Differences About Which There is Doubt | Differences Shown to be False |
| --- | --- | --- |
| Males are generally more aggressive then females. | Females are more timid and anxious (?) | Females are more sociable than males. |
| Females have greater verbal ability than males. | Males are more active than females (?) | Females are more suggestible than males. |
| Males excel in visual-spatial ability. | Males are more competitive than females (?) | Females have lower self-esteem than males. |
| Males excel in mathematical ability. | Males are more dominant than females (?) | Females lack motivation to achieve. |
| | Females are more passive than males (?) | Males are more "analytic" in cognitive style than females. |

Based on data from Maccoby and Jacklin, 1974.

43.  According to Piaget's theory of moral development, children
     initially have an _____ moral orientation.          objective
     During this stage acts are judged as good or bad primarily on
     the basis of their _____. At about age              consequences,
     seven the child supposedly develops a _____           subjective
     moral perspective. At this point acts are judged as good or bad
     depending on the goodness or badness of the _____.       intentions

44.  It appears that Piaget's hypothesis that all children go from
     the objective to the subjective moral orientation is _____      correct
     (correct/not correct). However, contrary to Piaget's theory,
     the speed of moral development _____ (can/can not) be        can
     affected by the influence of the social environment (e.g.,
     models).

45.  Kohlberg's theory of moral development suggests that children
     go through _____ stages of moral growth. The first two stages  six
     form the _____ level of morality.          preconventional
     At this level children evaluate acts in terms of their
     _____. The next two stages form the        consequences
     _____ level of morality. At this level     conventional
     actions are judged in terms of their approval by others (stage 3)
     and in terms of respect for law and authority (stage 4).

46.  Stages 5 and 6 make up the _____           post-convention-
     level of morality. Individuals in these stages evaluate acts     al
     in terms of _____ _____              universal, moral
     principles.

## KEY CONCEPTS AND TERMS

       After you have finished your Guided Review, fill in the meaning of
       the following terms in your own words. Check on your accuracy
       by consulting your text on the pages indicated or the Glossary.

period of the ovum  (p. 258)


period of the embryo  (p. 258)


period of the fetus  (p. 259)


neonate  (p. 259)

androgen (p. 261)

estrogen (p. 261)

puberty (p. 265)

holophrastic (p. 270)

telegraphic (p. 270)

overgeneralization (p. 270)

overdifferentiation (p. 270)

Language Acquisition Device (p. 273)

assimilation (p. 275)

accommodation (p. 275)

sensory motor stage (p. 276)

object permanence (p. 276)

preoperational stage (p. 276)

period of concrete operations (p. 277)

period of formal operations (p. 278)

attachment (p. 280)

sex-typing (p. 280)

objective moral orientation  (p. 290)

subjective moral perspective  (p. 290)

preconventional level of morality  (p. 291)

conventional level of morality  (p. 292)

postconventional level of morality  (p. 292)

## A PERSONAL QUIZ

After you are about finished with your studies but still have some time left for review, take this quiz to check on your mastery. Fill in your answers in the spaces provided and after you are finished check their correctness with the answers provided.

___ 1. Which one of the following is not one of the stages of parental development? (p. 258-259)
   a. the period of the ovum
   b. the period of the uterus
   c. the period of the embryo
   d. the period of the fetus

___ 2. The inner layer of cells of the ovum develops into _____ while the outer layer develops into _____. (p. 258)
   a. child, life sustaining structures
   b. embryo, umbilical cord
   c. embryo, life sustaining structures
   d. fetus, nervous system

___ 3. The blood of the embryo and the mother exchange nutrients in the (p. 258)
   a. umbilical cord
   b. placenta
   c. embryo's circulatory system
   d. both a and b

___ 4. Poor nutrition has its effects primarily during (p. 259)

   a. the embryonic stage
   b. period of the ovum
   c. the early part of the fetal stage
   d. the later part of the fetal stage

___ 5. Which of the following can have harmful effects on the circulatory system? (p. 260)
   a. psychoactive drugs
   b. cigarette smoking
   c. excessive aspirin
   d. thalidomide

___ 6. Motor development seems to occur in a _____ fashion. (p. 262)
   a. head-to-toe
   b. center-of-the-body-outward
   c. both a and b
   d. none of the above

___ 7. Research has shown that infants can discriminate _____ at birth. (p. 264)
   a. pitch
   b. color
   c. brightness
   d. all of the above

8. Research on famous Americans has found that _____ expected died in the month prior to their birthday. (p. 268)
   a. a larger number than
   b. a smaller number than
   c. about as many as
   d. only one-half as many as

9. Which of the following is not a characteristic of early speech? (p. 270)
   a. lack of grammar
   b. holophrastic
   c. overgeneralization
   d. overdifferentiation

10. Research on differences in language development between members of different racial and economic groups has found that (p. 272)
    a. such differences do not exist
    b. lower socioeconomic groups are deficient in language mastery
    c. these differences may reflect the use of a different language
    d. none of the above

11. The Language Acquisition Device (LAD) is part of _____ theory of language development. (p. 273)
    a. Chomsky's
    b. Skinner's
    c. the observational learning
    d. the cognitive

12. The LAD (p. 273)
    a. is innate
    b. is a neural system
    c. enables an intuitive grasp of grammar
    d. all of the above

13. According to Piaget, cognitive growth is the result of tension between the processes of (p. 275)
    a. overdifferentiation and overgeneralization
    b. abstract reasoning and logical thinking

    c. assimilation and accommodation
    d. emotionality and abstract reasoning

14. During the preoperational stage children exhibit (p. 276)
    a. observational learning
    b. logical thought
    c. knowledge of the principle of conservation
    d. an understanding of relational terms

15. The stage of formal operations is reached at about age (p. 278)
    a. 5
    b. 7
    c. 10
    d. 12

16. Studies by Harlow on attachment in monkeys have shown that attachment of monkeys to their mother depends primarily on (p. 282)
    a. nourishment by the mother
    b. contact comfort
    c. fear reduction by the mother
    d. social stimulation

17. Early social isolation has been shown to produce (p. 283-284)
    a. permanent cognitive and social deficiencies in humans
    b. social and sexual deficiencies in monkeys which are difficult to reverse
    c. produce easily reversible sexual deficiencies in monkeys
    d. none of the above

18. Research on differences between males and females has found that (p. 289)
    a. sexual stereotypes are generally correct
    b. males are more active and competitive than females
    c. males are more aggressive than females

d. males are more analytical than females

___ 19. The objective moral orientation (p. 290)
a. involves judging acts in terms of their consequences
b. involves judging acts in terms of intentions
c. is a mature stage of moral development
d. develops around age 7

___ 20. According to Kohlberg's theory of moral development, the stage at which individuals evaluate acts in terms of

their approval by others is the ___ level of morality. (p. 292)
a. postconventional
b. conventional
c. preconventional
d. none of the above

Answers:

| | | | |
|---|---|---|---|
| 1. b | 6. c | 11. a | 16. b |
| 2. a | 7. d | 12. d | 17. b |
| 3. b | 8. b | 13. c | 18. c |
| 4. d | 9. a | 14. a | 19. a |
| 5. c | 10. c | 15. d | 20. b |

## PSYCHOLOGY IN ACTION: PROJECTS AND DEMONSTRATIONS

### Preoperational Thought - When the Same is Less (or More)

See your text for the details of this demonstration (p. 279). You might want to repeat this type of demonstration with beakers and water as shown in Figure 8-10 in your text.

### Child Morality

Piaget suggests that children prior to the age of seven have an objective moral orientation. They evaluate the goodness or badness of actions on the basis of the consequences of those actions (good or bad). At about age seven, children develop a subjective moral orientation which involves evaluation of behavior in terms of whether the intentions were good or bad. You can demonstrate this to yourself by reading the pairs of stories provided on the next page (the first pair is from your text) to a number of children who are five years old and a number who are eight years old. After reading each pair of stories you should ask the children who did the naughtier thing? You should find that the younger children will judge the person who produces more bad consequences as naughtier, while the older children should judge the person with the bad intentions as naughtier.

Stories

### Story A

John was in his room when his mother called him to dinner. John goes down, and opens the door to the dining room. But behind the door was a chair, and on the chair was a tray with fifteen cups on it. John did not know the cups were behind the door, but the door hits the tray, bang go the fifteen cups, and they all get broken.

126

## Story B

One day when Henry's mother was out, Henry tried to get some cookies out of the cupboard. He climbed up on a chair, but the cookie jar was still too high, and he couldn't reach it. But while he was trying to get the cookie jar, he knocked over a cup. The cup fell down and broke.

## Story A

Dan was playing on his swing in his backyard. His sister was also playing there. She decided to go over to the sandbox and play. As she walks past the swing, Dan tries to kick her but misses.

## Story B

Chris was watching TV. His sister was playing nearby. He hears one of his friends playing outside and gets up to run outside to play with him. As he is running he bumps into his sister. She falls down, her nose begins to bleed, and she starts to cry.

## Story A

Suzy was riding her brother's tricycle in front of her house. She was trying to see how fast she could ride it. All of a sudden the tricycle fell over, breaking its horn and mirror, bending its wheels, and scratching its paint.

## Story B

Mary was playing in her sandbox behind her house. Her mother called for her to come in for a nap. As she walked by her brother's tricycle on the way into the house, she pushed it over, scratching the paint.

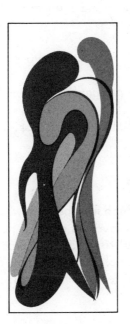

Chapter 9

# PERSONALITY:
Understanding the
Behavior
of Individuals

# LEARNING OBJECTIVES: WHAT YOU SHOULD KNOW

After reading this chapter you should:

Know the basic features of Freud's theory of personality.

Understand Freud's conception of psychosexual development.

Be able to discuss Rogers's self-theory of personality.

Know the basic concepts of Jung's theory.

Be able to dexcribe Sheldon's classification of body types and related temperaments.

Know Erickson's eight stages of the life cycle.

Be able to discuss the different types of personality tests and their advantages and disadvantages.

Know the differences between the Type A and Type B personality types.

Know the various characteristics of the authoritarian personality.

Be able to discuss the use of personality tests as predictors of behavior.

# STUDY TIPS: A HELPING HAND

There are a number of points in this chapter which may be somewhat difficult for you to master. The section on psychosexual development involves a lot of new terms and ideas. Be sure you know each stage and the types of personalities they may produce. The Oedipal period for both males and females is an especially complex set of events and should be studied carefully. Sheldon's classification of body types and temperaments will also require some extra effort for mastery in order to avoid confusion.

# STEP-BY-STEP: A GUIDED REVIEW

After you have read the chapter, mentally fill in each of the blanks in the following section while covering the answers in the margin. Check your answer with that in the margin as you go along. While in many cases your answer should be the same as that in the margin, in other cases a word of similar meaning is acceptable. Do not write in the spaces until you are doing your final review.

1. An individual's characteristic patterns of behavior is called
_____. The first model of personality was          personality
developed by _____. He proposed a          Hippocrates
_____which classified all behavior into four          typology

catetories or _____. Whenever there was an excess
of four bodily fluids or "humors", certain temperaments would
result. An excess of blood supposedly led to _____,
an excess of black bile _____, an excess
of yellow bile to _____, and excess of phlegm to
_____.

types

cheerfulness

depression

anger

apathy

2.  The first comprehensive personality theory was the
    _____ theory developed by
    _____. He proposed that mental functioning
    involved three states of consciousness. The _____
    state is whatever one is thinking of at the moment. The
    _____ is all the stored memories which
    can be brought into consciousness. The _____
    contains all the memories of which we are unaware. Much of
    the material in the unconscious has been _____
    because it produces anxiety when brought to consciousness. Some
    of these unconscious desires may be expressed in dreams.

psychoanalytic

Freud

conscious

preconscious

unconscious

repressed

3.  Freud later dealt with mental function primarily in terms of three
    basic constructs, the _____, the _____, and the
    _____. The primary region is the _____. This
    region is present at birth and is totally _____.
    The id is oriented completely to the immediate _____
    of desires without regard to _____ and what
    is possible.

id, ego

superego, id

unconscious

gratification

consequences

4.  As a consequence of early frustration of the desires of the id,
    the individual begins to learn the limitations imposed by _____.
    This signals the development of the _____. This region in-
    volves the perception, reasoning, and learning necessary to
    interact effectively with the world. The ego involves primarily
    _____ and _____
    states. The ego too strives for satisfaction and is concerned with
    aiding the satisfaction of the id guided by reality.

reality

ego

conscious, pre-
conscious

5.  The _____ develops as children are exposed to the
    moral values of their parents. The child learns to internalize the
    parental views of ideal behavior ( _____ ) and sense
    of right and wrong ( _____ ). The superego
    spans all three levels of consciousness.

superego

ego-ideal

conscience

6.  Freud viewed human development as a series of stages distin-
    guishable by the way bodily pleasure is obtained. Adult per-
    sonality depends on what happens during these stages. If someone
    does not progress beyond a particular stage he is said to be
    _____ at this stage. Going back to an earlier stage
    when things go badly is termed _____.

fixated

regression

7.   The first source of pleasure is _____. The oral stage       oral
     is a relatively passive one. Overindulgence at this point
     supposedly produces an oral personality type that is trusting,
     conforming, happy, _____, and likes to            dependent
     _____. Frustration and anxiety during the oral stage was      eat
     expected to produce a _____ and verbally              tense
     _____ individual. Research on the relation         aggressive
     between early oral experiences and personality type _____     has not
     (has/has not) supported these ideas.

8.   The period during which toilet training is undertaken is the
     _____ stage. This is the first time the child encounters   anal
     interference with his pleasure (defecation), and the anal per-
     sonality reflects the individual's reaction to this interference.
     The anal characters become obsessed with _____       saving
     and _____. They show a concern for               collecting
     _____ and _____.                  neatness, order-
     Since this stage allows for rebellion against parents by not     liness
     cooperating with the toilet training, the anal adult can also
     be characterized by _____ or                    stubborness
     _____. Empirical support                        aggressiveness,
     (exists/does not exist) for the hypothesized characteristics     exists
     of oral and anal types.

9.   At the third year there is a brief _____ stage         urethral
     based on concern with the control of urination. The adult
     urethral type is supposedly _____ but not very   ambitious
     persistent in the face of difficulty.

10.  When the child first discovers the pleasure of manipulating the
     genitals, he/she enters the _____ stage. The boy's    phallic
     sexual urges become directed toward the mother and this
     constitutes the _____ period. He fears the punishment  Oedipal
     by the father in the form of _____.             castration
     This fear is the basis for the development of the _____
     in that the most reasonable solution is for the boy to give up his superego
     lust for his mother and _____ with his father. The
     identification involves adoption of all of the father's _____ identify
     If the Oedipal conflict is not resolved the phallic adult may    values
     become _____ or _____.
                                                                     promiscuous, homo-
                                                                     sexual
11.  For the female the first sexual object is the _____.   mother
     When she discovers that she does not have the male penis, she
     develops _____ and blames her mother for        penis envy
     her inadequacy. Because females do not have castration fears,
     females are not forced to develop a strong superego according to
     Freud. This _____ (has/has not) been supported by       has not
     subsequent research.

12. The female Oedipal conflict is resolved when the child rejects the mother in favor of the father. If this conflict is not resolved, the adult phallic female may be a flirtatious teaser or a castrating female oriented toward a career. _____ is considered to be an extreme version of the unresolved conflict.

    Homosexuality

13. By the age of _____ the basic personality characteristics have supposedly developed through the experiences of the psychosexual stages. From that point until puberty, the child is in the _____ period in which there is a loss of interest in sex and involvement with friends of the same sex. The mature person reaches the _____ stage at which point sexual desire becomes associated with _____ and adult roles are taken on.

    six

    latency

    genital

    affection

14. While some of Freud's ideas appear to be correct, many are wrong. Others are either untestable or do not allow prediction of behavior.

15. Rogers developed a _____ theory of personality. His basic notion is that people are naturally open, honest, and in contact with their feelings. They have the natural capacity for _____ and _____ development. Difficulties arise only when others interfere and force individuals to _____ reality.

    self

    growth

    psychological

    distort

16. In analyzing human behavior Rogers tries to see the world from the individual's point of view. This is the _____ approach. The primary motive of the individual is the _____ tendency, which is the motive to maintain or improve oneself.

    phenomenological

    actualizing

17. Psychological health and adjustment depend on a _____ self concept that is congruent with reality. Discrepancies between one's self and one's experiences produce _____ and _____ and can lead to breakdowns.

    realistic

    maladjustment

    anxiety

18. According to Rogers, children have a need for _____ regard. This need is a crucial one for the development of the self since children may be forced by parents to accept values and perceptions that do not fit their own experiences and feelings in order for the child to receive approval. The development of a realistic and healthy self concept in children requires that the parent _____ the child's feelings and maintain positive regard for the child while disapproving of unacceptible behaviors.

    positive

    accept

19. Research has shown that the self concept is not necessarily a permanent structure but can be changed to a more positive self image by _____ and a more negative self image by _____.

    success

    failure

20. One of the basic concepts of Jung's theory is the
_____ **collective un-**
which is the individual's mental record of memories about the **conscious**
experiences of the human race. Evidence for this is supposedly
found in the independent creation of similar _____ **myths**
and artistic symbols in different cultures. The collective unconscious also contains _____ which are **archetypes**
universal symbols which appear frequently in art, literature,
myth, and religion. However, these universal themes and ideas
could be explained in terms of common experiences.

21. Jung also proposed the existence of the _____ **introversion-**
_____ dimension of personality. Indi- **extroversion**
viduals who are primarily concerned with themselves are
_____. Those who are primarily concerned **introverts**
with the outside world are _____. **extroverts**

22. Sheldon believes that the _____ **bodily constitu-**
is a major determinant of our behavior. He developed a classifi- **tion**
cation of the individual's body type or _____ **somatotype**
since this was believed to be related to one's basic temperament.

23. The classification involved three components. The component
which consists of a soft and rounded appearance is _____. **endomorphy**
An extreme endomorph would be classified as _____. The **7-1-1**
related temperament is _____. This **viscerotonia**
includes love of physical comfort and sociability.

24. The second component is _____ and consists **mesomorphy**
of a strong and muscular anatomy. The related temperament
is _____ which includes the love of **somatotonia**
physical activity and aggressiveness. An extreme mesomorph
would be classified as _____. **1-7-1**

25. The third component is _____, reflecting **ectomorphy**
a thin and delicate anatomy. The extreme ectomorph is classified
as _____. The accompanying temperament is **1-1-7**
_____, which involves love of privacy **cerebrotonia**
and intellectual activity.

26. Evidence _____ (supports/does not support) Sheldon's **supports**
suggested relationships between somatotype and temperament. Other
research suggests that _____ are most likely to **endomorphs**
develop disorders involving extreme variations in emotion,
_____ are likely to become paranoid, and **mesomorphs**
_____ are likely to become schizophrenic. **ectomorphs**
It has also been found that juvenile delinquents are more likely
to be _____ or a combination of **mesomorphic**
_____ and _____ than **endomorphic,**
nondelinquents. **mesomorphic**

27. Erikson proposed that there are _____ stages through        eight
which one must pass in order to reach maturity. Each stage has
a characteristic conflict, and the manner of its solution determines the type of person one will be. Table 9-1 below summarizes
these developmental periods.

**TABLE 9-1  Erikson's Eight Stages of Life and the Crises to be Faced in Each**

1. The *sensory stage* occurs during the first few months of life. The infant is totally dependent on others, and the crisis involves learning to trust or to mistrust other people. For example, if a mother is unkind or undependable in meeting the infant's needs, he would be expected to spend a lifetime mistrusting his fellow human beings.

2. The *muscular development stage* comes next and occurs during the period of toilet training. The crisis is between developing a sense of confidence and independence versus shame and self-doubt. The crucial determinant here is whether the child experiences primarily success or failure in learning to control his own bodily functions.

3. The *locomotor control stage* develops as the child learns to move about in his world and to assert his own needs. As in Freud's phallic stage, there is sexual desire for the parent of the opposite sex. The crisis involves initiative and expressing one's own desires versus guilt. Unless the individual can discover a socially acceptable way to express his or her sexual needs, he or she will be obsessed with guilt throughout life.

4. The *latency stage* occurs during the early school years, during which the child finds that he is competent or that he is a failure in comparison with his peers. Success during this period results in an industrious, hard-working adult, while failure leads to a pervasive sense of inferiority.

5. In the *puberty stage*, the problem is not simply one of sexuality but rather the problem of finding one's own identity. With regard to sex, social interactions, and plans for the future, the individual must develop and accept his personal identity. Otherwise, he will remain confused about just who he is and what his role in life might be.

6. The *young adulthood stage* coincides with the period in which most people seek to form a personal intimate relationship with someone. Success here involves the establishment of intimacy with another human being; failure results in a sense of isolation. The fact that an individual gets married is not necessarily an indication that this crisis has been resolved in favor of intimacy; two individuals can spend a lifetime together and yet be psychologically isolated.

7. In the *adulthood stage*, during our middle years, the crucial choice is the "growth crisis"—whether one becomes a productive and useful human being or settles into a pattern of complacency and stagnation.

8. The final stage is *maturity*, and it can be reached only by those who have been successful in resolving the crises at the previous seven stages. It is at this time that one must face the unthinkable realization of death. With a history of success at the other stages, the individual has a sense of integrity and a sense of self-worth, so that even death can be accepted. Previous failures leave an individual with a sense of despair and the feeling that life has been a foolish waste.

28. Let's briefly check your knowledge of the material in Table 9-1. The stage at which the child learns to move about and assert his/her needs is the _____ _____       locomotor con-
stage. The search for identity is the primary focus of the _____      trol
_____ stage. The establishment of psycho-      puberty
logical intimacy is important in the _____ _____      young adulthood

stage. The final stage is _____ and can be     maturity
reached only after successful solution of crises at the other
stages. The _____ stage occurs during the     sensory
first few months of life. The                            muscular
_____
_____ stage centers around the               development
control of bodily functions. Learning about one's degree of
competence occurs during the _____ stage.     latency
The crucial "growth" crisis is encountered in the _____     adulthood
stage.

29.  Tests which present ambiguous stimuli or pictures to elicit res-
     ponses from subjects which may reflect unconscious motives or
     problems are called _____ tests. One          projective
     which employs ink blots is known as the _____     Rorschach
     test.

30.  One test which was designed to allow objective prediction of
     behavior based on verbal responses to questions is the _____.     MMPI
     This test was designed by determining to what extent psychiatric
     groups and normals gave different responses to different questions.

31.  Recent research has related personality types to heart trouble.
     Individuals who are prone to heart trouble are called _____.     Type A
     These individuals are competitive, achievement oriented,
     aggressive, and impatient, while _____ individuals     Type B
     are not. _____ percent of the population is estimated     Forty
     to be Type A.

32.  Research has shown that only _____ individuals will work     Type A
     hard at an important task even if no deadline is set. Type _____     A
     individuals are likely to be involved in extracurricular activities.
     The development of the A or B types probably depends both on
     _____ and _____.     heredity, cul-
                                                    tural influence

33.  Since it is generally agreed that personality is too complex to
     be described in terms of a small number of types, some psycholo-
     gists have looked for the existence of numerous psychological
     _____. These are stable characteristics of behavior in     traits
     which people differ. Cattell tried to identify the most basic and
     important traits. He derived 16 basic _____ traits     source
     (e.g., dominance versus submissiveness) which are reflected in a
     variety of actual behaviors or _____ traits.     surface

34.  Some psychologists have focused on a single trait such as authori-
     tarianism. In the book, The Authoritarian Personality, Adorno and
     his colleagues proposed that this trait is characteristic of individuals
     from homes emphasizing obedience, respect, suppression of sex
     related topics or activities, and enforcement of conventional values.

136

This upbringing supposedly produces feelings of _____ towards parents. This hostility is supposedly directed toward inferior or different others and presumably explains the _____ supposedly characteristic of authoritarians. The test these investigators developed to measure authoritarianism was called the _____.

hostility

prejudice

F scale

35. Research _____ (has/has not) generally supported the above conception of the authoritarian personality. Authoritarians have also been found to be _____ in political and sexual matters.

has

conservative

36. Other studies suggest that authoritarians are more likely to employ aggression towards others, but only in situations where it is _____. This has been found for use of physical punishment with children and attitudes toward war.

justified

37. A simulated jury study found that authoritarians will recommend greater punishment than equalitarians, but only if the defendant is perceived as _____. A subsequent study found that this effect was due to the authoritarian's superior memory for details of the defendant's _____ and inferior memory for the details of the _____.

Another simulated jury study found that _____ were more severe with an authority figure defendant (policemen), while _____ were more severe with a nonauthority figure defendant. (See Figure 9-14 below.)

dissimilar

character
evidence

equalitarians

authoritarians

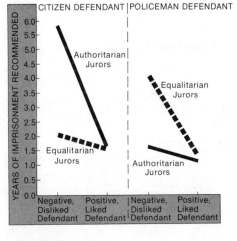

FIGURE 9-14 When an ordinary citizen is the defendant in a manslaughter case, authoritarians judge him on the basis of their feelings and recommend severe punishment if he has been described negatively. When a policeman is the defendant, however, it is the equalitarians who judge him on the basis of their feelings and recommend severe punishment if he has been described negatively. (Adapted from Mitchell, 1973.)

38. Research on personality tests as predictors of behavior has indicated that personality measures are generally _____ predictors of behavior, especially when one is trying to predict from one situation to a very _____ situation.

poor

different

39. Research on honesty has found that there _____ (is/is not) a great deal of consistency in this type of behavior across situations.

Is not

The relationship between measures of conscience (e.g., ability to delay gratification) and honesty has been found to be _____. weak

40. That situations are important in determining honesty was shown in a study in which individuals were more likely to report a robbery if they were _____ than if they were _____ _____. alone, with others

## KEY CONCEPTS AND TERMS

After you have finished your Guided Review, fill in the meaning of the following terms in your own words. Check on your accuracy by consulting your text on the pages indicated or the Glossary.

personality (p. 295)

four humors (p. 296)

psychoanalytic theory (p. 297)

conscious (p. 298)

preconscious (p. 298)

unconscious (p. 299)

repression (p. 299)

id (p. 299)

ego (p. 300)

superego (p. 300)

ego-ideal (p. 300)

conscience (p. 300)

fixation  (p. 300)

regression  (p. 300)

oral stage  (p. 300)

anal stage  (p. 301)

urethal stage  (p. 302)

phallic stage  (p. 302)

Oedipal period  (p. 302)

latency period  (p. 303)

genital stage  (p. 303)

self-theory  (p. 303)

positive regard  (p. 304)

collective unconscious  (p. 307)

archetypes  (p. 307)

introversion-extroversion  (p. 307)

somatotype  (p. 308)

endomorphy  (p. 308)

viscerotonia  (p. 308)

mesomorphy  (p. 308)

somatotonia  (p. 308)

ectomorphy  (p. 309)

cerebrotonia  (p. 309)

sensory stage  (p. 310)

muscular development stage  (p. 310)

locomotor control stage  (p. 310)

latency stage  (p. 310)

puberty stage  (p. 310)

young adulthood stage  (p. 310)

adulthood stage  (p. 310)

maturity  (p. 310)

projective tests  (p. 312)

MMPI  (p. 315)

Type A  (p. 318)

Type B  (p. 318)

source traits  (p. 319)

surface traits (p. 319)

authoritarian personality (p. 320)

## A PERSONAL QUIZ

After you are about finished with your studies but still have some time left for review, take this quiz to check on your mastery. Fill in your answers in the spaces provided and after you are finished check their correctness with the answers provided.

____ 1. The first model of personality was developed by (p. 296)
a. Freud
b. Rogers
c. Hippocrates
d. Kraepelin

____ 2. The psychoanalytic theory of personality was developed by (p. 297)
a. Rogers
b. Freud
c. Erikson
d. Sheldon

____ 3. The constitutional theory of personality was developed by (p. 308)
a. Jung
b. Erikson
c. Rogers
d. Sheldon

____ 4. The personality region which is primarily concerned with immediate gratification is the (p. 299)
a. id
b. ego
c. superego
d. preconscious

____ 5. The ego is primarily concerned with the demands of (p. 300)
a. bodily desires
b. reality
c. conscience
d. parents

____ 6. If someone does not progress beyond a particular psychosexual stage, this person is said to be (p. 300)
a. fixated
b. dependent
c. regressive
d. immature

____ 7. Which of the following is not characteristic of the anal personality? (p. 301-302)
a. orderliness
b. collecting
c. trusting
d. stubborness

____ 8. The Oedipal conflict of the male is resolved by (p. 302)
a. hatred for the father
b. the development of the superego
c. identification with the mother
d. none of the above

____ 9. In terms of the degree of support Freud's theory has received, it can be stated that (p. 302-303)
a. the theory has strong support
b. some support exists for the existence of oral and anal types
c. the theory is completely wrong
d. the theory is a good predictor of behavior

10. Rogers proposed that the primary human motive is (p. 304)
   a. the actualizing tendency
   b. sex
   c. power
   d. social intimacy

11. According to Rogers, psychological health depends on (p. 304-305)
   a. a realistic self-concept
   b. receipt of positive self-regard
   c. acceptance of a child's feelings by parents
   d. all of the above

12. Universal symbols which appear frequently in art, literature, and religion are termed_____by Jung. (p. 307)
   a. archetypes
   b. myths
   c. collective memories
   d. none of the above

13. The component of the body type which consists of a strong muscular anatomy is called_____by Sheldon. (p. 308)
   a. ectomorphy
   b. endomorphy
   c. mesomorphy
   d. viscerotonia

14. The temperament which is associated with endomorphy is (p. 308)
   a. somatotonia
   b. viscerotonia
   c. endotonia
   d. cerebrotonia

15. According to Erikson, the life stage at which the child learns that she is competent or a failure relative to her peers is the (p. 310)
   a. puberty stage
   b. locomotor control stage
   c. latency stage
   d. muscular development stage

16. A test which was designed to objectively predict behavior from verbal responses to questions is the (p. 315)
   a. MMPI
   b. Rorschach
   c. TAT
   d. projective test

17. Which of the following statements about the Type A individuals is not correct? (p. 318)
   a. they are aggressive
   b. they are impatient
   c. they are likely to be involved in extracurricular activities
   d. they constitute 60% of the population

18. Authoritarians tend to be characterized by (p. 320)
   a. liberalism
   b. dislike of war
   c. hostility toward inferior others
   d. having come from warm affectionate homes

19. Simulated jury studies have found authoritarians will recommend the highest level of punishment if the defendant is_____and an authority figure. (p. 322-323)
   a. dissimilar; is not
   b. similar; is not
   c. dissimilar; is
   d. similar; is

20. As predictors of behavior, personality measures appear to be (p. 324)
   a. quite good
   b. rather poor
   c. quite good in very similar situations
   d. good even across different situations

Answers:

| | | | |
|---|---|---|---|
| 1. c | 6. a | 11. d | 16. a |
| 2. b | 7. c | 12. a | 17. d |
| 3. d | 8. b | 13. c | 18. c |
| 4. a | 9. b | 14. b | 19. a |
| 5. b | 10. a | 15. c | 20. b |

## PSYCHOLOGY IN ACTION: PROJECTS AND DEMONSTRATIONS

### Personality and Overpopulation

This project involves taking the questionnaire on page 145 to determine attitudes concerning overpopulation. As suggested in your text you can administer this to yourself, score it, and compare your scores to those presented in Table 9-2 in your text. You might also consider giving this questionnaire to your parents and some of your older relatives to see if they score lower than you or the students in Table 9-2. If you get much lower scores, what might be some reasons? Another group you might be interested in testing is some feminist group on campus to see if they score higher. If you want to get even more ambitious, you could administer the questionnaire to a number of campus groups which you expect to differ in their overall attitudes toward overpopulation. You should formulate your hypotheses about the groups ahead of time so that you can evaluate your ability to predict. Your instructor might be willing to make available his/her department's reproduction facilities so that you can have the necessary number of questionnaires. Your instructor might even let you present your findings to the class.

The scoring key is reproduced below. You will notice that different items make up different parts of the scales. The test measures five components, which are labeled Birth Control, Abortion, Family Planning, Population Management, and Modernity. The total score on each scale can range from 5 to 40. Some of the items are added to 24 and others are subtracted. Make sure that you remember that in subtracting a negative number it becomes a positive number. Note the example below.

$$24 + (1-2+0-1) - (-2 + 1-1-1) = 24 - 2 + 3 = 25$$

To determine your scores on the five dimensions, use the following key:

1. Birth Control: Add 24 to the sum of your scores on items 1, 11, 21, 26 and 31; then subtract the sum of your scores on items 6, 16, and 36.

2. Abortion: Add 24 to the sum of your scores on items 3, 13, 23 and 33; then subtract the sum of your scores on items 8, 18, 28 and 38.

3. Family Planning: Add 24 to the sum of your scores on items 5, 15, 25 and 35; then subtract the sum of your scores on items 10, 20, 30 and 40.

4. Population Management: Add 24 to the sum of your scores on items 7, 17, 27, and 37; then subtract the sum of your scores on items 2, 12, 22, and 32.

5. Modernity: Add 24 to the sum of your scores on items 9, 29, and 39; then subtract the sum of your scores on items 4, 14, 19, 24 and 34.

Type A and Type B

It is currently popular in psychology to label people who are highly competitive, impatient, and achievement oriented as Type A, whereas those who do not have these characteristics are labeled as Type B. The Type A individual apparently has a higher chance of heart trouble than the Type B individual. We have provided a questionnaire on page 147 (adapted from Bortner, 1969) which you can use on yourself and your friends.

In scoring the questionnaire, you will need to invert the scores on items 2, 3, 4, and 6 since high scores on these items indicate Type A behavior, while the reverse is true with the other items. So if a person marks 1 on these four items, this should be scored as a 7. A 2 should be scored as a 6, a 3 as a 5, a 4 stays the same, a 5 should be scored as a 3, a 6 as a 2, and a 7 as a 1. After you have inverted the scores simply add up the seven scores and divide by seven to get a mean. People with relatively low mean scores (below 2.5) tend toward a Type A personality, while those with high mean scores (above 2.5) tend toward Type A personality.

Don't take the questionnaire too seriously since it certainly isn't a perfect predictor of heart trouble, and it takes a qualified clinical psychologist to interpret the results accurately. Just tell your friends that questionnaires like this have been used to determine which individuals are highly competitive and impatient, and that although such individuals may have a slightly higher chance of heart trouble, this is certainly not a sure thing. Many other factors besides competitiveness determine one's potential for heart trouble.

REFERENCE

Bortner, R.W., A short rating scale as a potential measure of pattern A behavior. J. of Chronic Diseases, 22, 1969, pp. 87-91.

# Population Policy and Social Attitude Questionnaire

Instructions: Read each statement below and then give your reaction on the line in front, using the following scale:

+2 = agree strongly
+1 = agree somewhat
0 = neutral or uncertain
-1 = disagree somewhat
-2 = disagree strongly

___ 1. Birth control methods should be made available to anyone who wants them.

___ 2. The world could easily support twice as many people as it now does.

___ 3. Abortion should be permitted if there is substantial risk that the baby will be born defective.

___ 4. It is better to live pretty much for today and let tomorrow take care of itself.

___ 5. Having a baby every year is bad for the mother's health.

___ 6. The disadvantages of birth control outweigh the advantages.

___ 7. Families with more than three children should be required to pay higher taxes.

___ 8. The decision to ask for an abortion must be in part a moral decision.

___ 9. A person should try to keep aware of the major events taking place all over the world.

___ 10. People should not "plan" on whether to have a child; such things are best left to fate or luck.

___ 11. Birth control increases the happiness of married life.

___ 12. In some parts of the world, the problem is underpopulation, not overpopulation.

___ 13. With the newer and safer methods of inducing abortion, there is no reason why a woman should not use abortion routinely as a birth control method.

___ 14. My preference is for the old dependable ways of doing things.

___ 15. If a couple is in poor economic circumstances, having a child should be postponed until its financial situation improves.

___ 16. The use of birth control devices involves a sort of risky tampering with nature.

___ 17. Overpopulation in the world is just as serious a problem today as crime and poverty.

___ 18. Abortion should be prohibited by law.

___ 19. There is nothing really new under the sun.

___ 20. Limiting the number of children in a family is something that works in favor ot those already financially well-to-do and against those in poorer circumstances.

___ 21. A birth control operation (vasectomy) should be given without charge to any man who requests one.

___ 22. There is no reason to fear a continued increase in population; the human race will find some way to cope with this problem.

___ 23. Abortion should be free of any and all legal restrictions.

___ 24. I tend to feel uncomfortable when I am with people who are much older than I am.

___ 25. Childless couples should be encouraged to adopt a child.

___ 26. It is difficult to think of any rational reason for opposing free release of birth control information.

___ 27. Unless population is controlled, mankind will never be able to live in peace.

___ 28. A married woman should be permitted to have an abortion only if both husband and wife request it.

___ 29. I would like to live for a time in at least three or four foreign countries.

___ 30. I would be unhappy if I were to have less than three children.

_____ 31. Birth control information and services (pill, etc.) should be available without cost to all married women.

_____ 32. In places where the population is decreasing, people should be encouraged to have more children.

_____ 33. Abortion should be permitted if the pregnancy is the result of rape or incest (intercourse between close relations).

_____ 34. I do not know whether my family and I will be better or worse off in the future than we are now; even when you work hard you never know what is going to happen.

_____ 35. Couples should wait to have children until they are financially able to take care of the child.

_____ 36. The decision to use birth control methods is in part a moral decision.

_____ 37. The world would be better off if the human population could be reduced by 50 per cent in the next 100 years.

_____ 38. Abortion is morally wrong, whatever may be its economic or medical benefits.

_____ 39. The traditional ways from the past are not always the best; they need to be changed.

_____ 40. The economic advantages of having small families are not as great as family planning advocates claim.

## Questionnaire

Below are listed several dimensions along which people vary. Please circle the number which best represents your position along this dimension.

1. Never late      1 2 3 4 5 6 7      Casual about appointments

2. Not competitive      1 2 3 4 5 6 7      Very Competitive

3. Always rushed      1 2 3 4 5 6 7      Never feel rushed, even under pressure

4. Take things one at a time      1 2 3 4 5 6 7      Try to do many things at once, always thinking about what you're going to do next

5. Fast (eating, walking, etc.)      1 2 3 4 5 6 7      Slow doing things

6. "Sit" on feelings      1 2 3 4 5 6 7      Express feelings

7. Many interests      1 2 3 4 5 6 7      Few interests outside work

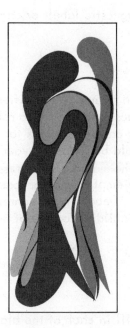

# Chapter 10

# MALADJUSTED PATTERNS OF BEHAVIOR

# LEARNING OBJECTIVES: WHAT YOU SHOULD KNOW

After reading this chapter you should:

Know the three different models of abnormality.

Be able to discuss the different defense mechanisms.

Be able to describe the different types of neuroses and their possible causes.

Know the different types of psychoses, their characteristics, and possible causes.

Be able to discuss the psychopathic personality.

Know the various effects of alcohol consumption.

Understand the problems associated with the use of diagnostic labels or categories.

# STUDY TIPS: A HELPING HAND

Your most difficult task in this chapter will be to memorize the different types of disorders, their characteristics, and causes. Again the best approach is to rehearse these facts for each disorder before going on to the next. In most cases the labels for the disorders directly reflect the nature of the disorder, and this should be an aid in your memorization process (e.g., the schism aspect of schizophrenia and the manic and depressive aspects of manic-depressive psychosis). Mnemonic tricks should also be employed. For example catatonic schizophrenia involves a "cat like" stiff posture. The "hebe" in hebephrenic sounds like a child's word and hence may help to remind you of the childish feature of hebephrenic schizophrenia.

# STEP-BY-STEP: A GUIDED REVIEW

After you have read the chapter, mentally fill in each of the blanks in the following section while covering the answers in the margin. Check your answer with that in the margin as you go along. While in many cases your answer should be the same as that in the margin, in other cases a word of similar meaning is acceptable. Do not write in the spaces until you are doing your final review.

1. A socially inappropriate pattern of behavior which results in unhappiness for the individual and/or for others is called

   _____. _____    maladjustment,
   behavior is a rather serious interference of normal functioning    Neurotic
   and involves a great deal of stress and _____.    anxiety
   Severe psychopathology that involves extreme distortions in
   perception, thought, and speech is termed _____    psychotic
   behavior.

2. In early times abnormal behavior was often attributed to
_____ and _____ _____.          witchcraft, evil
These perspectives were gradually displaced by a _____          spirits, medical
model which viewed insanity as a mental illness and was concerned
with classifying abnormal behavior into diagnostic categories. The
founder of the modern system of classification was _____.          Kraepelin

3. The _____ model of abnormality holds          psychological
that mental processes are involved in the production of abnormal
behavior. Conceptions of this type often are based on the idea
that _____ plays a major role in the development of          learning
abnormal behavior.

4. When certain situations, events, or ideas make us feel uncomfortable we may employ _____ mechanisms to feel          defense
more comfortable. The basic defense mechanism, _____,          repression
involves making the thoughts _____. The          unconscious
repressed impulses may be expressed in indirect or disguised form.

5. Other defense mechanisms represent ways in which the repressed
impulses are expressed. When someone expresses the opposite of
an impulse, she is using _____ _____          reaction forma-
Socially acceptable reasons given to explain one's behavior are          tion
_____.          rationalizations

6. When a strong emotion is vented upon a less threatening source
than the one which instigated it, _____          displacement
is said to occur. The target of the displacement is the
_____. _____          scapegoat,
involves attributing one's own unacceptible impulses to others.          Projection

7. Behavior is labeled as _____ when the anxiety is          neurotic
too high for defense mechanisms to work or the defenses become
very disruptive. One type of neurotic behavior is
_____ which involves the          hypochondriasis
exaggerated concern with one's health or body. Hypochondriasis may function to take one's mind off other problems, limit
interpersonal relations to a minimum, or to gain attention and
sympathy.

8. Extraordinary fears of objects or places are called _____.          phobias
These phobias can be the result of a _____          traumatic
incident. More often, however, the phobia is directed toward
some common element in the person's environment (e.g., birds,
horses, etc.). Such fears can be interpreted as _____          substitutes
for other more vague or frightening concerns. Such a
_____ fear is not easily eliminated. There          displaced

also appears to be some evidence that inborn tendencies
to develop certain types of fears may exist.

9.  Another neurotic behavior called _____ _____      obsessive reac-
    involves a thought that occurs repeatedly without being under the     tion
    person's control.  When individuals engage in some behavior re-
    peatedly they are exhibiting a _____ reaction.           compulsive
    Obsessive-compulsive reactions may serve to reduce _____          anxiety
    or may serve as a mild self-punishment for guilt.  Although Freud
    argued that the development of such reactions is related to the
    _____ stage and related pressures to be neat and clean, they     anal
    may involve accidental association between the compulsive be-
    havior and reward.

10. In _____ reactions the individual seems to               dissociative
    be setting aside some aspect of his personality.  One type is
    _____ in which an individual loses memory of             amnesia
    personal details of his life.  If the person also travels to another
    place, he is said to be in a _____ state.  Another type is        fugue
    frequent sleepwalking or _____.  The rarest              somnambulism
    form of dissociative reaction is _____                   multiple
    _____ in which two or more complete                      personality
    personalities are alternatively expressed by the individual.

11. _____ _____ involves                       Reactive depres-
    overreaction to stressful events in such a way that unhappiness        sion
    or sadness continues indefinitely and interferes with the
    individual's everyday life.  One reason for this reaction according
    to Freud is the existence of _____ or                    ambivalence
    conflicting feelings about what happened.  Seligman has proposed
    that such depression may be due to _____                 learned
    _____ induced by stressful experiences                   helplessness
    over which the person has no control.

12. When an individual has a feeling of fear, loss of self-control,
    and physiological responses as if the body were preparing to meet
    a physical danger, this individual is having an _____            anxiety
    _____.  This occurs when an individual can no            reaction
    longer cope with the pressures and strains of his or her life.  A
    similar reaction produced in war time or civilian disasters are
    labeled as _____ neurosis.                               traumatic

13. _____ involves symptoms which are so severe that         Psychosis
    the individual is likely to be unable to function in his or her
    personal life and usually requires hospitalization.  The individual
    may not recognize the problem, evaluates reality different from
    others, and may be dangerous to herself and others.

14. One symptom of psychosis is the occurrence of perceptions which do not correspond to external stimuli. These are called _____. Psychotics also exhibit distorted thinking. This may involve strongly held and defended but unrealistic beliefs called _____. These delusions are not open to logic or disconfirming evidence. One frequent delusion is that of _____ by others. A delusion that others are always referring to you is called _____ ____ _____. The belief that one is someone of very special importance is called the delusion of _____.

hallucinations

delusions

persecution

ideas of refer-
ence

grandeur

15. Another characteristic of psychotics is that they exhibit _____ emotion and speech. Their emotions are often inappropriate or uncalled for by the situation. The patient may express only the last element of a rapid series of free associations. Speech may involve meaningless repetition of the last word that is heard or _____, and the creation of new words or _____.

distorted

echolalia
neologisms

16. _____ _____ psychosis involves periodic changes in mood. This type of psychosis is also frequently accompanied by _____. A predisposition to manic-depressive reactions may be _____ and is also more likely with those at _____ socioeconomic levels. Learning also plays a strong role in manic depressive psychosis in that individuals raised in families which favored a strong _____ development were more likely to develop this psychosis. Early in life, manics tended to be ambitious, concerned about social expectations, and _____ oriented. Depressives tended to be anxious, obsessive, and _____. Manic-depressive psychosis is most often precipitated by the death of a loved one, job difficulty, and interpersonal problems.

Manic-depressive

delusions

inherited
higher

conscience

achievement
moralistic

17. Individuals who have highly organized conceptual systems which are characterized by delusions of persecution and reference are exhibiting a _____ _____. However, the various elements of the delusion do not appear to fit together well to others. The individual tends to function well in other areas.

paranoid disor-
der

18. One interpretation of paranoid ideas is that they represent an extreme form of _____ of one's own impulses and a _____ of them onto others. The tendency toward paranoia is believed to be formed _____ in life. Freud traces its origins to the _____ stage of development in

denial
projection
early
anal

153

which rigidity and hostility are prominent. Paranoid individuals
tend to come from homes in which the parents were _____
and _____.

cold
neglectful

19. The psychosis which involves a split between emotion and behavior
or reality and fantasy is _____. It is
the most common and severe of the psychoses. About _____
of the hospitalized mental patients are schizophrenics.

schizophrenia
half

20. Schizophrenia can take various forms. _____
schizophrenia is characterized by apathy and withdrawal from
society. _____ schizophrenia involves
grotesque silliness and childish behavior. _____
schizophrenia is characterized by bodily immobility. _____
schizophrenia involves bizarre paranoid delusions, while
_____ schizophrenia involves features of manic-
depressive psychosis.

Simple

Hebephrenic
Catatonic
Paranoid

affective

21. All five types of schizophrenia have certain common characteristics.
The most general one is _____. The patients
appear to have slower reaction times and to be unable to select
important from unimportant information. Their tendency to be more
concerned with their own thoughts, wishes, and fantasies than
objective reality is called _____. They also frequently
exhibit delusions, hallucinations, and distortions of speech.

withdrawal

autism

22. Schizophrenia often begins when the individual is quite _____.
Sometimes schizophrenia is categorized as inherited or _____
schizophrenia and learned or _____ schizophrenia.
Only the _____ type responds well to treatment. Evidence for a genetic basis comes in part from studies of twins in
which it was found that the incidence of schizophrenia for both
twins is much higher for _____ twins than _____
twins.

young
process
reactive
reactive

identical, fra-
ternal

23. Schizophrenia is more common at _____ socio-economic levels
than _____ ones. Families in which parents continually put
children into a _____ also tend to produce
schizophrenic children. This is a situation in which the parents
make conflicting or inconsistent demands on the child (e.g., don't
fight/be brave).

low
high
double-bind

24. Schizophrenics appear to be relatively unaffected by _____
_____ such as praise or approval. However,
research suggests that they can be taught to respond to praise.

positive
reinforcers

25. Behavior patterns which are not necessarily neurotic or psychotic but are harmful to others and society are called _____ _____. When an individual fails to acquire an internal code of values, is not able to feel remorse or guilt, cannot tolerate delayed gratification, and is superficial in relations to others, he is termed a _____ _____. Depending on the circumstances, these individuals may become very successful socially and economically or may turn to a life of crime.

conduct disor-ders

psychopathic personality

26. Psychopaths are impulsive and restless, apparently because they have a greater need for new _____. They also have lower _____ levels than normals and as a result have difficulty in learning to avoid _____.

stimulation
anxiety
pain

27. The origin of psychopathic behavior appears to lie in _____ _____ experiences. The parents of psychopaths tend to be _____. They often have lost a parent early in life. The fathers tended to alcoholism or left the family through divorce or dissertion.

early
childhood
neglectful

28. Alcoholism is a conduct disorder which may result in part from the ability of alcohol to reduce _____. Alcohol is a _____ drug that acts on the central nervous system, producing initial feelings of elation and energetic activity. There is also a lessening of self-criticism and increased concern with prestige, aggression, sex, and _____.

anxiety
depressant

power

29. Cultural factors _____(influence/do not influence) the incidence of alcoholism. Alcoholism occurs at very different rates in different countries and is more common among those with _____ class than _____class backgrounds.

influence

middle, lower

30. The moderate drinker has been found to have a _____ (longer/shorter) life expectancy than heavy and light drinkers. However, even moderate amounts of alcohol can interfere with perceptual and motor skills. Alcohol is involved in over _____ % of automobile accidents. Pregnant women who drink heavily are more likely to have children with _____ _____ than are nondrinking women. Chronic drinking can lead to psychotic behavior, and withdrawal of alcohol at this stage can result in _____ _____.

longer

50

birth defects

delirium tremens

31. The label of alcoholism is currently applied to about _____ million individuals in the U.S. An alcoholic can be described as someone who drinks _____, is unable to

five

excessively

_____ how much is drunk, becomes _____     control, confused
as a result of drinking, and whose work and interpersonal relations
suffer from the drinking.

32. Jellinek has suggested the existence of five types of alcoholism.
The _____ type involves heavy drinking to produce     Alpha
the psychological effects of alcohol and may cause only interpersonal problems. The _____ type is similar to the alpha     Beta
type but is accompanied by some personal distress. The _____     Gamma
type involves both physical and psychological dependence on
alcohol. The _____ type is similar to the Gamma except     Delta
there is no loss of control over drinking, but the individual con-
stantly craves a drink. The _____ type goes on long     Epsilon
sporadic drinking bouts. Jellinek's classification is shown below
so you can review it if necessary.

**TABLE 10-1   Classification of Alcoholism**

| Type of Alcoholism | Typical Behavior |
| --- | --- |
| Alpha | Heavy drinking based on the psychological effects of alcohol. The individual can control the amount consumed and shows no tendency to increase his intake over time; the only problems this causes are interpersonal ones. |
| Beta | Similar to the alpha type but causes the individual some personal distress, such as chronic indigestion or cirrhosis of the liver. Thus, there is damage to the person's nutrition, interferences with his work, and a decrease in his life span. |
| Gamma | Some physical as well as psychological dependence, as indicated by loss of control and drinking self into stupor, craving for alcohol, and withdrawal symptoms when alcohol is not available. Larger and larger amounts must be consumed to have any effect. This is the most common type of alcoholism in the United States and Canada. |
| Delta | Similar to the gamma type except that there is no loss of control over drinking but the individual constantly craves drink. In wine-drinking countries, such as France, this type of alcoholism is the most common. |
| Epsilon | The individual goes on long drinking bouts that last for days or even weeks and then sobers up and drinks nothing until the next drinking spree. |

The five types of alcoholism and the behavior associated with each, as defined by
Jellinek (1960).

33. There may exist physiological differences in susceptibility
to alcohol. Rats can be bred to like or dislike alcohol.
_____ deficiencies may also account for     Nutritional
individual differences in response to alcohol. Jellinek has
suggested that while the _____ type may have a psycho-     Alpha
logical origin, the other types may have a physiological basis.
Evidence _____ (does/does not) support the notion     does not
that one drink automatically leads an alcoholic to continue
drinking.

156

34. A field study by Rosenhan found that when normal individuals were admitted to a mental hospital, they _____ (were/ were not) detected as being normal by the staff members.

were not

35. Although diagnostic labels are frequently employed, _____ people actually fit these categories. These labels should be taken as representing common maladaptive behaviors instead identification of distinct groups.

few

36. Therapists often disagree about the application of these labels to people. The use of labels may also serve as a self-definition for the individual and may shape her subsequent behaviors to beconsistent with the label. Labels may also induce others to respond to the patient in ways which influence the patient to behave consistent with the label. The medical model implied by the use of diagnostic labels also incorrectly suggests that either an individual has a certain pathology or he does not. A more appropriate perspective is that maladjustment falls along a _____ of degrees of pathology.

continuum

37. The basis for psychopathology appears to be certain learned and inherited predispositions which when combined with _____ produce certain "abnormal" responses. Sometimes these "abnormal" responses may be normal responses to an abnormal situation.

stress

## KEY CONCEPTS AND TERMS

After you have finished your Guided Review, fill in the meaning of the following terms in your own words. Check on your accuracy by consulting your text on the pages indicated or the Glossary.

neurotic behavior (p. 332)

psychotic behavior (p. 332)

psychological model of abnormality (p. 336-337)

medical model of abnormality (p. 334-336)

repression (p. 337)

reaction formation (p. 338)

rationalization (p. 338)

displacement (p. 338)

projection (p. 338)

hypochondriasis (p. 340)

phobias (p. 342)

obsessive reaction (p. 343)

compulsive reaction (p. 344)

dissociative reaction (p. 346)

amnesia (p. 346)

fugue (p. 346)

somnambulism (p. 346)

multiple personality (p. 346)

reactive depression (p. 347)

ambivalence (p. 347)

learned helplessness (p. 347)

anxiety reaction (p. 348)

traumatic neurosis (p. 349)

hallucinations (p. 350)

delusions (p. 351)

echolalia (p. 352)

neologisms (p. 352)

manic-depressive psychosis (p. 353)

paranoid disorder (p. 355)

schizophrenia (p. 357)

hebephrenic schizophrenia (p. 357)

catatonic schizophrenia (p. 357)

paranoid schizophrenia (p. 357)

affective schizophrenia (p. 357)

autism (p. 357)

process schizophrenia (p. 358)

reactive schizophrenia (p. 358)

double-bind (p. 358)

conduct disorder (p. 359)

psychopathic personality (p. 360)

Alpha type  (p. 364)

Beta type  (p. 364)

Gamma type  (p. 364)

Delta type  (p. 364)

Epsilon type  (p. 364)


A PERSONAL QUIZ
--------------

After you are about finished with your studies but still have some time
left for review, take this quiz to check on your mastery.  Fill in your
answers in the spaces provided and after you are finished check their
correctness with the answers provided.

___ 1.  Severe psychopathology that in-
        volves extreme distortions in per-
        ception, thought and speech is
        (p. 332)
        a.  neurotic behavior
        b.  anxiety
        c.  psychotic behavior
        d.  none of the above

___ 2.  The model of abnormality which
        emphasizes mental processes is
        the (p. 336)
        a.  psychological model
        b.  medical model
        c.  learning model
        d.  experiential model

___ 3.  When someone expresses the opposite
        of an impulse, this person is ex-
        hibiting (p. 338)
        a.  repression
        b.  reaction formation
        c.  rationalization
        d.  displacement

___ 4.  Attributing one's own unaccepptible
        impulses to others is called (p.338)
        a.  rationalization
        b.  projection
        c.  displacement
        d.  scapegoating

___ 5.  When a thought occurs repeatedly
        without being under the control of
        the individual, this person is
        having (p. 343)
        a.  a phobia
        b.  hypochondriasis
        c.  a compulsive reaction
        d.  an obsessive reaction

___ 6.  The rarest form of dissociative
        reaction is (p. 346)
        a.  amnesia
        b.  fugue
        c.  multiple personality
        d.  somnambulism

7. Which of the following has been proposed as a cause of reactive depression? (p. 347)
   a. anxiety reactions
   b. pressures of the anal stage
   c. guilt
   d. learned helplessness

8. Which of the following is not characteristic of psychotics? (p. 350-352)
   a. very precise speech
   b. delusions
   c. hallucinations
   d. distorted perceptions

9. Manic depressives tend to come from homes which emphasize (p. 354)
   a. warmth
   b. cleanliness
   c. conscience development
   d. intellectual activities

10. Individuals who have highly organized conceptual systems involving delusions of persecution and grandeur are having (p. 355)
   a. a manic-depressive reaction
   b. a paranoid disorder
   c. schizophrenia
   d. neurosis

11. Schizophrenia which is characterized by body immobility is called (p. 357)
   a. simple
   b. hebephrenic
   c. paranoid
   d. catatonic

12. The most frequent type of psychosis is (p. 357)
   a. schizophrenia
   b. manic-depressive
   c. paranoid
   d. conduct disorder

13. Which of the following statements about schizophrenia is false? (p. 357-359)

   a. it often begins when the individual is young
   b. it is more common among the lower socio-economic groups than the high ones
   c. it does not appear to have a genetic base
   d. it tends to be characterized by withdrawal from reality

14. Which of the following homes is most likely to produce a schizophrenic? (p. 358)
   a. a cold, neglectful one
   b. one in which conflicting demands are made upon the child
   c. a highly achievement oriented home
   d. one in which there are few if any siblings

15. Individuals with psychopathic personalities are characterized by all but one of the following: (p. 360-361)
   a. lack of internal code of values
   b. inability to feel remorse or guilt
   c. impulsivity
   d. ability to tolerate delay of gratification

16. Psychopaths tend to (p. 360-362)
   a. be less anxious than normals
   b. have less need for stimulation than normals
   c. not to be successful socially
   d. have above average ability to learn to avoid pain

17. Alcohol tends to lead to (p. 362)
   a. lessening of interest in sex
   b. self-criticism
   c. increased anxiety
   d. increased concern with power

18. Heavy drinking or alcoholism has been related to (p. 363)
   a. cultural influences
   b. decreased life expectancy
   c. increased automobile accidents

d.  all of the above

___ 19. The type of alcoholic who goes on
       long sporadic drinking bouts is termed
       a(n)_____type by Jellinek. (p. 364)
       a.  Beta
       b.  Epsilon
       c.  Gamma
       d.  Alpha

___ 20. According to your text, the use of
       diagnostic labels (p. 367)
       a.  may serve to produce the very
           behaviors implied by the label

b.  is justified by the medical
    evidence
c.  is consistent across therapists
d.  may help identify distinct
    groups of patients

Answers:

| 1. c | 6. c | 11. d | 16. a |
|------|------|-------|-------|
| 2. a | 7. d | 12. a | 17. d |
| 3. b | 8. a | 13. c | 18. d |
| 4. b | 9. c | 14. b | 19. b |
| 5. d | 10. b | 15. d | 20. a |

## PSYCHOLOGY IN ACTION:  PROJECTS AND DEMONSTRATIONS

### Deviant Behavior

   In this chapter you are exposed to a discussion of a wide variety of deviant behaviors
and behavior disorders.  These range from neurotic and psychotic behavior to the behavior of
the psychopath.  Since these types of behavior are often dramatically different from behavior
usually observed in people, occurrences of these behaviors frequently make the daily news-
papers.  Scan your major regional newspaper one week for stories of bizarre behaviors.  Can
you classify the individuals involved as being neurotic, psychotic or psychopathic?  Also
look for some of the specific behaviors discussed in your text such as paranoia, phobias,
withdrawal, delusions, amnesia, obsessive reaction, etc.  This may be a good way to make
yourself learn the various disorders discussed in your text.  A form is provided on the next page
to help you in doing this.

## Survey of Deviant or Bizarre Behavior

| Behavior | General Type (psychotic, neurotic, or psychopathic) | Specific Type (e.g., delusions, amnesia, depression, paranoia, or withdrawal) |
|---|---|---|
| 1. _____ | _____ | _____ |
| 2. _____ | _____ | _____ |
| 3. _____ | _____ | _____ |
| 4. _____ | _____ | _____ |
| 5. _____ | _____ | _____ |
| 6. _____ | _____ | _____ |
| 7. _____ | _____ | _____ |
| 8. _____ | _____ | _____ |
| 9. _____ | _____ | _____ |
| 10. _____ | _____ | _____ |
| 11. _____ | _____ | _____ |
| 12. _____ | _____ | _____ |
| 13. _____ | _____ | _____ |
| 14. _____ | _____ | _____ |
| 15. _____ | _____ | _____ |
| 16. _____ | _____ | _____ |
| 17. _____ | _____ | _____ |
| 18. _____ | _____ | _____ |
| 19. _____ | _____ | _____ |
| 20. _____ | _____ | _____ |
| 21. _____ | _____ | _____ |
| 22. _____ | _____ | _____ |

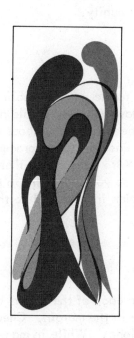

Chapter 11

# PSYCHOTHERAPY:
## Altering
## Maladjusted
## Behavior

# LEARNING OBJECTIVES: WHAT YOU SHOULD KNOW

After reading this chapter you should:

Know the different types of bio-therapy and their effects.

Be able to discuss the technique of psychoanalysis and its effectiveness.

Know the basic features of client-centered therapy, its aims, and for whom it works best.

Be able to describe the various techniques of behavior modification and their use.

Know the different types of group therapy.

Be able to discuss some of the recently popular therapies.

Be able to discuss the application of psychology in the community.

# STUDY TIPS: A HELPING HAND

Since the topics in this chapter are of great interest to the general public, you may already have encountered a good deal of this material. However, you should not take this chapter lightly since there are a number of facts you will need to master about each of the various therapies. Generally for each therapy you should know its aims, procedures, and its effects (both good and bad) as demonstrated by research. Also some of the therapies work better for certain disorders or certain types of individuals, so you should try to keep those facts straight. If you approach the chapter with those general aims in mind and do the appropriate rehearsal, you should do well.

# STEP-BY-STEP: A GUIDED REVIEW

After you have read the chapter, mentally fill in each of the blanks in the following section while covering the answers in the margin. Check your answers with that in the margin as you go along. While in many cases your answer should be the same as that in the margin, in other cases a word of similar meaning is acceptable. Do not write in the spaces until you are doing your final review.

1. _____ is the application of psychological            Psychotherapy
techniques by professionally trained individuals to change a
socially inappropriate pattern of behavior into a more appropriate
one. The use of bodily treatments to cure psychopathology is

_____.                                                  biotherapy

2. One type of biotherapy is shock treatment or _____            electrocon-
therapy. It has not proved to be a very reliable type of treatment.         vulsive
One undesirable effect of this procedure is that memory for material

learned as long as _____ years before treatment may be          three
impaired. Today this technique is used primarily in cases of
psychotic _____ and other disorders involving          depression
acute mood changes.

3.  Another biological technique is psychosurgery. This technique
    involves _____ _____              prefrontal lo-
    which is the cutting of the nerve pathways between the brain's  botomy
    prefrontal lobes and the _____ in order to interrupt thalamus
    existing thought patterns and fixed ideas.

4.  Although there were some reports that this technique was very
    successful, the outcomes of this procedure appear to be very
    _____ and serious side effects may occur. Some       uncertain
    of these side effects are _____, increased   hyperactivity
    _____, reduced ability to _____,          distractibility,
    overeating, and even death.                                     learn

5.  In the early 1950's tranquilizers and energizing drugs were intro-
    duced to treat emotional disturbances. The use of drugs has
    primarily served to reduce _____ and                 anxiety
    _____ in patients and thus make them                 aggression
    more susceptible to psychotherapy. However, tranquilizers may
    also have undesirable effects such as low blood pressure, _____ depression
    and _____. Energizing drugs may bring about          ulcers
    high blood pressure and _____.                       anxiety

6.  Another group of therapies are concerned with developing the
    patient's insight into his problems. The technique developed by
    Freud is called _____. One aspect           psychoanalysis
    of this technique is _____ _____        free association
    which involves the patient speaking freely about anything that comes
    to his mind. The analyst responds to this with her _____.    interpretations

7.  The goal of psychoanalysis is _____. This involves   insight
    making unconscious material conscious and having the patient's be-
    havior come under the control of the _____. Only_____  ego, emotional
    insight but not _____ insight is assumed to          intellectual
    be therapeutic.

8.  During the analytic session powerful feelings become directed to-
    wards the analyst. Such feelings are called _____.   transference

9.  Research on the effectiveness of psychoanalysis suggest that it works
    better with _____ than severely disturbed individuals. neurotics
    _____ educated individuals respond more favorably to psycho-  Well
    analysis than _____ educated individuals.            poorly

10. According to Carl Rogers, the goal of therapy is to have the
client develop an altered _____ so that
the client can respond to her experience in an _____
way.

self-concept

accurate

11. In Rogers's approach, the therapist must experience and express
_____ for the client's thoughts, feelings and
values and should try to be _____
and follow the client's leads. The therapist needs to provide

_____ _____
_____ by showing liking and respect for the
client without attaching conditions. Under these types of conditions the client can move toward _____ .

empathy

non-directive

unconditional

positive regard

self-actualiza-
tion

12. In contrast to psychoanalysis, client-centered therapy focuses not
on the _____ but the _____ feelings of the client.

past, present

13. Research has shown that those who go through client-centered
therapy do indeed show positive changes in _____ .
Changes in self-concept have also been related to improved social
functioning.

self-concept

14. Research has found that client-centered therapy works best for
_____ controlled patients, while directive
therapy works best for _____ controlled patients.
Other studies indicate that client-centered therapy works best if
therapists are extremely _____ , the patients
are _____ , and the patient and therapist are
_____ in social and educational backgrounds.

internally

externally

understanding

verbal

similar

15. Some studies have suggested that therapy sessions may involve the
functioning of learning principles. For example, several studies
have shown that the usage of certain classes of words can be increased by saying "mmm-hmm" each time they are used or responding in some other favorable way. That is, the therapist may be
acting as a _____ . This process has been shown
to take place in actual therapy sessions as shown in Figure 11-7
below.

reinforcer

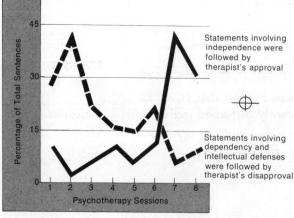

Statements involving
independence were
followed by
therapist's approval

Statements involving
dependency and
intellectual defenses
were followed by
therapist's disapproval

FIGURE 11-7 What a patient discusses during psychotherapy sessions is influenced by the reinforcements provided by the therapist. Over a series of eight
one-hour sessions, this patient was "punished" for
talking about dependency and using intellectual defenses, and these elements appeared less and less
frequently. There was "reward" for talking about independence, and this topic appeared with increased
frequency over the sessions. (Adapted from Murray,
1964.)

16. A learning procedure in which the therapist manipulates
    conditions in order to alter the behavior of the patient is called
    _____ _____.  **behavior mod-
                                                  ification**

17. Procedures which involve the association of a new response to
    a stimulus that previously elicited a problematic response are
    called _____. This technique      **countercondi-
    was used by Wolpe with various fears and called         tioning**
    _____ _____.            **systematic den-
                                                            sitization**
    His patients learn to associate feelings of calm with formerly
    frightening stimuli by moving gradually from mildly to strongly
    _____ stimuli.                              **feared**

18. Another type of counterconditioning which involves the association
    of negative feelings with an unacceptible stimulus or thought is
    called _____ conditioning.                  **aversive**

19. Others have employed the shaping procedures of _____     **operant**
    conditioning. In this procedure, the individual is required to emit
    increasingly accurate approximations of a desired response in order
    to gain a _____. This procedure has been used to    **reward**
    increase intellectual skills of retardates and to produce increasingly
    appropriate social and non-social behaviors among patients on a
    psychiatric ward. A system in which all the patients on a ward can
    earn plastic tokens for specific activities which later can be used
    to obtain extra privileges is called a _____ _____.   **token economy**
    The results of one such system are shown in Figure 11-10 below.

FIGURE 11-10 Psychiatric patients in a token economy were compared with a matched control group of
patients receiving standard hospital treatment. Observations before and after the 15-week experimental
program indicated that the token economy procedures
led to increases in positive behaviors and decreases
in negative behaviors. (Adapted from Schwartz and
Bellack, 1975.)

20. Some therapists have employed _____ in which    **modeling**
    patients observe others and then are able to copy their behavior.
    Studies by Bandura and his colleagues have used such procedures
    to reduce _____ of dogs and snakes. Those who watched   **fears**
    models exhibit _____ _____.               **increasingly
                                                              bold**

activities with dogs or snakes exhibited marked reductions
in fearful behavior.

21. Another popular form of therapy is group therapy. Moreno developed one technique in which members of a group act out or im-
provise various scenes from their lives. This is termed _____.
        psychodrama

22. The _____ _____ group
or T-group was designed to make each participant more aware of
his or her _____ and emotional impact on others.
        sensitivity
        training
        emotions

23. The _____ group evolved as a blending of T-
groups and client-centered groups. This type of group emphasizes
_____ and _____ and focuses
on the expression of _____ and the learning of how
one is perceived by others. These groups sometimes use exercises
such as touching and removal of clothes to get things started.
        encounter

        honesty, open-
        ness, feelings

24. One problem with encounter groups is that the honesty learned in
the group may not be _____ outside of the
group. Also, some individuals may become very anxious during
the session and may be unable to deal with this anxiety.
        appropriate

25. Only in well run encounter groups is there evidence of overall
positive effects. Such groups have been shown to lead to
increased _____ in personal relationships, better
_____, and greater _____
and consideration. Increased self-acceptance and reduced prejudice have also been obtained. Finally, encounter groups on sex
have led to increased sexual _____.
        sensitivity
        communication,
        relaxation

        tolerance

26. A number of other therapies are popular today. _____
therapy stresses the healthy functioning of the body. Rollo May
and Maslow have developed _____
_____ which stresses learning to trust and love
others and fulfillment of one's potential. _____
therapy by Perls stresses concentration on the present moment and
the discovery of one's projection tendencies.
        Bio-energetic

        existential
        analysis
        Gestalt

27. _____ therapy by Bindrim assumes that people will express their
feelings more honestly without clothing. The approach which stresses
the release of unpleasant emotions which individuals felt as children
is _____ therapy. In _____
_____ it is assumed that individuals express
various parts of their personality in the social games they play with
one another.
        Nude

        primal, trans-
        actional analy-
        sis

28. Psychotherapy encounters two problems of generalizability. First, it is frequently not clear that _____ changes are related to actual changes in behavior. Secondly, changes in the _____ situation may not generalize to changes in the patient's life situation.

verbal

therapy

29. _____ psychology is an approach which takes therapy to the situation where the individual lives and works. It has been applied with success in instances of community disasters. Disasters such as tornadoes lead to initial reactions of fear, grief and _____, but there are also long term effects. For some period of time after the disaster individuals may feel _____ and develop _____ illnesses. Family disturbances, problem drinking and feelings of _____, _____, and _____ may also persist. Finally the victims may _____ that the disaster happened.

Community

anxiety

apathetic,
psychosomatic
anger, guilt,
hopelessness,
deny

KEY CONCEPTS AND TERMS

After you have finished your Guided Review, fill in the meaning of the following terms in your own words. Check on your accuracy by consulting your text on the pages indicated or the Glossary.

psychotherapy (p. 371)

biotherapy (p. 372)

electroconvulsive therapy (p. 372)

prefrontal lobotomy (p. 374)

tranquilizers (p. 376)

energizers (p. 376)

psychoanalysis (p. 377)

free associations (p. 378)

interpretations (p. 378)

transference (p. 380)

client-centered therapy (p.

unconditional positive regard (p. 381)

self-actualization (p. 381)

behavior modification (p. 385)

counterconditioning (p. 386)

systematic desensitization (p. 387)

aversive conditioning (p. 388)

operant conditioning (p. 389)

token economy (p. 392)

modeling (p. 393)

psychodrama (p. 397)

sensitivity training group (p.398)

encounter group (p. 398)

bioenergetic therapy (p. 402)

existential analysis (p. 402)

gestalt therapy  (p. 402)

nude therapy  (p. 402)

primal therapy  (p. 403)

transactional analysis  (p. 403)


## A PERSONAL QUIZ

After you are about finished with your studies but still have some time left for review, take this quiz to check on your mastery. Fill in your answers in the spaces provided and after you are finished check their correctness with the answers provided.

___ 1. Apparently the most successful form of biotherapy is  (p. 376)
   a. shock treatment
   b. psychosurgery
   c. drug therapy
   d. hydrotherapy

___ 2. Electroconvulsive therapy is used primarily with  (p. 374)
   a. paranoid disorders
   b. psychotic depression
   c. schizophrenia
   d. none of the above

___ 3. Which one of the following is not one of the typical side effects of psychosurgery?  (p. 375)
   a. loss of appetite
   b. hyperactivity
   c. distractability
   d. reduced ability to learn

___ 4. The goal of psychoanalysis is  (p. 380)
   a. emotional insight
   b. intellectual insight
   c. transference
   d. self-actualization

___ 5. Which of the following is not characteristic of psychoanalysis?  (p. 378-380)
   a. transference
   b. free association
   c. interpretations
   d. nondirective therapy

___ 6. Roger's client-centered therapy involves all but one of the following:  (p. 381)
   a. nondirectiveness
   b. a concern with the past
   c. unconditional positive regard
   d. empathy

___ 7. The goal of client-centered therapy is  (p. 381)
   a. insight into one's past
   b. control of one's unconscious motives
   c. self-actualization
   d. the development of empathy

___ 8. Which of the following characteristics of a patient would facilitate the effectiveness of client-centered therapy?  (p. 383)

a. internal control, highly verbal
b. internal control, nonverbal
c. external control, highly verbal
d. external control, nonverbal

9. The technique of systematic desensitization was developed by (p. 387)
   a. Skinner
   b. Hull
   c. Bandura
   d. Wolpe

10. The technique which involves the association of negative feelings with an unacceptible stimulus or thought is called (p. 388)
    a. systematic desensitization
    b. aversive conditioning
    c. fear conditioning
    d. operant conditioning

11. Shaping is part of the technique of (p. 389)
    a. modeling
    b. aversive conditioning
    c. operant conditioning
    d. systematic desensitization

12. Which of the following statements about operant conditioning is not correct? (p. 391-393)
    a. it appears to be part of the procedure of the insight therapies
    b. it does not work well with retardates
    c. it has been used successfully as a therapeutic device
    d. the effects of this procedure on a ward may not generalize to the real world

13. Bandura has used modeling as a therapeutic device to (p. 393)
    a. reduce depression
    b. reduce paranoia
    c. increase interpersonal sensitivity
    d. reduce fears

14. Exercises such as touching and removal of clothes are most likely to be found

in (p. 398)
   a. encounter groups
   b. T-groups
   c. psychodrama
   d. behavior modification

15. The goal of sensitivity training or T-groups is (p. 398)
    a. to examine one's past
    b. intellectual insight
    c. to increase sensitivity to interpersonal games
    d. to increase awareness of one's emotions

16. Which one of the following is not characteristic of encounter groups? (p. 398-399)
    a. openness
    b. concern with feelings
    c. a directive leader
    d. honesty

17. Learning to trust and love others and the fulfillment of one's potential is the primary goal of (p. 402)
    a. existential analysis
    b. Gestalt therapy
    c. transactional analysis
    d. primal therapy

18. The type of psychotherapy which is concerned with the social games people play is (p. 403)
    a. Gestalt therapy
    b. transactional analysis
    c. primal therapy
    d. bio-energetic therapy

19. Which of the following is not a problem with psychotherapy? (p. 405)
    a. the lack of sufficient research on its effectiveness
    b. production of verbal changes but not changes in actual behavior
    c. too little concern with internal mental processes

d. generalization from therapy to the
   real life situation

___ 20. Disasters such as tornadoes can have
   a number of psychological effects.
   Such effects (p. 406-408)
   a. have been dealt with successfully
      by community psychologists
   b. are generally short term
   c. cannot be dealt with through
      psychological intervention
   d. lead to increased family cohesion

Answers:

| | | | |
|---|---|---|---|
| 1. c | 6. b | 11. c | 16. c |
| 2. b | 7. c | 12. b | 17. a |
| 3. a | 8. a | 13. d | 18. b |
| 4. a | 9. d | 14. a | 19. c |
| 5. d | 10. b | 15. d | 20. a |

# PSYCHOLOGY IN ACTION: PROJECTS AND DEMONSTRATIONS

The Power of Positive Reinforcement -- Say It Again Sam

The project in your text involves trying to increase another's usage of a particular sentence. Find a friend who has not taken a psychology course and an isolated area either in your own room, an empty classroom, or the library. Tell your friend that you are studying language and ask him/her to make up 100 different sentences. Have this person sit in a comfortable chair out of your line of vision so that you will provide no clues in the form of smiles, frowns, nods, and so forth. Before you start explain that you will not be able to talk during the session and that you will not be able to answer questions until the session is over.

You will have to select a particular type of sentence to reinforce. For example, you might reinforce sentences which have plural nouns, are in the past tense, are very long, make positive self-references, or, as your text suggests, you can reinforce sentences which begin with "I" or "we". Of course if the difference between the reinforced and nonreinforced sentences is too subtle, your project may fail since your friend may not be able to discriminate the difference.

For the first 20 sentences (base rate phase) every time your friend gives the appropriate sentence, simply mark a + on the scoring form provided. When your friend does not give this type of sentence, mark a - on the scoring form. For the next 50 sentences (acquisition phase), say "mmm-hmm" whenever your friend gives the appropriate sentence and mark a + on the form, and when another type of sentence is given say nothing and mark down a -. For the last 30 sentences (extinction phase), again say nothing and simply mark plusses and minuses.

Be sure to say "mmm-hmm" as naturally as possible so that your friend will not become suspicious. When you are finished, ask your friend to state his/her ideas about the experiment. Try to determine if your friend realized what you were trying to do. A number of studies suggest that this effect may not occur unless the subject is aware of what you are trying to do. Finally, explain the experiment fully to your friend.

To examine your data, determine the total number of plusses which occurred in each of the groups of 10 trials and make a mark at the appropriate point on the graph provided. You should find little if any change in sentence usage during the acquisition phase, an increase in appropriate sentence usage during acquisition, and a decrease during extinction. Compare your results with those of your classmates. You might combine their results with yours so that you can get a more representative picture of the effects of verbal reinforcement.

Many different types of therapy are available. These may of course be differentially effective for different types of problems. One factor which may affect this effectiveness in the patient's feelings about the potential effectiveness of therapy. You may want to poll some of your friends to see if they are biased in favor of certain therapies for certain problems. You might present them with four main types of therapy discussed in your text -- biotherapy (surgery, shock, drugs), insight therapy, behavior therapy (operant conditioning), and group therapy. Explain these briefly then ask them which of these would be best for each of the following problems.

1. smoking habit
2. depression
3. withdrawal
4. extreme fears
5. impotency
6. paranoia
7. conduct disorder

You may have to briefly explain what you mean by each of these. Indicate the choice of your subject after each behavior. Do you find any consistency? Do you think they are right? What does your text suggest? This exercise should help you in mastering some of the text material.

Data Recording Form

1. ___  11. ___  21. ___  31. ___  41. ___  51. ___  61. ___  71. ___  81. ___  91. ___

2. ___  12. ___  22. ___  32. ___  42. ___  52. ___  62. ___  72. ___  82. ___  92. ___

3. ___  13. ___  23. ___  33. ___  43. ___  53. ___  63. ___  73. ___  83. ___  93. ___

4. ___  14. ___  24. ___  34. ___  44. ___  54. ___  64. ___  74. ___  84. ___  94. ___

5. ___  15. ___  25. ___  35. ___  45. ___  55. ___  65. ___  75. ___  85. ___  95. ___

6. ___  16. ___  26. ___  36. ___  46. ___  56. ___  66. ___  76. ___  86. ___  96. ___

7. ___  17. ___  27. ___  37. ___  47. ___  57. ___  67. ___  77. ___  87. ___  97. ___

8. ___  18. ___  28. ___  38. ___  48. ___  58. ___  68. ___  78. ___  88. ___  98. ___

9. ___  19. ___  29. ___  39. ___  49. ___  59. ___  69. ___  79. ___  89. ___  99. ___

10. ___  20. ___  30. ___  40. ___  50. ___  60. ___  70. ___  80. ___  90. ___  100. ___

Total
Plusses

___    ___    ___    ___    ___    ___    ___    ___    ___    ___    ___

Graph of Data

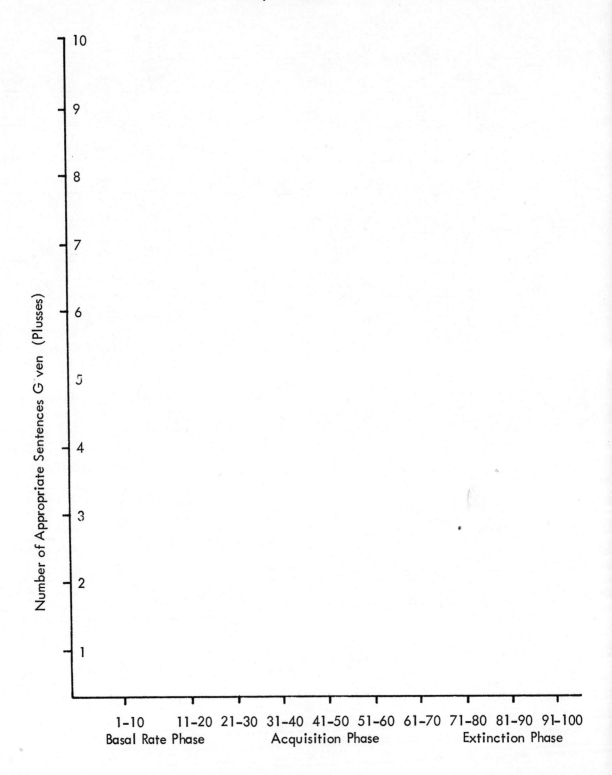

Trials

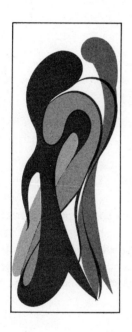

Chapter 12

# THE PROCESS
# OF
# SOCIAL INFLUENCE:
Changing Attitudes
and
Altering Behavior

## LEARNING OBJECTIVES: WHAT YOU SHOULD KNOW

After reading this chapter you should:

Know what attitudes are and how they are acquired.

Know the research on the effects of persuasive communications.

Be able to discuss the issues and findings associated with the controversy about the attitude-behavior relationship.

Be able to describe the various findings on the effect of attitude-discrepatant behavior and the dissonance theory interpretation of these findings.

Know the research on conformity, compliance, and obedience.

Be able to describe the different effects of models.

Know the social facilitation effect and its interpretation.

Understand the concept of deindividuation and the sources and effects of this psychological state.


## STUDY TIPS: A HELPING HAND

In this chapter you are primarily confronted with the task of mastering sets of research findings. Most of this material should not be difficult to master with the appropriate rehearsal. However, there are a few points at which the material becomes somewhat abstract and will demand some extra effort. Some of these points are the section on fear arousal and attitude change, the section on dissonance theory as related to attitude discrepant behavior, the theory of social facilitation of Zajonc, and the concept of deindividuation. There are also a number of findings which appear to be somewhat contrary to common sense expectations and may require some extra rehearsal. Be sure to watch for these.


## STEP-BY-STEP: A GUIDED REVIEW

After you have read the chapter, mentally fill in each of the blanks in the following section while covering the answers in the margin. Check your answer with that in the margin as you go along. While in many cases your answer should be the same as that in the margin, in other cases a word of similar meaning is acceptable. Do not write in the spaces until you are doing your final review.

1.  Efforts directed toward changing someone's behavior, feelings, or thoughts are known as _____ _____.                social influences

    One type of social influence is attitude change. Attitudes are
    defined as enduring organizations of _____, _____,      feelings, beliefs
    and _____ tendencies relating to any object,     behavior

person, issue, or group. Alteration of attitudes involves changing at least one of the three tendencies or components of the attitude. Often changing one of the components produces changes in the _____ .

others

2. Acquisition of attitudes usually involves the processes of

_____ _____,

_____, and

_____ _____ .

classical conditioning, imitation
instrumental conditioning

3. Most attempts to change attitudes involve _____ communications. Research on the effectiveness of such communications has shown that the more _____ the person who delivers them is, the more attitude change.

persuasive

credible

4. Three factors which influence credibility are _____,

_____ and _____ .

High expertise tends to _____ attitude change. Individuals who argue against their own interest are seen as more trustworthy and tend to produce _____ attitude change than those whose positions appear to be motivated by self-interest. Attractive communicators are _____ successful in producing attitude change than unattractive communicators.

expertise

trustworthiness, attractiveness
facilitate

more

more

5. Research has shown that a _____ message is more effective if the audience is already favorable towards the message, while a _____ message is better if the audience is initially unfavorable towards the communicator's view.

one-sided

two-sided

6. The greater the discrepancy between the communicator's position and that of the audience, the _____ is the attitude change up to a point when attitude change may _____ (a "boomerang" effect). _____ credible communicators can advocate relatively extreme positions with little reduction in persuasive impact, while this is not true for _____ credible communicators. This fact is demonstrated in Figure 12-6 below.

greater
decrease
Highly

low

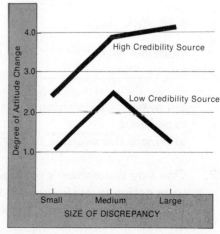

FIGURE 12-6 The effects of communicator-audience discrepancy size upon persuasion. Attitude change increases with increasing discrepancy size for high-credibility communicators, but may first increase and then decline in the case of low-credibility sources. See text for further explanation. (Based on data from Aronson, Turner, and Carlsmith, 1963.)

7. Individuals also differ in their persuasibility. This difference in susceptibility to persuasion appears _____ (to be/not to be) consistent across various situations.

to be

8. Persuasion appears to be _____ by good feelings on the part of the recipients, such as those induced by food and music.

enhanced

9. Research has shown that strong fear messages tend to induce _____ attitude change than weak ones. Strong fear appears to function best when followed by _____ _____ for avoiding the depicted negative outcomes. This effect may be due to the _____ effects on attitude change produced by fear reduction which accompanies the acceptance of the recommendations. (See Figure 12-9 below).

greater
clear
recommendations
reinforcing

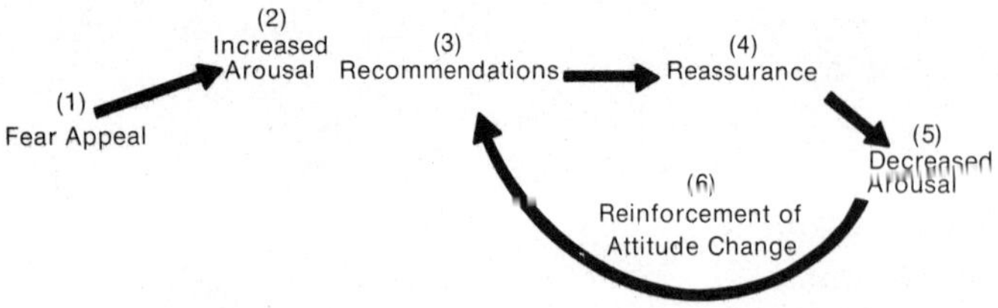

FIGURE 12-9 The drive-reduction explanation for the effectiveness of fear appeals. According to this view, fear communications (1) lead to increased arousal (2). Recommendations following the fear appeal (3) then lead to reassurance on the part of recipients (4), which serves to reduce their negative arousal (5). These reductions in arousal are reinforcing, and strengthen acceptance of the recommendations, thus producing attitude change (6).

10. Research indicates that in general attitudes _____ (are/are not) very closely related to overt behaviors. One reason for this may be that other factors such as _____ _____ or the desire to please others can lead an individual to behave contrary to his true feelings. Another reason may be the difficulty of accurately _____ attitudes.

are not

cultural norms

measuring

11. Some research suggests that accurate predictions from attitudes to overt behaviors can be made when attitudes toward a specific _____ of behavior and toward the _____ of that behavior are taken into account.

form, object

12. Festinger's theory of _____ _____ suggests that individuals have a strong preference for _____ _____ among their attitudes, opinions, and beliefs. Whenever individuals are aware of inconsistency between two related thoughts, they experience _____ and will strive to reduce or eliminate this aversive state.

cognitive dis-
sonance

cognitive con-
sistency

dissonance

13. One way dissonance is produced is when individuals perform some action inconsistent with their _____ . Individuals usually reduce this dissonance by changing their

attitudes

182

attitudes so that they are consistent with their _____.                behavior

So one way to induce attitude change is to induce behaviors

_____ with attitudes. This prediction                inconsistent

_____ (has/ has not) been supported in a number of                    has

laboratory studies.

14.  Another prediction derived from dissonance theory is that the

     _____ justification or reward we have for engaging in               less

     attitude discrepant behavior, the more attitude change will

     result. A high level of reward or justification provides a reason

     for engaging in the behavior and hence leads to _____               less

     arousal of dissonance than low levels of reward. This was

     supported in the study by Festinger and Carlsmith in which

     subjects were paid $1.00 or $20.00 to persuade another student

     that a boring task was interesting. Subsequently the $1.00 sub-

     jects reported liking the task _____ than the $20.00 subjects.      more

15.  The above type of dissonance effect seems to occur only if

     subjects perceive that they _____ to behave in the                  chose

     attitude discrepant fashion, and if they feel that important,

     foreseeable _____ have stemmed from their                 consequences

     actions.

16.  Formal or informal rules which indicate how individuals "ought"

     to behave are termed _____ _____. Actions                    social norms

     consistent with social norms are labeled _____.           conformity

     The tendency toward conformity is acquired during childhood by

     the _____ of adherence to accepted rules.                 rewarding

17.  A study by Asch suggests that individuals may change their behavior

     if they know they are not in accord with the accepted standards.

     Using a line judging task, _____ % of the subjects conformed to         75

     some extent to the wrong answers or norm set by a group of ex-

     perimental accomplices.

18.  The tendency to conform in this type of experiment seems to

     _____ with increases in the size of the group. The       increase

     presence of one person who does not conform greatly _____           reduces

     the conformity of the subjects. This effect _____         occurs even

     (occurs even/ does not occur) when the nonconforming person is

     low in prestige or competence.

19.  Early studies found that females conformed _____ than males.            more

     A later study found that this was due to the use of materials more

     familiar to _____ than _____. This study                     males, females

     found that females conformed more on _____               masculine

     items, males conformed more on _____ items,              feminine

     while they conformed equally on _____ items.             neutral

20. Attempts to make others like us are known as _____.  ingratiation
This technique may be used to induce others to agree to our
direct requests (i.e., _____).  One type of in-  compliance
gratiation is to _____ with the attitudes and suggestions  agree
of another.  Another way to increase someone's liking for ourselves
is to _____ him/her.  However if individuals  complement
become aware that such actions are designed to influence them,
they may react with _____.  anger

21. Another technique to induce compliance is to initially ask someone
for a small favor and then ask for a _____ one once  larger
the person has agreed.  This is called the _____  foot-in-the-door
technique.  Several studies have shown that such a technique
greatly _____ compliance with the larger request.  increases

22. A number of studies have shown that guilt produced by doing
something which harms another _____ the degree  increases
of compliance of the guilty party to subsequent requests from
others.

23. A study of children's neatness in the classroom found that the most
effective way to induce neatness was to suggest to the children
that they were _____.  neat

24. _____ is the social influence technique which  Obedience
consists of simply ordering another person to perform a particular
behavior.  The person requesting the obedience does not have
to be _____.  In a study by Milgram it was found  powerful
that ____ % of the subjects gave the maximum level of shock  65
possible to another person when ordered to do so by a relatively
powerless experimenter.

25. These results were not diminished when this experiment was
repeated in less prestigious settings and when the "victim" com-
plained about the painfulness of the shock.  When subjects were
asked to physically force the other person's hand on the shock
plate, ____ % fully obeyed the experimenter's orders.  30

26. Two factors appear to be important in counteracting obedience.
If an individual feels personally _____ for  responsible
the potentially harmful consequences of his actions, and if this
person is exposed to _____ _____,  disobedient
he will be less likely to obey.  models

27. Probably the most important type of unintentional social influence
is _____.  One effect of models is  modeling
_____ in that witnessing others  disinhibitory

184

engaging in an activity that we were afraid to perform may
_____ the probability of us performing such        increase

acts. In contrast, if a model receives negative consequences
for engaging in a prohibited act, the observer's _____            inhibitions
against engaging in this behavior will be strengthened.

28. In regard to actions not under the control of inhibitions, the actions
of others may stimulate similar actions on the part of the observers.
This is termed _____ _____.          response facili-
When we respond emotionally to another's emotional responses,          tation
we are exhibiting _____ _____          vicarious emo-
arousal. It appears that in many cases the unintentional effects        tional
of models yield _____ and _____          greater, longer-
effects than a number of the more direct techniques.                   lasting

29. Another type of unintential social influence is _____          social
_____, which involves the effects of                 facilitation
audiences on feelings and behavior. Research has shown that
audience presence can lead to increased _____.               arousal
Audiences also appear to facilitate the performance of
_____ tasks and hinder the performance of             well-learned
_____ tasks. Zajonc has suggested that               poorly-learned
this effect reflects the fact that arousal enhances the tendency to
perform _____ responses, whether they be incorrect           dominant
ones or correct ones. These effects have been found with both
humans and animals.

30. The fact that individuals will sometimes engage in anti-social
behaviors in the presence of many others that they would not
perform when alone is sometimes explained in terms of the
psychological state of _____.          deindividuation
This state involves feelings of _____          anonymity
in being part of a large group and a feeling of _____          shared
_____ for anti-social acts committed          responsibility
while others are present.

31. In one study of deindividuation Zimbardo found that groups of
students under relatively anonymous conditions showed          higher
_____ levels of aggression (delivery of electric shock)
than students in conditions in which anonymity was impossible.


KEY CONCEPTS AND TERMS

    After you have finished your Guided Review, fill in the meaning of the
    following terms in your own words. Check on your accuracy by con-
    sulting your text on the pages indicated and in the Glossary.

185

social influences (p. 412)

attitudes (p. 413)

communicator credibility (p. 415)

persuasibility (p. 418)

emotional appeals (p. 420)

cognitive dissonance (p. 421)

attitude-discrepant behavior (p. 424)

social norms (p. 427)

conformity (p. 427)

compliance (p. 432)

ingratiation (p. 432)

guilt (p. 434)

foot-in-the-door technique (p. 432)

obedience (p. 436)

modeling processes (p. 442)

disinhibitory effect (p. 442)

inhibitory effect (p. 443)

response facilitation  (p. 443)


vicarious emotional arousal  (p. 444)


social facilitation  (p. 444)


deindividuation  (p. 447)


## A PERSONAL QUIZ

After you are about finished with your studies but still have some time left for review, take this quiz to check on your mastery. Fill in your answers in the spaces provided and after you are finished check their correctness with the answers provided.

___ 1. Which of the following statements about attitudes is not correct? (p. 413)
   a. attitude change is a form of social influence
   b. attitudes involve feelings, belief, and behavior tendencies
   c. all three components of the attitude need to be changed to produce attitude change
   d. attitudes can be held toward persons, issues, and objects

___ 2. The general factors which influence credibility of the communicator as discussed in your text are (p. 415)
   a. speech, rate, size, and age
   b. expertise and looks
   c. expertise, trustworthiness, and attractiveness
   d. the issue and the manner of presentation

___ 3. In general it has been found that the most attitude change will be obtained by (p. 415)
   a. highly credible communicators
   b. moderately credible communicators
   c. intentional communicators
   d. both b and c

___ 4. A one-sided message is more effective if the audience is ____ towards the message, while a two-sided message is better if the audience is ____ towards the message (p. 417)
   a. neutral, favorable
   b. unfavorable, favorable
   c. favorable, neutral
   d. favorable, unfavorable

___ 5. In regard to the effect of the discrepancy between the position of the communicator and that of the audience it has been found that (p. 418)
   a. the greater the discrepancy, the greater the attitude change
   b. the greater the discrepancy, the greater the attitude change only for highly credible communicators
   c. the greater the discrepancy, the less the attitude change
   d. the greater the discrepancy, the less the attitude change only for moderately dredible communicators

___ 6. Strong fear messages tend to (p. 421)

a. inhibit attitude change
b. inhibit attitude change only with complex messages
c. facilitate attitude change when clear recommendations are made
d. facilitate attitude change only with simple messages

7. The fact that attitudes are often not very closely related to behavior suggests that (p. 422)
   a. individuals do not strive for consistency between their attitudes and behavior
   b. cultural norms may be affecting the behavior
   c. attitude measurement is often inadequate
   d. both b and c

8. Festinger's cognitive dissonance theory suggests that individuals (p. 421)
   a. have a strong preference for cognitive consistency
   b. find dissonance rewarding
   c. cannot live with cognitive consistency
   d. are often inconsistent in the way they act in different situations

9. According to dissonance theory the most attitude change will occur in cases where an individual engages in (p. 424)
   a. attitude-consistent behavior for a little reward
   b. attitude-discrepant behavior for a little reward
   c. attitude-consistent behavior for a large reward
   d. attitude-discrepant behavior for a large reward

10. The above dissonance effect will occur only under conditions of (p. 425)
    a. low choice, low consequences
    b. low choice, high consequences
    c. high choice, low consequences
    d. high choice, high consequences

11. In the study by Asch ____ % of the subjects conformed to some extent to norms of the group. (p. 429)
    a. 25
    b. 50
    c. 75
    d. 100

12. Research on group size and conformity suggests that (p. 430)
    a. group size increases conformity
    b. group size doesn't affect conformity
    c. group size decreases conformity
    d. group size increases conformity only up to groups of size three

13. In regard to the effect of sex on the subject on conformity, it has been found that (p. 431)
    a. females are more conformist
    b. males are more conformist
    c. male and female conformity depends on whether the items are masculine or feminine in nature
    d. none of the above

14. Which of the following is a technique which can be employed to tain compliance (p. 432-434)
    a. agreement
    b. complementing
    c. foot-in-the-door-technique
    d. all of the above

15. A study on neatness in the classroom found that the most effective technique was to (p. 435)
    a. tell the children they were neat
    b. demand neatness
    c. use persuasive appeal
    d. induce counterattitudinal behavior

16. In the Milgram study on obedience it was found that
    a. individuals only obey a powerful authority
    b. 65% of the subjects obeyed completely
    c. 30% of the subjects obeyed completely
    d. individuals obey only in a prestigious setting

17. Obedience in the Milgram situation can be reduced if (p. 438)
    a. the victim is far away
    b. others are present
    c. the subject feels personally responsible
    d. the experimenter sits close by

18. Which of the following is not a type of social influence exerted by models? (p. 442-444)
    a. social facilitation
    b. response facilitation
    c. response inhibition
    d. response disinhibition

19. The presence of an audience seems to (p. 445)
    a. decrease arousal
    b. facilitate learning
    c. hinder well learned responses
    d. none of the above

20. Deindividuation involves (p. 447)
    a. feelings of increased responsibility
    b. feelings of anonymity
    c. reduced feelings of aggression
    d. enhanced arousal

Answers:

| | | | |
|---|---|---|---|
| 1. c | 6. c | 11. c | 16. b |
| 2. c | 7. d | 12. a | 17. c |
| 3. a | 8. a | 13. c | 18. a |
| 4. d | 9. b | 14. d | 19. d |
| 5. b | 10. d | 15. a | 20. b |

## PSYCHOLOGY IN ACTION: PROJECTS AND DEMONSTRATIONS

### A Survey of Social Influence

This exercise involves conducting a survey of the various techniques of social influence you may encounter in your everyday life. On the next few pages you will find forms for recording information about seven different techniques of social influence. On these sheets you should note where the instance of social influence occurred, when it occurred (time of day), who was doing the influencing (influencing agent), who was the target of the influence (recipient), and whether or not the influence worked (result). Make additional sheets if necessary to record all of the influence attempts. Do this for two or three days or even a week if you like. At the end of the observation period you should note the frequency of each of the attempts of influence. Which types of influence were most frequent? Were they generally successful? Do you note any consistency in terms of the time of day and place of influence? For example, are influence attempts more frequent in formal settings than informal ones? Are certain types of people (e.g., males, older people, taller people) more frequent users of social influence than others? Are certain types of people more frequent recipients of social influence than others? Compare your findings with that of your classmates.

### Getting Your Foot In The Door

Several studies have shown that one way to get someone to do a large favor for you is to first get this person to do a small favor. You might want to try this with some of your classmates in other classes. Throughout the period of several weeks you might ask some students if you can borrow their class notes for a day. If they agree, the next time the class meets ask them for a larger favor (e.g., the loan of some money, help in studying for an exam, or a lift somewhere). Do this for five classmates and ask another five classmates for the larger favor without first borrowing their notes. Note for each of the students in the two groups whether they say "yes", "no", or "maybe". Unless you are the kind of person no one can refuse, you should find more willingness to let you borrow the car among the students who previously lent you their notes.

## Persuasive Appeals

| Where | When | Influencing Agent | Recipient | Result |
|---|---|---|---|---|
| 1. | | | | |
| 2. | | | | |
| 3. | | | | |
| 4. | | | | |
| 5. | | | | |
| 6. | | | | |
| 7. | | | | |
| 8. | | | | |
| 9. | | | | |
| 10. | | | | |

## Fear Communications

| Where | When | Influencing Agent | Recipient | Result |
|-------|------|-------------------|-----------|--------|
| 1. | | | | |
| 2. | | | | |
| 3. | | | | |
| 4. | | | | |
| 5. | | | | |
| 6. | | | | |
| 7. | | | | |
| 8. | | | | |
| 9. | | | | |
| 10. | | | | |

## Ingratiation

| Where | When | Influencing Agent | Recipient | Result |
|-------|------|-------------------|-----------|--------|
| 1. | | | | |
| 2. | | | | |
| 3. | | | | |
| 4. | | | | |
| 5. | | | | |
| 6. | | | | |
| 7. | | | | |
| 8. | | | | |
| 9. | | | | |
| 10. | | | | |

Foot-in-the-door-technique

| | Where | When | Influencing Agent | Recipient | Result |
|---|---|---|---|---|---|
| 1. | | | | | |
| 2. | | | | | |
| 3. | | | | | |
| 4. | | | | | |
| 5. | | | | | |
| 6. | | | | | |
| 7. | | | | | |
| 8. | | | | | |
| 9. | | | | | |
| 10. | | | | | |

## Guilt Induction

| Where | When | Influencing Agent | Recipient | Result |
|-------|------|-------------------|-----------|--------|
| 1. |  |  |  |  |
| 2. |  |  |  |  |
| 3. |  |  |  |  |
| 4. |  |  |  |  |
| 5. |  |  |  |  |
| 6. |  |  |  |  |
| 7. |  |  |  |  |
| 8. |  |  |  |  |
| 9. |  |  |  |  |
| 10. |  |  |  |  |

## Direct Commands

| Where | When | Influencing Agent | Recipient | Result |
|-------|------|-------------------|-----------|--------|
| 1. | | | | |
| 2. | | | | |
| 3. | | | | |
| 4. | | | | |
| 5. | | | | |
| 6. | | | | |
| 7. | | | | |
| 8. | | | | |
| 9. | | | | |
| 10. | | | | |

## Conformity Pressure

| | Where | When | Influencing Agent | Recipient | Result |
|---|---|---|---|---|---|
| 1. | | | | | |
| 2. | | | | | |
| 3. | | | | | |
| 4. | | | | | |
| 5. | | | | | |
| 6. | | | | | |
| 7. | | | | | |
| 8. | | | | | |
| 9. | | | | | |
| 10. | | | | | |

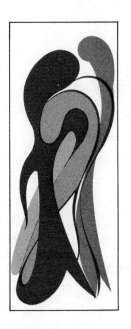

Chapter 13

SOCIAL
BEHAVIOR:
Interacting
with
Others

## LEARNING OBJECTIVES: WHAT YOU SHOULD KNOW

After reading this chapter you should:

Understand nature of the attribution process and how it functions to increase our accuracy in identifying traits.

Know how we form unitary and consistent impressions.

Know the effect of physical attractiveness on impression formation.

Be able to discuss the various ways facial expressions, eye contact, bodily position, posture, and movement provide information about a person's mood state.

Know how people can deceive us about their emotions, and how we can detect such deceit.

Know the major factors which determine interpersonal attraction.

Understand Rubin's concept of romantic love and the effect of parental interference on romantic couples.

Know the factors which inhibit and enhance helping behavior and the possible reasons for these effects.

Be able to describe the factors which facilitate or reduce the occurrence of aggression.

## STUDY TIPS: A HELPING HAND

In this chapter you will be exposed to the research and concepts in the areas of person perception, interpersonal attraction, altruism, and aggression. Again, it will probably be best during the rehearsal phase of your studying to try to master one of these sections before going on to the next. This should facilitate your integrating all of the research in each of the areas. A few topics will require some special attention. First, be sure you understand the differences between the averaging and the adding rules of impression formation. Second, the section on nonverbal cues contains a lot of facts which may be easily confused. Finally, the section on altruism presents a number of explanations for each phenomenon discussed. Try to keep the explanations associated with the appropriate phenomenon.

## STEP-BY-STEP: A GUIDED REVIEW

After you have read the chapter, mentally fill in each of the blanks in the following section while covering the answers in the margin. Check your answer with that in the margin as you go along. While in many cases your answer should be the same as that in the margin, in other cases a word of similar meaning is acceptable. Do not write in the spaces until you are doing your final review.

1. The process by which we come to know and understand other persons is known as _____ _____. This process involves the determination of the major _____ possessed by others and combining this information into consistent pictures of their personalities.

person perception
traits

2. The primary way in which individuals infer the traits possessed by others is by _____ others' behavior. The process of inferring the characteristics or traits of others from their overt behavior is called _____.

observing
attribution

3. Two problems with the attribution process are the ability of others to _____ us and the influence of _____ factors. Thus attribution often involves determining whether the causes of the actions of others stem from external or internal causes.

deceive, external

4. Research has found that we view the action of others as stemming largely from _____ factors, while perceiving our own actions as being caused by _____ factors. One consequence of this is that we often _____ victims of serious accidents, disasters, or rape for the fates they suffer.

internal
external
blame

5. In order to increase our accuracy in identifying traits we tend to focus on those actions for which individuals could have had only at most a _____ _____ reasons since this provides more useful information than behavior for which they could have had _____ reasons. For the same reason we also tend to pay a lot of attention to those aspects of another's behavior which are _____ from the usual patterns of behavior exhibited by others.

few distinct
many
different

6. In trying to combine a variety of information about a person into a unitary impression we appear to employ a _____ _____ rather than an _____ technique. In averaging information about others we tend to give more weight to _____ _____ and information derived from _____ sources.

weighted
average, adding
first impressions
credible

7. In initial encounters physically attractive individuals are generally liked more than unattractive ones. Physically attractive individuals also tend to be rated _____ on such characteristics as kindness, intelligence, and potential for success in work and marriage. These characteristics _____ (do/ do not) give a true picture of highly attractive individuals. This fact may account for the finding that extremely attractive

positively
do not

individuals are often _____ popular than those who are            less
less physically attractive.

8.  In trying to determine the individual's mood state we often
    rely on _____ cues such as facial expres-          nonverbal
    sions, eye-contact, and bodily position and movement.
    Research has shown that individuals _____(can/ cannot)          can
    determine inward feelings from observation of frowns, smiles,
    and tears.  Further these expressions appear to be recognized
    by children at a very young age and people all over the world.

9.  In many cases individuals may try to deceive us about their
    emotions.  They may _____ their expression by         qualify
    adding another expression as a comment upon it (e.g., a
    smile after an expression of anger).  They may also _____        modulate
    or adjust their expressions to show more or less emotion than is
    actually being experienced.  Finally, they may _____            falsify
    by pretending to experience feelings they do not have.

10. There are a number of ways one can detect such emotional
    deceit.  Individuals may only display part of the total pattern
    associated with a particular emotional reaction.  Or they may
    time their reactions inappropriately, such as reacting too
    slowly.  Deceit can also be detected from _____       micro-expressions
    which are very brief reactions which reveal a person's true
    emotions.

11. Eye contact is also used as an index of another's feelings.  The
    more an individual gazes at us, up to a point, the more
    _____ this individual is assumed to feel, and          positive
    the more this individual is assumed to _____ us.  However,       like
    continuous gazing or staring is often interpreted as a sign of
    _____.  For example, staring at people in            hostility
    cars leads to escape responses, such as driving off quickly.

12. Much information can be derived from someone's bodily posture,
    position, and movements.  A large amount of body movement
    can indicate _____, a clenched fist _____,          arousal, anger
    covering of the eyes _____, and rubbing hands               shame
    together _____.                                     excitement

13. If someone leans forward to you while conversing, this can be
    taken as a sign of _____ for you.  However if this per-       liking
    son orients her body away and backwards, she is indicating
    _____.  Also, if someone is very attentive and       dislike
    nods frequently while we speak, _____ feelings       positive
    are indicated, while shaking of the head in disagreement and
    staring away indicates _____ reactions.  Sexual     negative
    interest can also be indicated through bodily reactions.

14. One important determinant of interpersonal attraction is the
    extent to which others hold _____ similar          attitudes
    to ours. Studies have shown that the greater the _____       proportion
    of agreement between oneself and a stranger, the greater the
    liking. This tendency _____(is/ is not) found to be true across   is
    cultures and age levels.

15. In general, our liking for others closely _____        matches
    their expressed liking for us. This is the rule of _____.   reciprocity
    We are also very sensitive to changes in expressed liking for
    us, so we appear to like individuals best if they _____     increase
    their expressed liking for us but least if they _____       decrease
    their liking for us.

16. In first meetings involving young persons _____        physical
    _____ seems to overwhelm the influence       attractiveness
    of all other factors such as personality, intelligence, and simi-
    larity. While in casual dating situations individuals seem to
    seek the _____ attractive partners, long-term romantic        most
    choices seem to be based on a _____ rule.             matching

17. In a study of the attractiveness of a woman who plays hard to
    get, it was found that the type of woman who reacted
    _____ to the subject but _____      favorably, unfavor-
    to others was liked most.                                        ably

18. Everyday experience suggests that liking affects interpersonal
    behaviors such as hiring, voting, and helping. Moreover,
    recent studies have shown that defendants who are liked by
    members of a simulated jury received more _____        lenient
    sentences than disliked defendants.

19. According to Rubin the most central components of romantic
    love (as measured by his love scale) are the desire to be
    _____,_____                                 with one's lover,
    towards one's lover, and a willingness to place one's lover's    possessiveness
    _____ above one's own. High scores for         interests
    couples on the love scale have been related to increased a-
    mounts of time spent in _____ _____.          mutual gazing

20. Parental interference has been found to _____          increase
    the reported feelings of love of married and unmarried couples.
    In contrast, feelings of _____ decreased and           trust
    _____ _____ increased            critical feelings
    with increased parental interference, suggesting that such
    interference may be detrimental in the long run.

21. A number of studies have shown that the presence of bystanders _____ helping in emergencies. In          inhibits
fact, some studies have shown that the greater is the _____    number
of bystanders present, the less the degree of helping.

22. Two factors often cited as operating to produce this reduction in
helping are diffusion of _____ and              responsibility
fear of _____ in the presence of others.        embarassment
Studies have shown that increasing the _____    responsibility
of the observers by getting a prior commitment to help increases helping. Reducing _____, and hence      ambiguity
fear of embarassment, by making the nature of the victim's
plight clear and making other observers' concern clear also
increases helping.

23. Models who make donations or assist individuals in need of
help have been shown to lead to _____ responses    similar
on the part of observers. This finding may be due to reduced
fears of _____, increased feelings of          embarassment
_____ _____, or simply           social obligation
_____ facilitation in the observer.            response

24. Individuals experiencing _____ emotional states    positive
appear to more willing to help others and donate to charity.
This finding may reflect either the _____      generalization
of these positive feelings to feelings towards others or the
fact that positive mood states enhance one's feelings about
_____.                                          oneself

25. Individuals react _____ to aid from friends    positively
and react _____ to aid from adversaries.           negatively
Another study demonstrated that individuals prefer aid which
requires _____ repayment over aid which requires           equal
_____ repayment or repayment in excess of that donated (see   no
Figure 13-18 below). The negative reactions to aid requiring
no repayment may be due to the violation of the norm of
_____, _____ or interpretation    reciprocity, suspi-
of the aid as _____.                            cion, charity

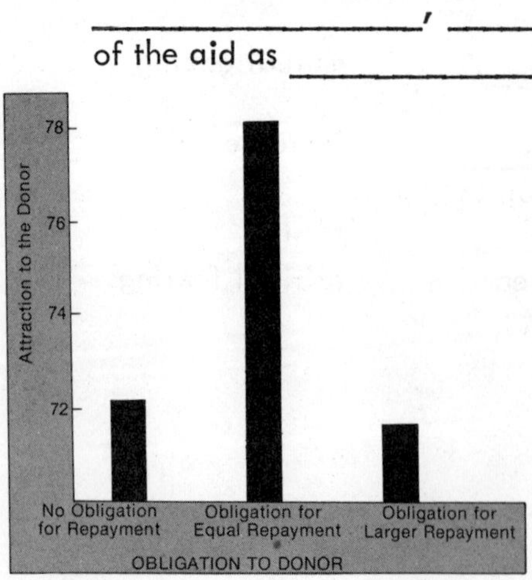

FIGURE 13-18 Reactions to aid from others. Individuals
seem to react most positively to aid which carries with it the
obligation to make equal repayment to the donor. They
react less favorably to aid which carries with it no obligation
of repayment or an obligation to pay back even more than
was received. (Based on data from Gergen et al., 1975.)

26. _____ is the behavior which seeks to        Aggression
inflict harm or injury on others. Although some hold that
aggression has biological or genetic causes, many psychologists hold that much of aggression is determined by
_____ and _____ conditions     learning, stimulus
and is strengthened by _____ .                  reward

27. Three situational factors which have been related to the
occurrence of aggressive behavior are _____ ,     frustration
_____ , and _____ models.       attack, aggressive

28. One popular hypothesis on aggression known as the _____     frustration –
_____ hypothesis suggested that frustration     aggression
_____ leads to aggression and aggression is _____     always, always
the result of frustration. This hypothesis has been shown to be
_____ . A revised view suggests that frustration     false
_____ leads to aggression and is only _____     sometimes, one
of many different determinants of such behavior. However,
other studies suggest that frustration often has _____     no or only a weak
effect on aggression.

29. The factor which may be the most powerful elicitor of aggression
is physical or verbal _____ . This does not actually     attack
have to be received since the mere knowledge that someone
intended to harm us may be sufficient to elicit aggression.

30. Research has shown that both adults and children can learn
novel aggressive behaviors by observing live or filmed models.
Many studies have shown that television violence _____     heightens
aggression in children, while others have shown that children
are more willing to _____ another child after watching an     hurt
aggressive show.

31. Heat and crowding may _____ aggression if indivi-     enhance
duals become irritated or annoyed. Heightened arousal due to
other sources such as exercise may _____ aggres-     enhance
sion if this arousal is interpreted as _____ .             anger

32. In a series of studies on the effects of alcohol and marijuana
upon physical aggression it was found that small doses of
alcohol seemed to _____ aggression, while larger     inhibit
doses _____ aggression. Small doses of         facilitate
marijuana had little effect on aggression, while large doses
_____ it. These findings are shown in Table     reduce
13-3 on the top of the next page.

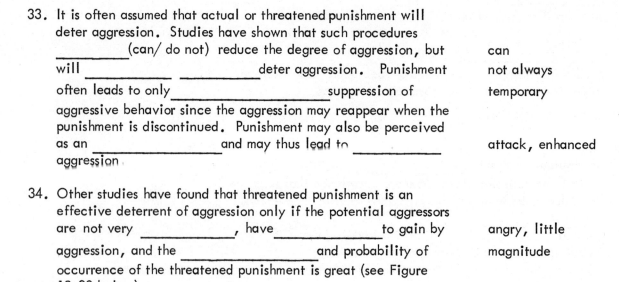

**TABLE 13–3  The Effects of Alcohol and Marijuana on Physical Aggression**

| Dose | Average Strength of Shocks (with no drugs, shock level = 3.9) | |
| --- | --- | --- |
| | With Marijuana | With Alcohol |
| Small | 3.1 | 2.1 |
| Large | 1.0 | 5.4 |

As shown here, small doses of alcohol seem to inhibit aggression, while larger doses facilitate such behavior. In contrast, small doses of marijuana have little effect upon aggression, while larger doses reduce it. (Numbers shown represent the average strength of the shocks set by subjects for their opponent.)

(Based on data from Taylor et al., 1976.)

33. It is often assumed that actual or threatened punishment will deter aggression.  Studies have shown that such procedures _____ (can/ do not) reduce the degree of aggression, but will _____ _____ deter aggression.  Punishment often leads to only _____ suppression of aggressive behavior since the aggression may reappear when the punishment is discontinued.  Punishment may also be perceived as an _____ and may thus lead to _____ aggression.

can

not always

temporary

attack, enhanced

34. Other studies have found that threatened punishment is an effective deterrent of aggression only if the potential aggressors are not very _____, have _____ to gain by aggression, and the _____ and probability of occurrence of the threatened punishment is great (see Figure 13-22 below).

angry, little

magnitude

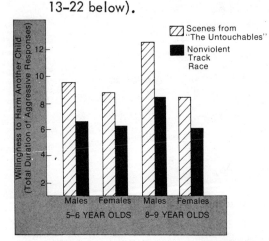

FIGURE 13-22  When individuals can obtain rewards through aggression, even the threat of strong punishment for such behavior is often ineffective in preventing its occurrence. In the study illustrated here, subjects in the reinforcement condition (top line) were led to believe that they could make a good impression on the experimenter by behaving in an aggressive manner, while those in the nonreinforcement group (lower line) were not provided with such information. As expected, subjects in the reinforcement condition were not deterred from aggressing even by a high probability of punishment. (Based on data from Baron, 1974b.)

35. The _____ hypothesis suggests that if angry individuals are allowed to blow off steam through various indirect aggressive activities, they subsequently will have a _____ tendency to aggress against the source of

catharsis

lessened

their anger.  This hypothesis _____ (has/ has not)          has not
been supported.  Evidence suggests that prior aggression against
the individual will _____ the tendency to aggress          increase
against this person at a later time.

36.  Several studies have shown that humor and mild sexual arousal
     may_____aggressive behavior.  Apparently the          inhibit
     emotional states produced by humorous and sexual stimuli are
     _____ with anger.  Strong sexual      incompatible
     arousal produced by very erotic stimuli appears to _____       increase
     aggression.

## KEY CONCEPTS AND TERMS

After you have finished your Guided Review fill in the meaning of the
following terms in your own words.  Check on your accuracy by consulting your text on the pages indicated or the Glossary.

person perception  (p. 453)


attribution  (p. 455)


internal factors  (p. 456)


external factors  (p. 456)


weighted average technique  (p. 459)


adding technique  (p. 458)


nonverbal cues  (p. 461)


qualifying  (p. 462)


modulating  (p. 462)


falsifying  (p. 462)

micro-expressions (p. 463)

Matching rule (p. 469)

love scale (p. 472)

the "Romeo and Juliet" effect (p. 472)

diffusion of responsibility (p. 475)

norm of social reciprocity (p. 479)

aggression (p. 478)

frustration-aggression hypothesis (p. 482)

cartharsis hypothesis (p. 487)


## A PERSONAL QUIZ

After you are about finished with your studies but still have some time left for review, take this quiz to check on your mastery. Fill in your answers in the spaces provided and after you are finished check their correctness with the answers provided.

____ 1. Individuals tend to attribute the causes of (p. 456)
    a. behavior to external factors
    b. behavior to internal factors
    c. their own behavior to internal factors
    d. their own behavior to external factors

____ 2. Victims of serious accidents or disasters (p. 456)
    a. are often blamed for the fates they suffer
    b. always receive empathy

    c. usually attribute their fate to internal causes
    d. none of the above

____ 3. In order to increase one's accuracy in identifying traits one should focus on (p. 457)
    a. multiple behaviors
    b. usual patterns of behaviors
    c. actions which have few distinct reasons
    d. actions which have multiple reasons

4. In forming a uniform impression of others we tend to employ a(n) _____ rule. (p. 458)
   a. weighted-average
   b. averaging
   c. adding
   d. multiplicative

5. Which of the following statements about physically attractive individuals is not true? (p. 461)
   a. they are liked
   b. they are independent
   c. extremely attractive individuals are most popular
   d. extremely attractive individuals are rated likely to be successful

6. Individuals may try to deceive us about their emotions by doing all but one of the following to their emotions: (p. 462)
   a. qualify
   b. regulate
   c. modulate
   d. falsify

7. In examining the effect of eye contact, the most positive interpersonal feelings will result if one (p. 464)
   a. gazes continuously at the other person
   b. gazes very little
   c. gazes moderately
   d. does not gaze at all

8. If one wants to indicate one's liking for someone with bodily cues one should (p. 465)
   a. exhibit a lot of movement
   b. rub one's hands together
   c. lean backwards
   d. lean forward

9. The effect of agreement on attraction is that
   a. agreement reduces attraction
   b. agreement increases attraction
   c. too much agreement may reduce attraction

   d. both b and c

10. In casual dating situations individuals tend to choose _____ partners; individuals making long-term romantic choices will choose _____ partners. (p. 467-68)
    a. the most attractive; equally attractive
    b. equally attractive; the most attractive
    c. the most attractive; the most attractive
    d. equally attractive; equally attractive

11. Research suggests that defendants who are liked will receive (p.473)
    a. lenient sentences
    b. harsh sentences
    c. the same sentences as disliked defendants
    d. more lenient sentences than disliked defendants only in misdemeanor cases

12. Parental interference seems to _____ among married and unmarried couples. (p. 472)
    a. increase feelings of love
    b. increase feelings of trust
    c. increase critical feelings
    d. both a and c

13. If one is being mugged, under which of the following conditions will one be most likely to receive help? (p. 474)
    a. there is one bystander
    b. there are two bystanders
    c. there are four bystanders
    d. there are six bystanders

14. Which of the following has been shown to increase helping? (p. 475-78)
    a. embarassment
    b. positive mood states
    c. unhelpful models
    d. ambiguity

15. Individuals seem to prefer aid (p. 479)
    a. which requires no repayment
    b. which requires payment with interest
    c. which requires equal repayment
    d. from an adversary

16. It appears that frustration (p. 482)
    a. often has only a weak effect on aggression
    b. always produces aggression
    c. is the cause of all aggression
    d. reduces aggression

17. The most powerful determinant of aggression appears to be (p. 483)
    a. frustration
    b. crowding
    c. genetic malfunctioning
    d. verbal or physical attack

18. Television violence generally appears to (p. 484)
    a. increase aggression
    b. reduce aggression
    c. have no effect on aggression
    d. affect aggression only in children

19. It appears that punishment will
    a. always deter aggression
    b. can increase aggression
    c. is an effective deterrent only if person is angry
    d. is an effective deterrent only if it is mild

20. Which of the following techniques does not appear to reduce aggressive tendencies? (p. 489)
    a. humor
    b. mild sexual arousal
    c. blowing of steam
    d. punishment

Answers:

| 1. d | 6. b | 11. a | 16. a |
|------|------|-------|-------|
| 2. a | 7. c | 12. d | 17. d |
| 3. c | 8. d | 13. d | 18. a |
| 4. a | 9. b | 14. b | 19. b |
| 5. c | 10. a | 15. c | 20. c |

## PSYCHOLOGY IN ACTION: PROJECTS AND DEMONSTRATIONS

### The Matching Game: Similarity in Physical Attractiveness

In this project you will try to determine if couples who differ in the degree to which their relationship is long-lasting differ in the degree to which they are similar in physical attractiveness. Select 10 couples you know who are married, 10 who are engaged or dating steadily, and 10 who are dating casually. Sheets are provided for you to list each person and rate this person's physical attractiveness. For example, the male member of the first married couple is inserted after number 1 on the married male rating sheet, while the female member is listed after number 1 on the married female rating sheet. The other married couples are then listed in order, and this procedure is repeated for the engaged and the casual couples on the appropriate rating sheets. Next, go back and rate each person in terms of his/her physical attractiveness. Rate all of the persons on one sheet before going on to the next. You may not be sure about your answers at times but rate everyone anyway. After you have rated everyone, transcribe these ratings to the data analysis form and determine the differences in ratings for each couple (e.g., if the man in a couple is rated 2 and the woman 5, the difference is 3) and the average difference for the couples in each of the three categories. Do you find that couples who have a more permanent relationship are more similar in attractiveness? Compare your findings with those of some of your classmates.

## Analyzing TV violence

For five days carefully watch two hours of programs shown on the three major networks (ABC, CBS, NBC) during prime time. As you watch, keep count of both (1) the number of violent incidents (e.g., beatings, shootings, stabbings, etc.) and (2) the number of cooperative, helpful incidents (e.g., one person assists another, works together with others to achieve some goal, etc.). Use the data sheet below for this purpose.

At the end of the week, add the number of violent incidents you have observed on each day and the number of helpful, cooperative ones. If you have kept careful records, you should find that the number of aggressive episodes greatly outnumbers the number of cooperative ones.

| Name of Show | Number of Aggressive Episodes | Number of Cooperative Episodes |
|---|---|---|
| | | |
| | | |
| | | |
| | | |
| | | |
| | | |
| | | |
| | | |
| | | |
| | | |
| | | |
| | | |
| | | |
| | | |
| | | |
| | | |
| | | |

## Married Males Ratings

|  | Unattractive |  |  |  |  |  | Very Attractive |
|---|---|---|---|---|---|---|---|
| 1. _____ | 1 | 2 | 3 | 4 | 5 | 6 | 7 |
| 2. _____ | 1 | 2 | 3 | 4 | 5 | 6 | 7 |
| 3. _____ | 1 | 2 | 3 | 4 | 5 | 6 | 7 |
| 4. _____ | 1 | 2 | 3 | 4 | 5 | 6 | 7 |
| 5. _____ | 1 | 2 | 3 | 4 | 5 | 6 | 7 |
| 6. _____ | 1 | 2 | 3 | 4 | 5 | 6 | 7 |
| 7. _____ | 1 | 2 | 3 | 4 | 5 | 6 | 7 |
| 8. _____ | 1 | 2 | 3 | 4 | 5 | 6 | 7 |
| 9. _____ | 1 | 2 | 3 | 4 | 5 | 6 | 7 |
| 10. _____ | 1 | 2 | 3 | 4 | 5 | 6 | 7 |

## Married Females Ratings

|  | Unattractive |  |  |  |  |  | Very<br>Attractive |
|---|---|---|---|---|---|---|---|
| 1. _____ | 1 | 2 | 3 | 4 | 5 | 6 | 7 |
| 2. _____ | 1 | 2 | 3 | 4 | 5 | 6 | 7 |
| 3. _____ | 1 | 2 | 3 | 4 | 5 | 6 | 7 |
| 4. _____ | 1 | 2 | 3 | 4 | 5 | 6 | 7 |
| 5. _____ | 1 | 2 | 3 | 4 | 5 | 6 | 7 |
| 6. _____ | 1 | 2 | 3 | 4 | 5 | 6 | 7 |
| 7. _____ | 1 | 2 | 3 | 4 | 5 | 6 | 7 |
| 8. _____ | 1 | 2 | 3 | 4 | 5 | 6 | 7 |
| 9. _____ | 1 | 2 | 3 | 4 | 5 | 6 | 7 |
| 10. _____ | 1 | 2 | 3 | 4 | 5 | 6 | 7 |

Engaged or Steady Males Ratings

|  |  | Unattractive |  |  |  |  | Very Attractive |
|---|---|---|---|---|---|---|---|
| 1. _____ | 1 | 2 | 3 | 4 | 5 | 6 | 7 |
| 2. _____ | 1 | 2 | 3 | 4 | 5 | 6 | 7 |
| 3. _____ | 1 | 2 | 3 | 4 | 5 | 6 | 7 |
| 4. _____ | 1 | 2 | 3 | 4 | 5 | 6 | 7 |
| 5. _____ | 1 | 2 | 3 | 4 | 5 | 6 | 7 |
| 6. _____ | 1 | 2 | 3 | 4 | 5 | 6 | 7 |
| 7. _____ | 1 | 2 | 3 | 4 | 5 | 6 | 7 |
| 8. _____ | 1 | 2 | 3 | 4 | 5 | 6 | 7 |
| 9. _____ | 1 | 2 | 3 | 4 | 5 | 6 | 7 |
| 10. _____ | 1 | 2 | 3 | 4 | 5 | 6 | 7 |

# Engaged or Steady Females Rating

|  |  | Unattractive |  |  |  |  | | Very Attractive |
|---|---|---|---|---|---|---|---|---|
| 1. | _____ | 1 | 2 | 3 | 4 | 5 | 6 | 7 |
| 2. | _____ | 1 | 2 | 3 | 4 | 5 | 6 | 7 |
| 3. | _____ | 1 | 2 | 3 | 4 | 5 | 6 | 7 |
| 4. | _____ | 1 | 2 | 3 | 4 | 5 | 6 | 7 |
| 5. | _____ | 1 | 2 | 3 | 4 | 5 | 6 | 7 |
| 6. | _____ | 1 | 2 | 3 | 4 | 5 | 6 | 7 |
| 7. | _____ | 1 | 2 | 3 | 4 | 5 | 6 | 7 |
| 8. | _____ | 1 | 2 | 3 | 4 | 5 | 6 | 7 |
| 9. | _____ | 1 | 2 | 3 | 4 | 5 | 6 | 7 |
| 10. | _____ | 1 | 2 | 3 | 4 | 5 | 6 | 7 |

Casual Date Male Ratings

|   |  | Unattractive |  |  |  |  |  | Very Attractive |
|---|---|---|---|---|---|---|---|---|
| 1. | _____ | 1 | 2 | 3 | 4 | 5 | 6 | 7 |
| 2. | _____ | 1 | 2 | 3 | 4 | 5 | 6 | 7 |
| 3. | _____ | 1 | 2 | 3 | 4 | 5 | 6 | 7 |
| 4. | _____ | 1 | 2 | 3 | 4 | 5 | 6 | 7 |
| 5. | _____ | 1 | 2 | 3 | 4 | 5 | 6 | 7 |
| 6. | _____ | 1 | 2 | 3 | 4 | 5 | 6 | 7 |
| 7. | _____ | 1 | 2 | 3 | 4 | 5 | 6 | 7 |
| 8. | _____ | 1 | 2 | 3 | 4 | 5 | 6 | 7 |
| 9. | _____ | 1 | 2 | 3 | 4 | 5 | 6 | 7 |
| 10. | _____ | 1 | 2 | 3 | 4 | 5 | 6 | 7 |

Casual Date Female Ratings

|  | Unattractive | | | | | | Very Attractive |
|---|---|---|---|---|---|---|---|
| 1. _____ | 1 | 2 | 3 | 4 | 5 | 6 | 7 |
| 2. _____ | 1 | 2 | 3 | 4 | 5 | 6 | 7 |
| 3. _____ | 1 | 2 | 3 | 4 | 5 | 6 | 7 |
| 4. _____ | 1 | 2 | 3 | 4 | 5 | 6 | 7 |
| 5. _____ | 1 | 2 | 3 | 4 | 5 | 6 | 7 |
| 6. _____ | 1 | 2 | 3 | 4 | 5 | 6 | 7 |
| 7. _____ | 1 | 2 | 3 | 4 | 5 | 6 | 7 |
| 8. _____ | 1 | 2 | 3 | 4 | 5 | 6 | 7 |
| 9. _____ | 1 | 2 | 3 | 4 | 5 | 6 | 7 |
| 10. _____ | 1 | 2 | 3 | 4 | 5 | 6 | 7 |

## Data Analysis

| Scores for Married Couples | | | Scores for Engaged Couples | | | Scores for Casual Couples | | |
|---|---|---|---|---|---|---|---|---|
| Male | Female | Diff. | Male | Female | Diff. | Male | Female | Diff. |
| 1. ___ | ___ | ___ | ___ | ___ | ___ | ___ | ___ | ___ |
| 2. ___ | ___ | ___ | ___ | ___ | ___ | ___ | ___ | ___ |
| 3. ___ | ___ | ___ | ___ | ___ | ___ | ___ | ___ | ___ |
| 4. ___ | ___ | ___ | ___ | ___ | ___ | ___ | ___ | ___ |
| 5. ___ | ___ | ___ | ___ | ___ | ___ | ___ | ___ | ___ |
| 6. ___ | ___ | ___ | ___ | ___ | ___ | ___ | ___ | ___ |
| 7. ___ | ___ | ___ | ___ | ___ | ___ | ___ | ___ | ___ |
| 8. ___ | ___ | ___ | ___ | ___ | ___ | ___ | ___ | ___ |
| 9. ___ | ___ | ___ | ___ | ___ | ___ | ___ | ___ | ___ |
| 10. ___ | ___ | ___ | ___ | ___ | ___ | ___ | ___ | ___ |

Total Difference ___          Total Difference ___          Total Difference ___

Average ___          Average ___          Average ___

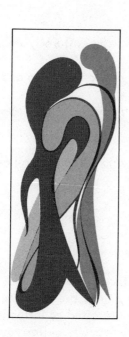

Chapter 14

# PSYCHOLOGY AND SOCIETY: Contributions and Controversies

# LEARNING OBJECTIVES: WHAT YOU SHOULD KNOW

After reading this chapter you should:

Be able to describe the various steps of the traditional personnel selection process and the problems associated with it.

Understand the racial and sexual biases in personnel selection and some of their causes.

Know the various factors which increase and decrease motivation to work.

Know the factors which increase and decrease job satisfaction.

Understand how inequity is produced and what its effects are.

Be able to discuss the basic features of the intelligence tests developed by Binet and Wechsler and their shortcomings.

Understand the problem of using intelligence tests with the culturally underprivileged.

Know the effects of the categorizations of bright and dull on students and teachers.

Be able to discuss the results of studies trying to determine the extent to which genetics and environment determine intelligence.

Know the research and conclusions in regard to black and white differences in intelligence.

Know the basic findings in advertising related research.

# STUDY TIPS: A HELPING HAND

You should find this chapter quite interesting since it covers topics closely related to our everyday lives. As with the other chapters, however, there are some sections which may require a little extra effort. The various factors which are cited as influencing work motivation can easily be confused with those influencing job satisfaction. After you have studied the work motivation and job satisfaction sections separately, compare the factors which are important in each case and their effects. You will note that while a potential factor may enhance work motivation, it may not enhance job satisfaction. So try to keep the findings in these two different areas straight. The section on inequity should also be read carefully since this is an important and somewhat complex concept. The section on intelligence presents a lot of details about intelligence tests and the results of studies on intelligence. You will need to review and rehearse the various portions of this section a number of times in order to master the material.

# STEP-BY-STEP: A GUIDED REVIEW

After you have read the chapter, mentally fill in each of the blanks in the following section while covering the answers in the margin. Check your answer with that in the margin as you go along. While in many cases your answer should be the same as that in the margin, in other cases a word of similar meaning is acceptable. Do not write in the spaces until you are doing your final review.

1.  Psychologists who examine different aspects of work and work
    settings are known as _____ psychologists.        industrial
    They focus on choosing the best person for the job
    (_____ _____), the                 personnel selection
    motives which lead workers to spend long hours at work (_____   work
    _____), and the rewards people both seek          motivation
    and find in their occupations (_____ _____).      job satisfaction

2.  The traditional approach to personnel selection involves _____   seven
    steps. The first step involves _____ _____        job analysis
    which is the determination of the specific behaviors required
    for the performance of a position. Next, preliminary ideas are
    formulated concerning the type of person most likely to succeed
    in its performance. Then a means for _____         selecting
    such persons from a larger group of applicants must be devised
    by the use of various tests. For example, the use of
    _____ _____                          biographical informa-
    _____ has gained popularity due to its ability     tion blanks
    to predict.

3.  The next phase involves administering measures to a large
    number of applicants. After the passing of a certain period of
    time, the psychologist gathers information on the performance
    of these applicants. This information is then _____   correlated
    with the information previously collected from the applicants to
    determine strength of the relationship between job performance
    and scores on the tests.

4.  A further step is the _____                        cross-validation
    of these findings through the repetition of the testing with
    another series of applicants. Only if the results of both corre-
    lational analyses are positive will specific recommendations
    be made regarding personnel selection.

5.  Some problems with this traditional approach is that it is
    _____ , works only in situations in                time-consuming
    which a lot of people perform the _____ job, and                same
    makes the unfounded assumption that the jobs and the people
    will not _____ over time.                          change

6.  While minority groups often perform _____ poorly than           more
    whites on personnel selection tests, they often perform _____   as well
    in the jobs.

7. There is a considerable bias in the selection of women for jobs. Part of this can be blamed on _____ in hiring and advancement, but this appears to be changing. Another factor, _____ _____ towards women, seems to be more resistant to change. Contrary to the facts, the belief that women are not _____ to their work persists. Women also tend to be judged as _____ _____than men even when they demonstrate identical levels of performance.

discrimination

negative attitudes

committed

less competent

8. Another factor is the tendency of women to develop a fear of _____ which leads to active avoidance of competition or advancement. In responding to stories, _____ % of the women will display hints of fear of success while _____% of the men display such a fear.

success

40 to 65

10

9. One of the major factors influencing motivation to work is the _____people expect to gain through such activities. This idea is an important part of the _____ theory of work motivation. This theory holds that an individual's effort on the job depends upon the _____ of such outcomes and the _____ of her expectancies that such effort will lead to various outcomes.

incentives

expectancy

balance, strength

10. Among the various incentives for working,_____ranks relatively low while_____, _____ _____, and _____ working conditions rank relatively high (see Table 14-1 below).

pay

advancement, job

security, good

TABLE 14-1   Factors Determining Work Motivation

| Factor | Rank |
| --- | --- |
| Opportunity for advancement | 1 |
| Job security | 2 |
| Opportunity to use ideas | 3 |
| Opportunity to learn a job | 4 |
| Opportunity for public service | 5 |
| Type of work | 6 |
| Supervisor | 7 |
| Company | 8 |
| Pay | 9 |
| Co-workers | 10 |
| Working conditions | 11 |
| Easy work | 12 |

The relative importance of various factors as determinants of work motivation. Somewhat surprisingly, pay ranks a poor ninth. (The larger the number shown, the less importance attached to a given factor.) (Based on a summary of data from studies reported in McCormick and Tiffin, 1974.)

11. Research has shown that when individuals are provided with external rewards for activities they already enjoy, their _____ motivation for engaging in these activ-     intrinsic
ities is _____ .     reduced

12. To determine whether they are treated fairly, individuals seem to compare the _____ they receive from their     benefits
jobs with the _____ they bring to it.     contributions
If the proportion between others' contributions and benefits equals one's own, job satisfaction may be _____ .     high
If these values are greatly discrepant, individuals will exper-
ience feelings of _____ . Although feelings     inequity
of inequity may also occur when individuals receive _____     more
benefits than they are entitled, such feelings are less intense in this case.

13. When individuals experience feelings of inequity, job satisfaction tends to _____ , and individuals often tend to     drop
remove or reduce these feelings. They may seek _____     adjustment
to their inputs or benefits from the job, they may _____     punish
their employers indirectly, or they may _____ .     quit

14. A large-scale study by Herzberg suggests that the factors
leading to job satisfaction are _____     different from
(the same as/ different from) those leading to dissatisfaction.
Factors important in positive attitudes toward work are
_____ / _____ ,     achievement, recog-
_____ / _____ ,     nition, advancement,
and the nature of the work. These are termed _____ .     responsibility, moti-
     vators

15. A second group of factors called _____ factors     hygiene
induce _____ reactions if they are absent and     negative
_____ reactions if they are present. These     neutral
factors are _____ / _____ ,     security, high pay
_____ , and     good working condi-
_____ with fellow     tions, pleasant rela-
workers. The validity of Herzberg's two-factor theory is     tions
somewhat in doubt, however.

16. In a study with West Point cadets it was found that those
given realistic expectations about the summer training period
were _____ likely to resign during this period than those     less
given no information.

17. A major concern of the educational and school psychologist is
with the objective measurement of intelligence. The first

objective test of intelligence was developed by _____ and _____. They viewed intelligence as the ability to _____, _____, and _____ well. Similarly, definitions today generally refer to intelligence as the abilities to adapt to _____ circumstances, deal with _____ materials, and solve _____ problems.

| | |
|---|---|
| | Binet |
| | Simon |
| | judge, comprehend |
| | reason |
| | new |
| | complex |
| | intellectual |

18. The Simon-Binet test contained different items for each age level. Items were assigned to an age level if _____ % of the children at that age level could pass it. This test was used to derive an I.Q. or _____ _____ score. This quotient was derived by dividing the person's _____ age by his or her _____ age and multiplying the result by 100. In determining mental age, the examiner would first determine the age level at which the person could answer all the items, termed the _____ age. Then _____ _____ of additional age credit were added for each item answered correctly at higher levels of the test.

| | |
|---|---|
| | 75 |
| | intelligence quotient |
| | mental, chronologi- |
| | cal |
| | basal |
| | two months |

19. One problem with this measure of I.Q. is that chronological age will keep increasing, while mental age will reach a maximum in the _____ _____. Consequently, this measure was replaced with the _____ I.Q. in which the individuals' scores reflect their performance relative to others their age.

| | |
|---|---|
| | early twenties |
| | deviation |

20. The test developed by Binet had two major problems. First _____ items were included at different age levels, making it possible that _____ types of intelligence were being measured at different age levels. Second this test ignores the possibility that intelligence may be reflected in _____ as well as verbal activities.

| | |
|---|---|
| | different |
| | different |
| | nonverbal |

21. Tests by _____ were designed to overcome these problems. He included items of the same type but varying in _____ at different age levels. In addition, he included nonverbal or _____ items as well as verbal ones. He also divided the two types of items into _____, each reflecting a different aspect of intelligence. This test is now the most widely used intelligence test.

| | |
|---|---|
| | Wechsler |
| | difficulty |
| | performance |
| | subscales |

22. The extent to which scores on a test are stable or dependable is termed _____. The degree of

| | |
|---|---|
| | reliability |

_____ of a test is the extent to which                 validity
it measures what it is designed to measure. This requires that
the test scores be related to some other aspect of behavior
called the _____ (e.g., academic success).             criterion

23. Although intelligence tests appear to be _____,        reliable
    there is some question about their _____.              validity
    The intelligence tests have been found to be related to school
    performance for middle-class _____ students but not for      white
    lower class _____ students. The black students may       black
    be lacking in _____ required by the tests        knowledge
    and there may be difficulties of language and communication.

24. Although psychologists have attempted to design culture-fair
    tests of intelligence, such tests still do not take into account
    differences in _____ and _____              motivation, test-
    skills.                                                          taking

25. Being designated as bright or dull on the basis of an I.Q.
    test may have effects on both students and teachers. Being
    categorized as dull may have negative effects on a child's
    confidence in herself and her _____. Teachers         ability
    appear to call more often on _____ students than      gifted
    _____. It was also found in a study that white        nongifted
    teachers directed more _____ to white students        attention
    than black students. Apparently they expected whites to do
    better than blacks.

26. Intelligence appears to be influenced by both _____          heredity
    and _____. Evidence for the                           environment
    influence of genetics comes from studies showing that the
    more closely related individuals are, the more _____        similar
    their intelligence (see Figure 14-14 on the top of the next
    page). Other studies have shown that the I.Q. of children
    is _____ closely related to their biological parents than   more
    their adoptive parents. Also, the I.Q. scores of twins remain
    _____ correlated even when reared in different homes. highly
    These findings suggest that the genetic inheritance from parents
    is a _____ (more/ less) important determinant of in-    more
    telligence than the environment.

27. The fact that the I.Q. of identical twins is correlated only
    _____ when reared together and _____ when reared        .90, .80
    apart suggests an effect of environmental factors. Studies have
    also shown that absence of environmental stimulation at an
    early age can _____ affect intelligence. Other        adversely
    studies have shown that such effects can be avoided and reversed
    by _____ programs.                              enrichment

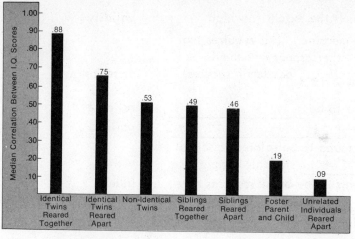

FIGURE 14-14 The more closely individuals are related, the more similar their IQ's tend to be. This fact provides strong support for the influence of genetic factors upon intelligence. (Numbers at the top of each bar represent the median correlations obtained in 52 different studies. Based on data from Erlenmeyer-Kimling and Jarvik, 1963.)

28. More evidence for the effect of the environment is provided by the finding that the _____ an individual is born in his or her family, the lower is his or her intelligence. Zajonc has proposed that this is due to the lowering of the quality of the _____ environment for later borns relative to early borns. That is, the average _____ of the family for the first or second born is _____ than it is for those born later.

later

intellectual

intelligence

higher

29. Recently developed techniques enable psychologists to estimate _____ of a characteristic or the extent to which variations in it are determined by genetic factors. The heritability of intelligence appears to be _____ percent. High heritability does not mean that this characteristic is not subject to modification.

heritability

75-80

30. Blacks tend to score _____ than whites on intelligence tests. Jensen has interpreted this as support for _____ differences between whites and blacks. More recent research suggests that this conclusion is _____. For example, a study has shown ____ I.Q. difference between blacks from mixed and unmixed racial heritage. Another study found that children born to white mothers and black fathers have _____ intelligence than children born to black mothers and white fathers, possibly due to rearing differences.

lower
genetic

false
no

higher

31. The branch of psychology which is concerned with consumer behavior is _____ _____. One of its major concerns is the effect of advertising on the consumer. Research has shown that ads which are _____, _____, and employ large type tend to be noticed more frequently than ads without these features. Other techniques such as the use of jingles, slogans, unexpected visual images, attractive models, and humorous situations also appear to be effective.

consumer psychology

large
colorful

226

32. A large number of studies has shown that repeated exposure to a stimulus leads to _____ liking. When a stimulus is presented a large number of times, _____ liking for the stimulus may result.

increased
decreased

33. Some studies have employed the process of _____ _____ by exposing individuals viewing a film to ads exposed for such a short time that they were not aware of their presence. The best conclusion one can draw from this research is that although such subliminal messages may have a mild influence on the subjects' _____, they do not affect their _____.

subliminal
perception

feelings
behavior

34. Research by Hess suggested that the pupils of the eyes _____ when someone is looking at something unpleasant. Subsequent research has shown that pupil dilations may be associated with _____ or _____ rather than positive feelings. Dilations can also be produced by mental _____. Furthermore the contraction of pupils in response to negative stimuli has been difficult to demonstrate.

dilate

attention
interest
effort

35. At present there is much pressure by consumer advocates for full disclosure of information about a product. A recent study has shown that, up to a point, increases in information led to more _____ choices based on the consumer's notion of the ideal product. However, beyond this point the ability to make accurate choices _____.

accurate

declined

KEY CONCEPTS AND TERMS

After you have finished your Guided Review fill in the meaning of the following terms in your own words. Check on your accuracy by consulting your text on the pages indicated or the Glossary.

personnel selection (p. 496)

work motivation (p. 496)

job satisfaction (p. 496)

traditional personnel selection (p. 497)

biographical information blanks  (p. 498)

cross-validation  (p. 499)

fear of success  (p. 502)

expectancy theory of work motivation  (p. 503)

intrinsic motivation  (p. 505)

inequity  (p. 506)

Herzberg's two-factor theory  (p. 508)

motivators  (p. 508)

hygiene factors  (p. 508)

intelligence  (p. 511)

the Stanford-Binet  (p. 512)

intelligence quotient  (p. 512)

mental age  (p. 512)

basal age  (p. 512)

deviation I.Q.  (p. 513)

Wechsler Scales  (p. 514)

reliability  (p. 515)

validity  (p. 515)

criterion  (p. 516)

culture-fair tests  (p. 516)

heritability  (p. 524)

subliminal-perception  (p. 529)


A PERSONAL QUIZ

After you are about finished with your studies but still have some time left
for review, take this quiz to check on your mastery.  Fill in your answers
in the spaces provided and after you are finished check their correctness
with the answers provided.

___ 1. The personnel psychologist is
primarily concerned with all but
one of the following:  (p. 496)
a. social influence
b. personnel selection
c. work motivation
d. job satisfaction

___ 2. Which one of the following is not
one of the steps involved in the
traditional approach to personnel
selection?  (p. 497-99)
a. selection of applicants
b. administration of tests
c. worker counseling
d. cross-validation

___ 3. One of the problems with the
traditional approach to personnel
selection is  (p. 499)
a. the use of small numbers of
applicants
b. lack of cross-validation
c. the failure to make specific
recommendations
d. that it is time consuming

___ 4. One of the reasons that women may
not show as much advancement in
their work as men is their  (p. 502)
a. lack of competence
b. lack of commitment
c. fear of success
d. negative attitudes toward work

___ 5. Which of the following does not
rank high as an incentive for
working?  (p. 504)
a. pay
b. advancement
c. job security
d. working conditions

___ 6. When individuals are provided
with external rewards for activities
which they already enjoy, their
intrinsic motivation for these activities (p. 505)
a. increases
b. stays the same
c. decreases
d. decreases only when the activities are relatively unimportant

7. Individuals' level of satisfaction will be highest if they receive (p. 506)
   a. more benefits than they deserve
   b. benefits appropriate to their efforts
   c. less benefits than they deserve
   d. a high level of benefits

8. If there is a discrepancy between a person's contributions and his benefits in a particular job, he will experience feelings of (p. 506)
   a. satisfaction
   b. jealousy
   c. accomplishment
   d. inequity

9. The study of Herzberg suggested that the factor(s) leading to job satisfaction (p. 508)
   a. are security and high pay
   b. is good working conditions
   c. is pleasant relations with fellow workers
   d. are different from those leading to dissatisfaction

10. The first objective intelligence test was developed by (p. 511)
    a. Freud
    b. Stanford
    c. Binet
    d. Wechsler

11. Which of the following is not generally considered to be part of present day notions of intelligence? The ability to (p. 511)
    a. deal with complex materials
    b. memorize complex materials
    c. solve intellectual problems
    d. adapt to new circumstances

12. Intelligence tests today generally provide (p. 513)
    a. intelligence quotients
    b. a basal quotient
    c. a mental age
    d. a deviation I.Q.

13. A problem with the early intelligence tests was (p. 513-14)
    a. the use of the intelligence quotient
    b. inclusion of different items at different age levels
    c. the failure to include non-verbal abilities
    d. all of the above

14. The Wechsler intelligence test (p. 514)
    a. is entirely verbal
    b. employs subscales
    c. can be employed only with young children
    d. is not reliable

15. Which of the following is not a reason mentioned in your text for the lack of relation between scores on intelligence tests and school performance of lower-class black children? (p. 516)
    a. reliability of the test
    b. lack of test taking skills
    c. lack of knowledge required by the tests
    d. lack of motivation for such tests

16. If certain students are labeled as bright and others as dull, teachers tend to (p. 518)
    a. be able to treat both groups equally
    b. pay more attention to the dull students
    c. pay more attention to the bright students
    d. select the dull students for individual study

17. Which of the following should be least similar in intelligence? (p. 520)
    a. siblings reared together
    b. foster parent and child
    c. twins reared together
    d. twins reared apart

18. Which of the following member(s) of a family should have the lowest intelligence level? (p. 522)
   a. the fourth born
   b. the first born
   c. the second born
   d. the parents

19. The heritability of intelligence appears to be about (p. 524)
   a. 30%
   b. 50%
   c. 75%
   d. 90%

20. Which of the following is not a finding in consumer psychology? (p. 526-529)

a. large colorful ads draw attention
b. a lot of exposure to an ad decreases liking for it
c. subliminal perception has an effect on consumer behavior
d. pupil dilation occurs in response to pleasant stimuli

Answers:

| 1. a | 6. c | 11. b | 16. c |
| 2. c | 7. b | 12. d | 17. b |
| 3. d | 8. d | 13. d | 18. a |
| 4. c | 9. d | 14. b | 19. c |
| 5. a | 10. c | 15. a | 20. c |

# PSYCHOLOGY IN ACTION: PROJECTS AND DEMONSTRATIONS

## Are You as Unbiased as You Think? A Do-it-Yourself Test for Sexism

See your text for this demonstration (p. 504).

## A Survey of Persuasive Techniques in Advertising

Survey the ads in a current magazine such as Time or Newsweek. Can you categorize these in terms of their use of certain persuasive techniques? The form on the next page can be used for this. For each ad which fits one of the categories provided place a mark in the appropriate block. Instead of simply placing a checkmark for each ad, you might want to write a 1 or 2, depending on whether the ad was one-sided or two-sided. You can substitute a survey of ads during one evening of TV viewing if you prefer. In fact, if you have time, you could survey both TV and a magazine and compare the frequency with which different types of ads occur. In making your comparison, determine the percentage of the time each type of ad occurs in the magazine and on TV.

# Persuasive Techniques Found in Ads

| | |
|---|---|
| 1. Sex Appeal | |
| 2. Emotional or Fear Appeal | |
| 3. Prestigious or Attractive Communicator | |
| 4. Expert Communicator | |
| 5. Emphasis on Personal Rewards | |
| 6. Educational | |

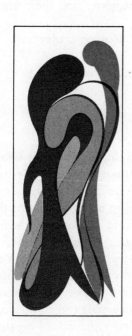

Chapter 15

ENVIRONMENTAL
PSYCHOLOGY:
Behavior
in the
Physical World

## LEARNING OBJECTIVES: WHAT YOU SHOULD KNOW

After reading this chapter you should:

Know the factors which affect personal space.

Be familiar with the research on the invasion of personal space.

Understand the concept of stress and the problems involved in defining this concept.

Be able to discuss the general effects of crowding on humans and animals.

Be able to describe the effects of noise on performance and the psychological factors involved.

Be able to discuss the effects of heat and air pollution.

Be familiar with the nature of cognitive maps, their measurement, and their use.

Know the factors responsible for the failure of many public housing projects.

Know the advantages and disadvantages of the city as an environment.


## STUDY TIPS: A HELPING HAND

As with the previous chapters, the best policy in studying the present chapter is to note the major findings of a section and actively rehearse these for a few minutes before going on to the next section. One part of the chapter which may be a little confusing is the effect of the sex of the individual or group on reactivity to crowding and the size of the personal space bubble. Be sure to compare these two sets of results and try to have them clearly in mind so that you won't be confused when you are asked a question about them. Another part of the chapter which you should make sure that you understand clearly is the Yerkes-Dodson law. This law is discussed in reference to the effects of both noise and heat and makes some nonintuitive predictions. Finally, to help you remember some of the lists of terms which you will encounter, let us make a few suggestions. You can remember the three stages of the general adaptation syndrome (alarm reaction, resistance, and exhaustion) by simply remembering the verb are which represents the first letters of the three stages. So the question, "The three stages of the adaptation syndrome are?" will provide its own answer. Similarly, Lynch's taxonomy of five elements of the cognitive map (path, edge, district, node, and landmark) can be remembered by thinking of a lead pen used in drawing such a map.


## STEP-BY-STEP: A GUIDED REVIEW

After you have read the chapter, mentally fill in each of the blanks in the following section while covering the answers in the margin. Check your answer with that in the margin as you go along. While in many cases your answer should be the same as that in the margin, in other cases a word of similar meaning is acceptable. Do not write in the spaces until you are doing your final review.

1.  Environmental psychology is defined as the study of man in
    his _____ _____.                                    physical setting
    Environmental psychology seems to have its primary roots
    in the areas of _____ psychology and _____                      social, engineering
    psychology.

2.  A number of investigators have been concerned with the
    study of personal space or _____. These                       proxemics
    investigators assume that individuals carry around some sort
    of psychological _____ designed to protect                         bubble
    them from the encroachment of others.

3.  The behavior used by the individual to stake out and defend
    a specific area against members of his or her own species
    is called _____. The existence of                             territoriality
    territoriality in animals _____ (can/cannot) be taken                 cannot
    as evidence that man is territorial in the same way. In
    fact, territorial behavior is often confused with
    _____ behavior which is intended                               jurisdictional
    to defend an area without presuming ownership.

4.  A study by Kinzel has shown that violent prisoners have
    considerably _____ (larger/smaller) personal                       larger
    space bubbles than nonviolent prisoners. While non-
    violent prisoners exhibited roughly the same size of per-
    sonal space area in front as in back, the violent prisoners
    had a _____ area behind them than in front.                          larger

5.  Sommer and others have argued that the primary function
    of personal space is to reduce _____ and control                     stress
    _____ among members of the same                                aggression
    species. Others have argued that the personal-space
    bubble is used to _____                                communicate
    _____ about a person's feelings                                information
    and attitudes.

6.  Hall has proposed that there are four distance zones for
    Americans. _____ distance ranges from 0 to                     Intimate
    18 inches and may involve physical contact, strong olfac-
    tory and heat stimuli, and reduced intensity of vocal be-
    havior. _____ distance corresponds to the                      Personal
    personal space bubble, while _____ distance                        social
    is used for conducting impersonal business in the range of
    four feet to twelve feet. The largest interpersonal distance
    range is called _____ distance.                                    public

7.  Attitudes toward spatial distances appear to culturally
    be related. Arabs generally requires _____ (more/less)          less
    interpersonal distance than Americans.

8.  In a study of seating patterns, Sommer found that indivi-
    duals prefer to sit _____ (at the end/near             at the end
    the middle) of an empty table in a library. However if
    students are interested in preventing others from sitting
    at the same table, they will select a(n)_____             middle
    chair.

9.  In a study of the effect of personal space invasion on
    urination it was found that subjects who had a person adja-
    cent to them took _____ time to start urinating and took       more
    _____ time to complete the act than subjects who did not       less
    have someone in the adjacent stall.

10. When an individual is stressed, his personal space bubble
    appears to _____ (increase/ decrease) in size.          increase

11. When one's personal space bubble is violated, the usual
    response is _____.  In other cases, such as            escape
    someone sitting near a water fountain, individuals tend to
    drink with less frequency the _____ the                  closer
    stranger is sitting to the water fountain.

12. Women generally have _____ bubbles than men.            smaller
    The exact size of the bubble depends on the sexual composi-
    tion of the groups. For _____ (males/females) the size         males
    of the bubble does not depend on the sex of the individual
    being approached. When females approach a male their
    bubble is _____ than in the case where females            larger
    approach a female.

13. In another study it was found that in mixed sex groups both
    males and females like the other members of the group_____        more
    (more/less) in a high density room than in a low density
    room. The _____ (same/reverse) is true for fe-           reverse
    males in same sex groups.

14. According to Selye, stress reactions involve a series of
    stages. First there is an _____ _____             alarm reaction
    which involves physiological changes. This stage is
    followed by the _____ stage in which                    resistance
    physiological reactions directly counter to those of the alarm
    stage occur. That is, while blood volume _____          diminishes
    and body weight _____ during the alarm reaction, these        drops
    processes are reversed during the resistance stage. The last

236

stage is _____ in which the body is       exhaustion
unable to resist aversive events. This series of three stages
has been termed the _____ _____       general adaptation
_____.       syndrome

15. A precise operational definition of stress is rather difficult
to come up with and involves numerous conceptual problems.
Hence concentrating on stressful _____       situations
rather than stress in the abstract would seem to be a better
approach. A stressful situation occurs when there is a
substantial _____ between demands im-       imbalance
posed upon an organism and the organism's ability to cope
with these demands. This imbalance can take the form of
both an _____ and an _____.       overload, underload

16. Research on crowding in rats by Calhoun showed that over-
crowding in rats can result in high levels of infant mortality
due to a breakdown in normal mothering as well as high
mortality rates for pregnant females, apparently due to
sexual abuse. The pathological condition produced by this
extreme crowding was attributed to the formation of a
_____ _____. Some rats became       behavioral sink
hyperactive, hypersexual, homosexual, and cannabalistic
and were called _____.       probers

17. Demographic studies have found that high levels of population density _____(do/do not) lead to increases       do
in social pathology such as mortality, fertility, juvenile
delinquency, and admissions to mental hospitals. The
measure of density which seemed to be the primary determinant of these pathologies was _____       number of persons
_____.       per room

18. Laboratory studies have shown that high density tends to
intensify _____ reactions. For example,       typical
pleasant situations were found to be more unpleasant when
crowded. Research has also shown that males are more
disturbed by _____spatial invasions,       face-to-face
while females respond more negatively to_____       side-by-side
invasions.

19. The standardized noise source used in laboratory studies
is called _____ _____. While noise       white noise
has little if any effect on many tasks, it appears that noise
does affect the performance of tasks which present high
rates of information and demand high degrees of_____.       attention

20. Noise _____(can/cannot) lead to both facilitation       can
and inhibition of performance on a task. Noise is generally
assumed to increase the general level of arousal. According

to the Yerkes-Dodson law, there exists a _____          curvilinear
relationship between arousal level and performance. As
shown in Figure 15-10 below, performance is best at moderate levels of arousal, and decreases when arousal is either
too high or too low.

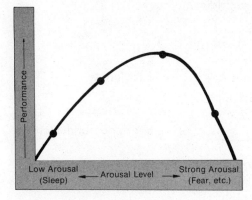

FIGURE 15-10   The Yerkes-Dodson law. Arousal level increases as we move to the right. The height of the function indicates the level of performance; performance gets
better as the curve gets higher. Note that performance is
best at an intermediate level of arousal and decreases
when arousal is either too low or too high.

21.   Noise also appears to have adverse aftereffects on individuals
      after the noise is removed.  These effects are especially
      likely to occur when the noise is _____ .          unpredictable
      Glass and Singer have argued that the detrimental aftereffects
      of unpredictable noise are mediated by a feeling of _____      helplessness
      resulting from one's inability to control this stressful environ-
      mental condition.

22.   Although heat has been shown to increase negative affect,
      some research suggests that the relationship between aggression
      and heat is of the _____ type.  One          Yerkes-Dodson
      study showed that the effect of combining heat and the receipt
      of a negative personality rating was to _____          decrease
      (increase/decrease) aggression relative to conditions involving
      only one of these stressors.  Reducing the level of arousal to
      a moderate level by giving the subjects a cooling drink
      tended to _____ aggression (see Figure 15-12          increase
      below).

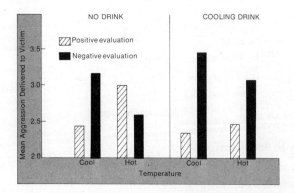

FIGURE 15-12   Effects of a cooling drink on
aggression. The left panel shows the amount
of aggression without a drink, and the right
panel shows the amount of aggression with a
cooling drink. When the temperature is cool,
drink has no effect. However, when the temperature is hot, a cooling drink reverses the
pattern between aggression and personality
evaluation. With a cooling drink, a negative
evaluation leads to more aggression, regardless of temperature. Without a drink, a negative evaluation leads to more aggression only
when the temperature is cool. (From Baron
and Bell, 1976.)

23. Research suggests that air pollution _____ (does/does not) lead to decreased mental efficiency.

    does

24. The term _____ has been suggested for the best habitat which can be attained in the real world.

    entopia

25. Mental images of the world at large are generally called _____ _____. Work on cognitive maps of the urban environment was initiated by _____. He formed a taxonomy involving five elements for the analysis of cognitive maps. These elements were _____, _____ / _____ / _____, and _____. A focal point within the city where transition between different activities occur or where activities are focused as a result of physical or functional features is called a _____.

    cognitive maps
    Lynch

    paths
    edges, districts, nodes
    landmarks

    node

26. In his research on cognitive maps of New York City, Milgram found that the recognizability of street scenes depended upon architectural and social _____ and _____ to population flow.

    distinctiveness
    centrality

27. The vandalism and deterioration of housing projects appears to be partly due to the lack of reasonable amenities and _____ space.

    defensible

28. Milgram has developed an information _____ model to account for the way in which the urban dweller copes with her environment. The urban dweller supposedly allocates less _____ time to incoming information, filters out _____ _____ inputs completely, and intentionally _____ the likelihood of social interaction.

    overload

    processing
    low priority
    decreases

29. The information-overload protection mechanisms seem to lead to _____ in social responsibility as reflected in willingness to help in emergencies.

    decreases

30. An abandoned car study found that the car was vandalized _____ (more/less) in a large city than in a small city. Zimbardo argues that this is due to the feelings of _____ of the residents of the larger cities which in turn lessen inhibitions about antisocial behavior.

    more

    anonymity

31. Research indicates that slum dwellers may be highly committed to their housing and may resist attempts at relocation. Many residents of one slum seemed to like living there and had a strong sense of _____.

    locality

32.	Jacobs has argued that old-fashioned city sidewalks
serve many useful social functions.  The merchants along
the sidewalks are seen as providing a model for _____		social
_____ when they take an interest		responsibility
in the welfare of the neighborhood children.  These merchants also can provide numerous social functions which
provide the basic social cement for the neighborhood.


## KEY CONCEPTS AND TERMS

After you have finished your Guided Review fill in the meaning of the
following terms in your own words.  Check on your accuracy by consulting your text on the pages indicated or the Glossary.

proxemics  (p. 536)


personal space bubble  (p. 536)


territoriality  (p. 536)


jurisdiction  (p. 537)


intimate distance  (p. 539)


personal distance  (p. 539)


social-consultive distance  (p. 540)


public distance  (p. 540)


general adaptation syndrome  (p. 547)


stressful situation  (p. 548)


behavioral sink  (p. 549)


probers  (p. 549)

arousal  (p. 554)

Yerkes-Dodson law  (p. 554)

cognitive map  (p. 559)

path  (p. 559)

edge  (p. 559)

district  (p. 559)

node  (p. 559)

landmarks  (p. 559)

entopia  (p. 558)

## A PERSONAL QUIZ

After you are about finished with your studies but still have some time
left for review, take this quiz to check on your mastery.  Fill in your
answers in the spaces provided and after you are finished check their
correctness with the answers provided.

___ 1.  The study of personal space is often
termed (p. 536)
   a.  eugenics
   b.  jurisdictional psychology
   c.  proxemics
   d.  environmental psychology

___ 2.  Territorial behavior in man is
often confused with (p. 537)
   a.  jurisdictional behavior
   b.  personal space behavior
   c.  proxemics
   d.  aggression

___ 3.  It has been found that violent prisoners have (p. 538)
   a.  smaller personal space bubbles
than nonviolent prisoners
   b.  larger personal space bubbles
than nonviolent prisoners
   c.  a larger personal space area in
front than behind
   d.  both b and c

___ 4.  Which one of the following has
not been proposed as a primary
function of personal space?(p. 539)

a. reduction of stress
b. reduction of interaction
c. control of aggression
d. communication of feelings about a person's feelings and attitudes

5. Which one of the following distance zones is used for conducting business? (p. 540)
   a. intimate
   b. social
   c. personal
   d. public

6. In regard to personal space it has been found that (p. 540-542)
   a. individuals prefer to sit in the middle chair of an empty table at a library
   b. Americans require less interpersonal distance than Arabs
   c. when one is stressed, one's interpersonal space bubble increases
   d. none of the above

7. Research on sex differences in personal space has shown that (p. 545-546)
   a. males have smaller bubbles than females
   b. for females the size of the bubble does not depend on the sex of the individual being approached.
   c. in mixed sex groups both males and females like other members of the group better in low density spaces than in high density spaces
   d. in same sex groups males like other males more in high density spaces than in low density spaces

8. The general adaptation syndrome (GAS) proposed by Selye involves all but one of the following: (p. 547)
   a. anticipation
   b. alarm reaction
   c. resistance

d. exhaustion

9. A study of gastric ulceration in response to stress produced by shock found that the most ulceration was shown by rats who (p. 548)
   a. could predict the onset of shock
   b. could not predict the onset of shock
   c. only heard a tone but received no shock
   d. received varying levels of shock

10. Calhoun's studies on crowding and pathology in rats found all but one of the following to be results of excessive crowding: (p. 549-550)
    a. deterioration of nestbuilding behavior
    b. cannibalism
    c. sexual aberration
    d. a reduction in pregnancy rate

11. Studies on population density and pathology in humans have shown that (p. 551)
    a. population density appears to be related to pathology
    b. the relationship between population density and pathology disappears when social factors are statistically controlled
    c. the number of rooms per housing unit seems to be the best predictor of pathology
    d. no relationship between population density and pathology exists

12. Laboratory research on crowding in humans suggests that (p. 551-552)
    a. males find side-by-side invasions most aversive
    b. females find face-to-face invasions most aversive
    c. high density seems to intensify typical behavior

d. effects of crowding do not depend on the sexual composition of the group

13. Research on the effects of noise on behavior has found that (p. 554-555)
   a. noise can affect the performance of ongoing tasks but has no aftereffects
   b. noise does not affect ongoing task performance but does have negative aftereffects
   c. noise can produce facilitation of performance on tasks
   d. the aftereffects of noise tend to be enhanced when the noise is predictable

14. Research on the psychological effects of heat have shown that (p. 557)
   a. heat increases aggression
   b. heat in combination with other stressors can actually lead to reduced aggression
   c. a cooling drink reduces aggression
   d. combining heat with a negative personality evaluation can produce a high level of aggression

15. Which one of the following is not one of the five elements in Lynch's taxonomy of cognitive maps? (p. 559)
   a. zenith
   b. path
   c. edge
   d. landmark

16. Milgram's research on cognitive maps assessed the recognizability of street scenes. Recognizability was found to depend on all but one of the following factors: (p. 560-561)
   a. architectural distinctiveness of a location
   b. centrality of a location to population flow
   c. resident status
   d. size of the structures

17. The Pruitt-Igoe housing project and others like it have been social disasters. The deterioration through vandalism of these structures is probably due to (p. 562-563)
   a. personality defects of the lower classes
   b. the lack of sturdiness of the structures
   c. their ugliness and lack of easy visual surveillance
   d. the fact that the tenants paid too little for their apartments and hence did not appreciate them

18. Milgram's information overload model of the urban dweller proposes that urban dwellers (p. 564)
   a. cannot cope very well with their environment
   b. adapt to their environment by using various cognitive techniques to reduce the level of information being processed
   c. seek high levels of social interaction
   d. tend to be highly responsive to their fellow urban dwellers

19. Research comparing the helping behavior of residents of cities and rural areas has shown that (p. 564)
   a. city residents are less helpful
   b. rural residents are less helpful
   c. city residents are more helpful with small requests and rural residents with large requests
   d. helping behavior is unrelated to the rural-urban dimension

20. A study of slum dwellers found that these individuals (p. 566)
   a. were very dissatisfied with their environment
   b. were highly committed to their dwelling
   c. had a weak sense of locality

d. liked their environment only if
they considered it as home

Answers:

| | | | |
|---|---|---|---|
| 1. c | 6. c | 11. a | 16. d |
| 2. a | 7. d | 12. c | 17. c |
| 3. b | 8. a | 13. c | 18. b |
| 4. b | 9. b | 14. b | 19. a |
| 5. b | 10. d | 15. a | 20. b |

## PSYCHOLOGY IN ACTION: PROJECTS AND DEMONSTRATIONS

### Mapping Personal Space

This exercise is designed to help you determine the shape of your personal space bubble. The first part of the exercise concerns changes in your feelings and subtle aspects of your behavior as the distance between you and a friend decreases. It would be best to select an area which minimizes distractions and social intrusions. An unused classroom with a tile floor might be a good place, but any other space with tiles will do. Do not tell your friend what you are interested in since this might affect the "naturalness" of his or her reactions. Start at a distance of about 15 feet. Stay at that distance and assess the volume of your conversations, degree to which you maintain mutual eye contact, and your own degree of personal comfort. After 20 seconds have your partner come about three steps closer. Reassess your feelings and behavior. Repeat this procedure until you are practically face-to-face. On the form provided you should note the points at which the conversation seems to decrease in volume, eye contact is reduced, and you start to feel uncomfortabe. Use the number of one-foot tiles between you and your friend as the measure of distance. Next, assess the conversation level and your degree of comfort in a similar fashion as your friend approaches you from the side and the rear. You will have to peek at the tiles at the appropriate measuring points. Repeat this entire series of procedures or a part of them you found most intriguing with a friend of a different sex, and strangers of the same and opposite sex. Be sure to pick individuals of the same age, race, and ethnic group for all of your participants.

### Assessing Interpersonal Distance

This exercise involves obtaining a measurement of the distances between you and people you encounter during the course of a typical day. You will need to carry a tape measure and the form contained on page 246 . As individuals approach you and stop in front of you to talk to you, ask them to stand still prior to engaging in conversation, and quickly measure the distance between your nose and that of the other person. Note the sex and age of this individual as well as his/her relationship to you (e.g., friend, stranger, and parent). Do this for an entire day or until you have a reasonable number of individuals in the various categories (about 39 or 40). You are obviously going to get some surprised reactions from your subjects. You might in fact note these and see if the reactions differ for individuals in the different categories. In any case this exercise should be fun. Determine the mean distance between you and the individuals in the various categories. That is, get the mean for the males and females, for the individuals above and below the average age of your sample, and for the individuals in the most substantial relationship categories. Compare your results with those reported in the text from a variety of studies and with those of your fellow classmates.

# Personal Space Mapping Sheet

| | | Friend | | Stranger | |
|---|---|---|---|---|---|
| | | Male | Female | Male | Female |
| **Front** | Uncomfortable | | | | |
| | Conversation Volume Reduced | | | | |
| | Eye contact Reduced | | | | |
| **Side by Side** | Uncomfortable | | | | |
| | Conversation Volume Reduced | | | | |
| **Back** | Uncomfortable | | | | |
| | Conversation Volume Reduced | | | | |

# Interpersonal Distance Sheet

|  | Subjects | Sex (M.F.) | Age | Relationship (Friend, Acquaintance, Teacher, Relative, Stranger etc.) |
|---|---|---|---|---|
| 1. | | | | |
| 2. | | | | |
| 3. | | | | |
| 4. | | | | |
| 5. | | | | |
| 6. | | | | |
| 7. | | | | |
| 8. | | | | |
| 9. | | | | |
| 10. | | | | |
| 11. | | | | |
| 12. | | | | |
| 13. | | | | |
| 14. | | | | |
| 15. | | | | |
| 16. | | | | |
| 17. | | | | |
| 18. | | | | |
| 19. | | | | |
| 20. | | | | |
| 21. | | | | |
| 22. | | | | |
| 23. | | | | |
| 24. | | | | |
| 25. | | | | |
| 26. | | | | |

Means: Males _____ Older _____ Friends _____ Strangers _____

Females _____ Younger _____ Acquaintances _____ Relatives _____

# Appendix A

# STATISTICS:
# Tool for Research

# LEARNING OBJECTIVES: WHAT YOU SHOULD KNOW

After reading this appendix you should:

Understand the different types of descriptive statistics and how to use them.

Know the different measures of dispersion and how to use them.

Be able to discuss the features and use of the normal curve.

Understand the technique of correlation.

Know the different ways statistics can be used to mislead or deceive.

# STUDY TIPS: A HELPING HAND

Statistics is a topic students often find difficult. Part of the problem may be that they expect the material and concepts to be difficult. So let me tell you right now that the material in this appendix is not difficult. In fact it is relatively simple and just requires that you read the material carefully. The illustrations provided should make most of the concepts clear but you should work through some of the problems illustrated so that you'll be sure to understand each of the statistics.

# STEP-BY-STEP: A GUIDED REVIEW

After you have read the appendix, mentally fill in each of the blanks in the following section while covering the answers in the margin. Check your answer with that in the margin as you go along. While in many cases your answer should be the same as that in the margin, in other cases a word of similar meaning is acceptable. Do not write in the spaces until you are doing your final review.

1. Psychologists use statistics to _____ large amounts of information in a conventient form, to _____ the behavior of groups of individuals, to _____ different traits, characteristics, or behaviors in order to determine whether they vary together in any systematic manner, and to _____ future behavior from present information.

    summarize
    compare
    relate



    predict

2. Statistics which summarize information are termed _____ statistics. When data is grouped and graphed in terms of the frequency of occurrence of various magnitudes of a variable, the result is termed a _____ _____.
Summary statistics which indicate the characteristics of the center of the distribution are measures of _____ _____. Those which indicate the degree

    descriptive



    frequency distribution


    central
    tendency

of spread around the center are termed measures of

_____.                                          dispersion

3.  One indicator of central tendency is the _____ or the          mode
    most frequently occurring score. If scores tie as the mode,
    the distribution is _____. The second measure         bimodal
    of central tendency is the _____, which is the         median
    point above which 50% of the distribution falls and below
    which 50% of the distribution falls. A third measure of
    central tendency is the arithmetic _____ which is deter-       mean
    mined by adding all the scores in the distribution and
    dividing by the total number of scores.

4.  When distributions have the same value for the mean and
    median, they are said to be _____. If                 symmetric
    they do not have the same value, the distribution is termed

    _____.                                                skewed

5.  The measure of dispersion which is the width of the distri-
    bution is the _____. This is the difference between   range
    the highest and the lowest number in the distribution. Gen-
    erally more useful measures of dispersion are the _____,       variance
    which is the average squared distance from the mean, and the

    _____ _____, which                          standard deviation
    is the square root of the variance. (Consult your text for the
    exact procedures if you are not sure.) The larger the vari-
    ance, the _____ is the spread of the scores           greater
    around the mean.

6.  A bell-shaped distribution which has the same value for the
    mean, median, and mode is the _____ _____.          normal curve
    This curve is characteristic of such features as height, weight,
    and intelligence. One characteristic of the normal curve is
    that _____ % of the scores fall between the mean and one       34
    standard deviation above or below it. The next standard devia-
    tion above or below it contains _____ %. The third contains    14
    _____ %. These characteristics of the normal curve are         2
    shown in Figure A-7 below.

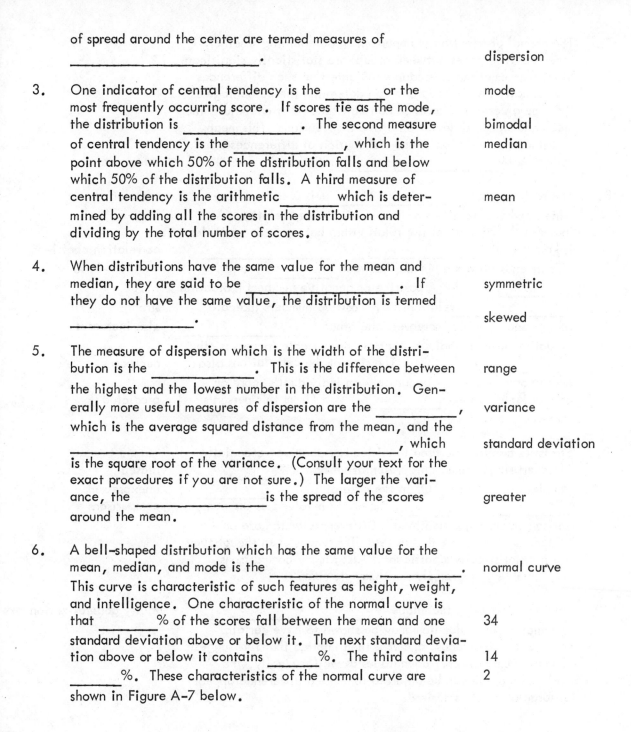

FIGURE A-7 A normal distribution showing the percentage
of scores falling into the areas bounded by 1, 2, and 3
standard deviation units above ($+1\sigma$, $+2\sigma$, $+3\sigma$) and below ($-1\sigma$, $-2\sigma$, $-3\sigma$) the mean.

7. The normal distribution is important in determining whether
   observed differences between groups are statistically significant.
   Since mathematical procedures indicate that such differences
   are normally distributed, one can determine the percentage of
   the time a certain difference can be expected if one knows the
   mean and standard deviation of the distribution. This mean
   and standard deviation of the distribution of differences are
   estimated by _____ statistics.          inferential

8. The technique of _____ is used to deter-      correlation
   mine to what extent two or more variables are related. An
   index of the strength of the relationship between the variables
   is known as the _____ _____.   correlation coeffi-
   This index is always a number between _____ and           cient, -1.00
   _____, with large positive or negative numbers indicating  +1.00
   a _____ relationship. Positive numbers indicate            strong
   that as one variable increases, the other _____.  also increases
   Negative numbers indicate that as one variable increases, the
   other _____. The size of the correlations also  decreases
   enable one to tell how accurately an individual's score on
   one variable can be _____ from this person's    predicted
   score on one or more others.

9. Statistics can also be used to mislead or deceive, especially
   in advertising. First, unrepresentative or _____  biased
   samples may be used. Or in the case of _____     unexpressed
   _____, the group involved as the com-            comparisons
   parison group is not mentined. Differences which are obtained may be represented as real differences even though they
   are not statistically significant. Also, many comparisons
   may involve an extremely small sample size.

10. Another misleading technique is _____ _____           faulty generalization
    in which a particular item may be shown to have certain
    features or advantages, and it is then implied that this suggests
    that the item has other advantages as well. Finally, the
    scale on a graph can be adjusted to make a difference appear
    as large or small as desired.


KEY CONCEPTS AND TERMS

          After you have finished your Guided Review fill in the meaning of the
          following terms in your own words. Check on your accuracy by con-
          sulting your text on the pages indicated or the Glossary.

descriptive statistics (p. 572)

frequency distribution  (p. 573)

measures of central tendency  (p. 573)

measures of dispersion  (p. 573)

mode  (p. 573)

bimodal  (p. 573)

median  (p. 574)

mean  (p. 574)

symmetric distribution  (p. 574)

skewed distribution  (p. 574)

range  (p. 575)

variance  (p. 575)

standard deviation  (p. 575)

normal curve  (p. 576)

inferential statistics  (p. 579)

correlation  (p. 579)

correlation coefficient  (p. 580)

biased samples  (p. 581)

unexpressed comparisons (p. 582)

faulty generalization (p. 583)

misleading graphs (p. 583)

## A PERSONAL QUIZ

After you are about finished with your studies but still have some time left for review, take this quiz to check on your mastery. Fill in your answers in the spaces provided and after you are finished check their correctness with the answers provided.

____ 1. Statistics which summarize information are called ____ statistics. (p. 572)
    a. inferential
    b. descriptive
    c. analytical
    d. modal

____ 2. The measure of central tendency which is the most frequently occurring score is called the (p. 573)
    a. frequency distribution
    b. mean
    c. median
    d. mode

____ 3. When distributions have the same mean and median they are called (p. 576)
    a. symmetrical
    b. normal
    c. skewed
    d. bimodal

____ 4. The measure of dispersion which is the average squared distance from the mean is the (p. 575)
    a. standard deviation
    b. range
    c. variance
    d. median

____ 5. In a normal curve distribution ____ % of the scores fall between the mean and one standard deviation above or below it (p. 577)
    a. 75
    b. 50
    c. 34
    d. 14

____ 6. The statistic used to determine to what extent two or more variables are related is (p. 579)
    a. symmetric analysis
    b. standard deviation
    c. the range
    d. correlation

____ 7. Which of the following numbers indicates a strong relationship between two variables in which increases in one are related to decreases in the other? (p. 580)
    a. -.12
    b. -.67
    c. +.33
    d. +.80

____ 8. One misleading use of statistics in which the "other group" is not specified is called (p. 582)
    a. unexpressed comparisons
    b. biased samples
    c. faulty generalization
    d. unreliable samples

**Answers:**

1. b    5. c
2. d    6. d
3. b    7. b
4. c    8. a

## Appendix B

# THE NATURE-NUTURE CONTROVERSY REVISITED:
# Innate Patterns of Behavior

# LEARNING OBJECTIVES: WHAT YOU SHOULD KNOW

After reading this appendix you should:

Understand the problem with the instinctual explanation of behavior.

Know the characteristics of instinctive behavior according to ethologists.

Be able to discuss the conflicting perspectives of the ethologists and psychologists.

Be able to describe the deprivation experiments and their implications.

Know the various ways in which ethology and psychology have become reconciled.

Know the characteristics of imprinting.

Understand Lorenz's view of aggression and the problems with it.


# STUDY TIPS: A HELPING HAND

Probably the most demanding task in trying to master the material in this appendix will be to keep straight the various differences between the ethologists and the psychologists mentioned throughout the appendix. A good idea would be to list the beliefs and approaches which have characterized the ethologists and the psychologists in two separate columns on a sheet of paper so that you can then easily review this material at a later time. Also, be sure you know how they have shifted their positions toward each other.


# STEP-BY-STEP: A GUIDED REVIEW

After you have read the appendix, mentally fill in each of the blanks in the following section while covering the answers in the margin. Check your answers with that in the margin as you go along. While in many cases your answer should be the same as that in the margin, in other cases a word of similar meaning is acceptable. Do not write in the spaces until you are doing your final review.

1.  Innate patterns of activity assumed to be universal in a species
    are called _____. One psychologist who con-          instincts
    tended that nearly all forms of human behavior are based
    upon instincts is _____. With the advent             McDougall
    of behaviorism, instincts came under attack as providing a
    _____ explanation of behavior. Instincts also        circular
    became unpopular since the psychologists were primarily con-
    cerned with the task of _____ _____.      changing behavior

2.  Scientists who study organisms in the open field under
    natural conditions are known as _____.              ethologists
    These scientists often noticed behavior patterns which are

_____ _____ in nature,        highly stereotyped

_____ in species, elicited by specific        universal

_____ _____, and which are _____        sign-stimuli, self

_____ in that they are not soon repeated        exhausting

after they have been performed. The mating behavior of

the male _____ is one example of this.        stickleback

3.    On the basis of the above observations the ethologists proposed that these behavior patterns were _____.        instinctive

     They contended that these patterns are both _____        innate

     (inherited in a direct fashion) and _____        unlearned

     (uninfluenced by experience). They often cited the results

     of _____ experiments in support of their        deprivation

     position. These studies reared animals so that they could not
obtain the typical life experiences early in life. A number
of such studies found that the behaviors of these animals as
adults _____(were/ were not) affected by this proce-        were not
dure.

4.    Psychologists have pointed out that many of the behaviors
described by the ethologists as innate may actually have been
_____. Further, in many case species specific        learned
behavior fails to develop in a normal manner when organisms
have been deprived of experiences they would normally
obtain during maturation.

5.    Ethologists and psychologists have recently moved to a
resolution of their discrepant points of view. Both groups
have come to realize that classifying behaviors as innate or
learned is of little value since all behaviors are influenced
by _____ _____. Some behaviors may        both factors
be predominantly determined by genetics, while others are
primarily shaped by experience. Ethologists now tend to
refer to species specific behavior as being relatively

_____ _____        environment resistant

rather than innate.

6.    Part of the past controversy between psychologists and
ethologists stemmed from their different usage of the term
_____. Ethologists tended to use the term        learning
to denote _____ and pointed out that many forms        practice
of species specific behaviors occur without practice. Psychologists used this term to refer to changes brought about by
_____ and argued that even during depriva-        experience
tion the animals were having some experiences which would
affect the occurrence of behaviors in maturity.

7. One example of the joint influence of learning and innate factors is _____, or the tendency for the organism to follow the first object it sees. For example, birds will utter cries of distress when _____, follow and remain with this object in preference to others, run to it when _____, and work hard to gain access to it if this is denied. This behavior seems to be innate since it does not require practice. Yet it can also be affected by experience (e.g., being reversed or eliminated).

imprinting

separated from it

frightened

8. Psychologists have also become increasingly aware of the important influence of innate predispositions on behavior. For example, organisms seem to be prepared to learn certain types of responses required for _____. Organisms also may be _____ for certain forms of learning which might interfere with their survival. For example, _____ fail to learn the songs of the different species of bird that may raise them, but retain their own distinct song.

survival
counterprepared

cowbirds

9. Psychologists have now come to believe that the kind of learning a particular species accomplishes most effectively becomes neatly matched over the course of evolution to the requirements of its particular style of life or _____ _____. Evidence suggests that specific forms of behavior are not inherited but that a complex pattern of physical characteristics which predispose organisms toward various forms of activities and learning may be inherited.

ecological demands

10. Some ethologists have generalized their findings with animals to humans. For example, Lorenz has suggested that humans have an _____ instinct. Yet psychologists point out that the mechanisms underlying similar behavior in different species may be quite _____. Further, in comparison to animals, human behavior is much more complex and diverse, largely as a result of the influence of experience. Psychologists are willing to accept that some patterns of behavior may be universal in mankind, such as _____ _____.

aggressive

dissimilar

facial expressions

## KEY CONCEPTS AND TERMS

After you have finished your Guided Review, fill in the meaning of the following terms in your own words. Check on your accuracy by consulting your text on the pages indicated or the Glossary.

instincts  (p. 587)

sign-stimuli  (p. 588)

self-exhausting behaviors  (p. 588)

deprivation experiments  (p. 590)

innate  (p. 591)

unlearned  (p. 591)

environment-resistive behavior  (p. 591)

imprinting  (p. 591)

counterprepared  (p. 593)

ecological demands  (p. 593)


## A PERSONAL QUIZ

After you are about finished with your studies but still have some time left for review, take this quiz to check on your mastery. Fill in your answers in the spaces provided and after you are finished check their correctness with the answers provided.

____ 1. A psychologist who contended that nearly all forms of human behavior are instinctual is (p. 587)
   a. Lorenz
   b. Tinbergen
   c. McDougall
   d. none of the above

____ 2. Those behavior patterns which are taken as evidence for instinctive behaviors by ethologists are characterized as being (p. 588)

a. self-exhaustive
b. elicited by sign stimuli
c. universal in the species
d. all of the above

____ 3. Deprivation experiments have shown that if organisms are deprived of certain typical experiences during maturation (p. 590)
   a. the organisms are generally not prevented from developing into normal adults

b. species specific behaviors may fail to develop in a normal manner
c. they will have a shortened life expectancy
d. they will be severely retarded in locomotor skills

4. The present relationship between the positions of the psychologists and ethologists can best be characterized as (p. 591)
a. one of reconciliation of views
b. showing a movement to a more instinctual approach
c. both moving toward a stronger learning position
d. one of mutual disrespect

5. Part of the controversy between ethologists and psychologists stemmed from their usage of the term learning. Psychologists used it to mean _____, while ethologists used it to mean _____. (p. 591)
a. experience, practice
b. practice, instinctual drift
c. experience, instinctual drift
d. practice, experience

6. Imprinting in birds results in all but one of the below reactions to the imprinted object: (p. 592)
a. following
b. distress when separated from it
c. running toward it when frightened
d. heightened arousal

7. Which of the following statements does not appear to have support? (p. 592-593)

a. organisms are prepared to learn certain responses required for survival
b. organisms may be counter-prepared for certain types of learning
c. specific forms of behavior are inherited
d. a species' ability for certain types of learning may be matched to its ecological demands

8. One pattern of behavior which appears to be universal in man is (p. 595)
a. the aggressive instinct
b. facial expressions
c. social behavior
d. child rearing

Answers:

| | |
|---|---|
| 1. c | 5. a |
| 2. d | 6. d |
| 3. b | 7. c |
| 4. a | 8. b |

NOTES

NOTES

NOTES

NOTES

NOTES

NOTES

NOTES

NOTES

NOTES